THE PARADOX
OF SUCCESS

The
PARADOX
of
SUCCESS

When Winning at Work
Means Losing at Life

A BOOK OF RENEWAL FOR LEADERS

BY JOHN R. O'NEIL

A Jeremy P. Tarcher/Putnam Book
published by
G. P. Putnam's Sons
New York

A Jeremy P. Tarcher/Putnam Book
Published by G. P. Putnam's Sons
Publishers Since 1838
200 Madison Avenue
New York, NY 10016

Library of Congress Cataloging-in-Publication Data

O'Neil, John R.
The paradox of success : when winning at work means losing at life:
a book of renewal for leaders / by John R. O'Neil.
p.   cm.
"A Jeremy P. Tarcher/Putnam book."
Includes index.
ISBN 0-87477-707-0 (hard : alk. paper)
1. Success—Psychological aspects.   2. Success in business—
Psychological aspects.   3. Executives—Conduct of life.
4. Leadership.   I. Title.
BF637.S80545   1993   92-26057
158.1—dc20   CIP

Design by Irving Perkins Associates

Printed in the United States of America

1   2   3   4   5   6   7   8   9   10

This book is printed on acid-free paper.

Acknowledgments

This book was born through the midwifery of mentors, associates, friends, and family. The longest-suffering of them were my children: Mike and Allison, Dana and Vince, and Megan and Tom. Their support and love made the dark stretches passable. Without them, no book. My wife, Patricia, and our extended families, have provided the daily sustenance of abiding generosity, belief, and affection. My colleague, Diana Landau, managed the many drafts with great editorial skill and good humor.

There have been so many kind people involved in the seven years of sweat and gestation that I dare not weigh and sort their contributions. Suffice it to say that the busiest, wisest people were unfailingly kind, remarkably available, and highly revealing to me. Among the many savants, friends, distinguished scholars, and leaders who have shaped my ideas and values are the following: John W. Gardner, Warren Bennis, John L. Levy, Joseph L. Henderson, Phillip Moffitt, Charles Handy, James O'Toole, Peter Carpenter, Nan and David Robinson, Christine T. Millikin, Donald Michael, Dick and Lois Gunther, Elsa Porter and Burt and Emily Marks, C. West Churchman, Sam Keen, Anita Roddick, Ben Cohen, Tom Peters, Ellen Langer, Ed Schein, Robert Perloff, Max DePree, Tony Athos, Peter Drucker, Rollo May, Michael Murphy, Francis Vaughan, and Roger Walsh.

I am deeply grateful to the team that magically spliced the DNA strands together that have become a book. They include Inez Burke; Morena Monterrosa; my editor, Connie Zweig; my agent, M. T. Caen; and Jeremy P. Tarcher, publisher and chief magician.

And, finally, I must acknowledge a very special debt to the many friends, associates, and clients who have told me their stories. The tales of their lives and tender confessions are the basis for any wisdom, wit, and grit the book contains. My own follies are an integral part of whatever moral spine this project has and the voice that I trust the reader will hear. I have masked the identities of those who opened their hearts to me, not as their therapist or kindly country vicar but as a fellow sufferer and aspiring learner.

Contents

PREFACE

Lighting the Dark Side of Excellence

"When I meet people who have had a great triumph, I tell them that I hope it doesn't hurt them too much."

C. G. JUNG

THE FIRST SEED OF THIS BOOK was planted one day in 1982 when I heard Tom Peters talk about his then-new book, *In Pursuit of Excellence*. The occasion, which took place at the vast Biddle-Duke estate on Long Island, was billed as a gathering of America's top 100 entrepreneurs. Other speakers and organizers included Peter Drucker, the grand master of management education, and leadership scholars and writers Warren Bennis of USC and Peter Senge of MIT's Sloan School of Management. I was attending in the role of a consultant on issues of leadership and organization dynamics, which grew out of my winding career path through management, venture capital, education, and psychology. I was also looking for wisdom to bring to my post as president of a pioneering graduate school, the California School of Professional Psychology.

Seated in the living room, we listened to Peters whip up his high-energy tales about leaders and their top-notch companies, and what made them that way. He led us on a whirlwind tour across the business landscape of the 1980s, and

11

pointed out excellence everywhere. Vibrating with his own excitement, he was utterly engaging.

I was enchanted by his vision and wanted very much to believe in it—but the longer I listened, the more troubled I grew. There was something missing from Peters's extravagant picture of contemporary success, or "excellence," as he called it. His optimistic analysis didn't fully describe the lives of the business and professional leaders whom I knew. In fact, I knew that some of the "excellent" leaders and companies he referred to had serious problems that were not being addressed.* And my personal experience had taught me that success is not always the glittering prize that it seems to be on the surface.

I didn't need to look far for evidence of the toxic problems lurking below public achievements. The previous night, a tough and highly successful entrepreneur, now seated three rows ahead, had told me about the "train wreck" of his personal life. His wife was threatening a vicious proxy fight for "his" company, and his two children were threatening to join her. Nearby sat a client and friend whose media empire sprawls across the Southwest. He was suffering from depression and required medication to get out of bed. Two others I knew in the audience were considering leaving high-level positions that they hated. They felt stuck, afraid to let go, and at a loss what to do next. They were starting to manifest ominous physical symptoms of extreme stress.

Furthermore, I knew that in that living room, and in offices around the country, countless other leaders were entering the early stages of career disenchantment. Men and women in top positions across America were drowning in work and bored by it, chronically overstimulated by pressure and understimulated by genuine challenge, growing daily more irritable and with-

---

* Tom Peters is an honest man. He would eventually acknowledge some of the shortcomings of the *Excellence* book and seek to remedy them in later books and speeches that delved more deeply into what constitutes lasting excellent performance.

drawn from their co-workers and families without know-ing why.

The presence of serious, suppressed problems among the conference group was no surprise to me. In the years that I have been a counselor to CEOs and other leaders of organiza-tions spanning business, finance, education, media, public ser-vice, and philanthropy, I've heard many of them. Sometimes the issues my clients bring up are straightforward organiza-tional ones, simply calling for sound strategic decisions about growth or restructuring, such as opening or streamlining communications channels or developing the next generation of leaders. But often the problems are more complex and unyield-ing to structural fixes. The culture of any organization reflects its dominant personalities, and all too often I find that beneath apparent structural problems lie human problems that leaders find terribly hard to admit, much less resolve.

Most of my consultations are with heads of organizations that appear sound from the outside. Once inside, though, I discover layer upon layer of stress, anxiety, stagnation, and communication problems which are eventually revealed by loss of market share, high turnover, or crippled productivity. Early conversations almost never come close to the real prob-lems, but as the comfort level grows, my discussions reveal serious splits in the top ranks about corporate values and goals, and a frightening lack of trust at every level. Often the infight-ing is so intense that really important subjects have become taboo. Secrets abound: secrets about relationships, perks, plans, and performance. Problems at the top filter downward and are soon reflected elsewhere. Totally incompetent or even destructive people are tolerated and ignored (but everyone knows who they are). Leaders are under siege, exhausted, and, most people suspect, dreaming of tall grass somewhere else. The environment for creativity and growth is terrible, and momentum alone seems to be keeping the company in motion (but no one dares to say the King has no clothes).

When organizational secrets are denied or downplayed, they

sap the vitality of the players and poison the entire enterprise. The glaring examples of business excesses in the eighties—the Drexel–Burnham–Milken debacle, Donald Trump's brush with disaster, the abuses of Ivan Boesky, Leona Helmsley, and the Keating S&L cabal—all thrived on secrecy and cover-up.

An essential part of the mystique of business success has been to present a corporate happy face and an image of solid strength to the public. The need to maintain an image of invulnerability and vitality is felt by successful individuals, too—men in particular, although women are by no means immune. But in a human life, success cannot be sustained over the long term by denying the existence of problems—problems having nothing to do with finding the best locations, computer system, or product manager, but with deeply personal matters such as the loss of passion, commitment, vision, and meaning.

The primary goal of any organization is to perpetuate itself, but the individual, human needs of its leaders and managers are far more complex than mere survival. After having attained the basic goals of security, respect, and ego fulfillment, personal needs arise. Less evident but no less urgent is the desire to realize emotional and creative potential, to achieve peace of mind, to serve the community, or to discover some sort of spiritual connection with one's work.

Men and women who have achieved high positions too often ignore these subtle but compelling needs. The pressure to devote oneself body and soul to maintaining outward success can be powerful, seductive, and all-consuming. It comes from the strokes and demands of those we work with, from the pleasant perks of position, from the potent drug of command, and from the basic human tendency to resist change and stay on the path that has led to success.

A fundamental lesson, however—taught by human experience, evolution, and myth—is that staying on one path must lead eventually to a dead end. If you are not breaking new ground, gaining new knowledge, you are risking being trapped in your success.

I was lucky to have run up against a dead end rather early in life. My experience with excellence in business began at AT&T, working in the company's New York headquarters more than twenty years ago. I directed the development of new large-scale communications systems for major customers. The (then) world's largest utility was run from a sedate little building on lower Broadway. The ethics were simple: work diligently, be modest and loyal, wear a white shirt and seasonal hat. If you fitted the mold, worked hard, and played by the rules, you were taken care of. Even though my co-workers were obviously anxious about their futures and preoccupied with being passed over, they never admitted their ambitions, never talked back, never raised ripples on the genteel surface or showed disappointment. They worked with their heads slightly bowed.

AT&T was routinely listed among the best-managed companies in America, but I never understood why. Many of my associates were bright and hardworking; many others were simply hanging on, waiting for retirement. And there were uncomfortable secrets under the veneer of respectability and excellence. Several of the top brass were known alcoholics, but no one ever commented about this or the problems it caused. One very senior executive was such a boorish bigot that he had to be kept away from the press and politicians. It was not an open-to-all company; it was a men's club: no Jews, Afro-Americans, hispanics, or Asians in evidence, except in service.

In spite of my discomfort, my time at AT&T was invaluable; it was there that I learned much about the basic art of leadership. I met my first mentor, John Gardner, who remains my wise friend and teacher today. There was a lot I didn't like. The institutionalized sexism and racism were dispiriting, but what drove me to leave, ultimately, was that AT&T was safe to the point of being stifling.

I didn't discover this without help, though. One of my perks was a company car and driver, and I was inordinately proud of this badge of success. I loved to give my associates rides—what's a perk without some strutting?—and I wanted my driver to be another friendly admirer, part of my supportive audience.

No matter how much I tried to chat him up, however, he remained distant, responding correctly but coolly. Finally, I asked him if there was a problem. Had I offended him in some way? He tried to duck the question but eventually responded with classic New York directness. He said, "All you seem to think about or do is work, and it doesn't even look like you enjoy yourself. I guess you're nice enough, but frankly, from my point of view your life is real boring."

The more I thought about this comment, the more it rankled. But I still couldn't help seeing my life in a less favorable light from then on. Seen through the driver's eyes, it *was* boring—and sometimes worse. I was hooked on work. I was like a train speeding along a very narrow track. Though we never spoke so frankly to each other again, the driver in a strange way became my mirror, a way for me to step back and observe myself from the outside.

I remember one scene in particular; one of my many early-morning departures to the airport for a business trip. As I prepared to leave, my two young daughters hung on to me, crying and saying, "Don't go, Daddy." I looked up to catch the driver's eye. He said nothing. He didn't have to.

My departure from AT&T was embarrassing for my colleagues: one simply didn't leave the club. I next tried my hand at venture capital and entrepreneurship, using my experience in systems development and management to help others start new companies. This move was a total shift in pace, style, and ethics, like moving from Wall Street to the theater district, from a Victorian parlor to a room of shiny chrome and mirrors. The new environment was high-octane, and the players were risk takers: quick, edgy, and articulate. People moved fast, swaggered over their victories, and shaved the edges of deals.

I was swept away both by the thrills of the work and by the high passions of that time, the late sixties. Caught up in career, I wasted little time on introspection. Responding to strident, urgent stimuli and demands from the outside, I almost entirely lost sight of my deepest personal values. My first marriage was the major casualty of that time.

The breakup of the family forced me to take some time off to be with my children, and this turned out to be the best move I could have made. During this mini-sabbatical I began exploring what had gone wrong. When you crash into a wall, you had better find out why it happened before you enter another race. First I just spent time thinking about the past and keeping notes on my observations. I had many long conversations with friends, urging and finally receiving honest critiques. The problems, it turned out, were in me rather than in the nature of AT&T, or the venture business, or other people. This realization was my first conscious step down a road of self-observation and periodic retreat that I have tried to follow ever since.

In 1970, seeking calmer waters, I entered academia. As a vice president of Mills College in Oakland, California, I pursued writing, lecturing, and consulting on behalf of the college and higher education. I also began to formulate my ideas about the failure of success. I set up a symposium series on problems in leadership, and immediately glimpsed one part of the difficulties: many of my gutsy business friends—men who spoke publicly and often about their triumphs—refused to go before the class and talk about errors or failures.

There were many more lessons. Helping to design and teach seminars for new leaders under the aegis of the Council for the Advancement and Support of Education, I met many newly appointed presidents, board chairs, and administrators, and admired those who could speak about their inner doubts and workaholic tendencies. For the National Endowment for the

Arts I examined the leadership of theater companies and observed the many masks of optimism in the performing arts. Serving on corporate, government, and community boards, I witnessed the gulf between the public performances of leaders and the secrets of their private feelings they so carefully concealed.

After seven years at Mills I became president of the California School of Professional Psychology, the nation's first private graduate school devoted to training doctoral-level clinical and organizational psychologists. I remain at that post and continue independently to advise clients on new ventures or the ancient problems of how to educate, motivate, and organize people. The school has served as a rich laboratory for investigating these issues—to my great good fortune.

Having embarked on this new path, an early priority was to study psychology and leadership intensely, from the inside. I read widely and searched for the best teachers, therapists, and mentors in these daunting, vexing, thrilling, and satisfying arts. The more I studied, the more apparent it became to me that the greatest problems of any leader lie deep inside the psyche—in the territory often called the *shadow*.

The term comes from Jungian psychology. Jung used it specifically to refer to "the dark aspects of the personality. . . . The shadow," he writes, "personifies everything that [one] refuses to acknowledge about himself and yet is always thrusting itself upon him. . . ." Both Jung and those who have expanded on his ideas also use "shadow" in a more general way to mean our "dark side."

Anything in our character or personal history that we try to repress because it is painful or makes us feel unworthy—memories of injury, terror, or humiliation at the hands of others; our own capacity for anger, deceit, frailty, or cruelty—forms the substance of the shadow. Also buried there are positive aspects of our personality: the wildness and impossible dreams of childhood, rich treasures that our families and others usually did not value and which we repressed but that ask for recognition and exercise in our daily life. Jung tells us that if we do not bring this shadow material to light sooner or later, it will tarnish all the glittering prizes and make sweet success taste like dust.

But most successful men and women are as reluctant to deal with shadow issues as they are to confess their failures. This became clear to me during a bimonthly seminar I attended, led by Warren Bennis. The participants were twenty-five business, religious, and military leaders. Guest speakers included John Gardner, Peter Drucker, Tom Peters, Tony Athos, Charles Handy, and Henry Kissinger. They spoke off the record and were urged to tell of their moments of doubt and skepticism, but they rarely mentioned anything but their brightest moments.

In the group's fifth year, Warren and I agreed to try to push the participants to be more self-revealing. I started things off by talking about aspects of my "shadow self" and shadow issues that I had discovered in years of working with leaders—institutionalized secret-keeping, executive self-inflation, closed systems of inquiry, and failures of individuals and organizations to grow and learn. Although the response was strong and a heated discussion ensued, the speaker who followed seemed unnerved by the topic. He assured the group that we could get back to business, and began to draw organizational charts. In the end, little of a personal nature was revealed that night.

There are many reasons why it's especially hard for the successful to confront their shadows. American leaders are trained to prize positive statements and firm measures. The image of strength and certainty of purpose is important to them—if they unbend enough to express doubts about what they're doing, it could undermine the whole enterprise. Also, they find it unbecoming to complain or acknowledge pain. They often feel guilty about their privileged status, as though it conferred an obligation to be happy, to shrug off hurts and disappointments. If they have triumphed over adversity to get where they are, they often want to leave it all behind, never looking back until some deeply buried demon trips them up.

I'm concerned chiefly with leaders, professionals, and other readers *as individuals*. We'll explore many ways of bringing shadow material into the light, of focusing your powers of observation on your own life. Though we will use the insights and vocabulary of psychology and its applied arts, what I engage in with my clients and urge you to practice is *not* psychotherapy but something more akin to philosophy, the examination of your life within its larger contexts of value and purpose. It is the exercise of probing and lighting those secrets, unmet aspirations, and dreams that have been packed away in the shadow—of seeking out what shaped your path, what you might be hiding from, what you have lost along the way. (I'm assuming that most readers of this book, while they may be feeling the shadow's chill, are basically functioning quite well. If that's not the case, you may need the help of a good therapist in your explorations.)

Going further, we want to find a definition and shape for success that can integrate different aspects of your personality and adapt to your changing needs—a kind of success that can be sustained over a lifetime. Fortunately, in this effort we have models to look to. These are people I call "long-distance winners" or "success sustainers." They have learned how to keep their pursuit of excellence in balance with their inner well-being. Such people can observe their own developmental needs, sniff out a decaying situation, relish the chaos (and even the pain) of new learning, and spot and quickly reduce the debilitating self-inflation that so often accompanies success. They understand the value of honoring their failures. They know that the successful road has potholes, detours, and junk food, as well as brilliant vistas, freedom, and feasts, and they have learned to prepare for the whole trip. Our persistent winners know how to illuminate and learn from the shadow.

While I emphasize helping individuals become success sustainers, our discoveries will have implications for organizations. Leadership and management training is fashionable in today's business world, but I know organizations that have spent millions on "corporate-culture improvements," internal-communications campaigns, or management courses only to find that the problems persist. Such programs can foster "groupthink," or, worse, split employees into the camps of believers and nonbelievers. Catchy slogans are a far cry from telling the truth to your associates or to yourself, and pre-packaged organizational remedies often mask the behavior of leaders who don't encourage real communication, fear candid input, and direct their energies toward entrenching their own position.

Real change on the organizational level has to begin with real change inside leaders. Success of a deeper kind and a different order than the currently accepted version requires that we see the shadow as a repository of vitality, vision, and renewal, as well as of mischievous and destructive impulses. This is the great promise of the work we are embarking on.

CHAPTER 1

Prisoners of the Office: The Paradox of Success

BEING A PRISONER of the office was only a figure of speech to me—until the early-morning phone call from the headquarters of a Fortune 500 corporation. "He's locked himself in that office and won't come out. It's been three days now," confided the executive vice-president in a tight, frightened voice.

He was the company's CEO, a man I had consulted with some years earlier. The office, reflecting all the power and privilege of its occupant, had a small apartment adjoining it, so Morgan could hold out there for a while—though he probably could have used a clean shirt. Food and mail were allowed in, but only curses came out in response to his staff's entreaties.

"How do we get him out?" was the first question the desperate vice-president asked me. And the second, nearly as urgent, was: "How can we make sure no one hears about this?"

Although I was shocked by the extreme form of Morgan's breakdown, I wasn't really surprised that something in him had snapped. Over the years I had observed from a distance as this talented, hard-driving leader became consumed by his own success, so enamored of his own achievements that the very qualities that had taken him to the top were by now obscured or abandoned.

The symptoms showed up in his work and personal life:

first, an obsessive reliance on quantitative reporting. He rejected any idea that didn't promise immediate bottom-line results. "Numbers, that was all that counted," recalled an employee. The problem was that the numbers were usually cooked or simply wrong; top staff had come to realize that their survival depended on feeding Morgan a steady diet of good news. He ignored the counsel of honest friends and colleagues and eventually cut them out of the charmed circle, relying on a shrinking cadre of "trustworthy" people who were either afraid to speak plainly or caught in the same spiraling updraft of success.

The business world and press had taken notice of Morgan's rapid rise, and he relished the spotlight, the perks, the heady society of other ultrasuccessful people. In consequence, any semblance of a truly rewarding private life was sacrificed; family members were allotted small increments of "quality time," which wasn't enough for them—or for him—to enjoy the benefits of intimacy. He had long since given up fishing trips with friends and golf as too time-consuming. Solitude was a casualty too. Even spectator sports like football had become occasions not for relaxing with family and friends but for lavish corporate entertainment in a sealed-off box.

The numbers finally did him in. When the good news stopped—when sales crashed in defiance of the rosy projections—so did Morgan's personal stock. Even someone with as much denial as he had could heed a possible heart-attack warning.

Morgan's dramatic behavior was unusual and extreme. Not many executives literally lock themselves in their offices. On the other hand, it provides a perfect metaphor for the trap in which many successful people find themselves. Their bodies may go home every night, but psychologically and spiritually they remain imprisoned by the roles they have worked so hard to construct for themselves.

They may feel exhausted, drained of the energy that propelled them so far, or suffer from unexplainable outbursts of anger or sarcasm. They may work themselves into illness or secretly engage in self-destructive behavior, abusing alcohol, drugs, their company's finances, or privileged information. Some develop an insatiable need for praise and affirmation. Some may feel fraudulent, undeserving of compliments and credits they have rightfully earned; others feel that the best, most creative part of themselves is mired in administrative quicksand: juggling financial statements, and stroking board members and key employees.

They may sense distance growing between themselves and old friends and family, between the image of who they would like to be and what they have become, yet feel powerless to do anything about it.

With all achievement comes a variety of pressures and demands, and each person reacts to them differently according to his or her psychic chemistry. When some people feel pressure, they simply bear down and tough it out; others respond by looking to escape or try to spread the weight around. A very common reaction of successful people, when problems and discontented rumblings arise, is to push them aside, ignore them, and concentrate on the positive.

This is easy to do. They want to believe that they're okay. They have evidence of their gifts and good fortune at close hand, and others, from families to stockholders, are looking to them for good news and reassurance. So a reservoir of secrets accumulates beneath the surface of their awareness—things they dislike about their work, their relationships, themselves—and when it gets full enough it spills over. They can no longer so easily shove it out of sight. They come to feel that they are living a lie. Like Morgan in his gilded cage, they are prisoners of the paradox of success.

THE DARK SIDE OF MYTHIC SUCCESS

Success can be defined in many ways, including the simple attainment of a goal or doing a good job at any endeavor. We can speak of being successful in a marriage, as a parent, a friend, a teacher. But these kinds of achievements are usually not the first thing that comes to mind when we call someone successful. In our society they lack the glamour and allure of what I call *mythic success*—a potent elixir compounded of wealth, power, privilege, and freedom from care.

The leaders of any flourishing enterprise experience the joys of high-level decision-making, creating, motivating, traveling, and making things happen that can reverberate throughout their industry, our society, and sometimes the world. Such experiences are exhilarating and enlarging, and the tangible rewards of wealth and privilege can be enormous and fun as well. In addition, today's media concoct flattering mythological portraits of winners, whether in politics, business, athletics, or entertainment.

And yet there is Morgan's story, and so many others I've heard in my career of counseling people in business and the professions. There are the familiar stories of "poor little rich girl" Gloria Vanderbilt, the troubled Kennedy clan, the ouster of Apple founder Steve Jobs from his own company. There are the well-chronicled tribulations of moguls Donald Trump, Michael Milken, Ivan Boesky, and Leona Helmsley. And there are hundreds of thousands of less well-known achievers in business, the professions, and academia who have made it, yet paid a higher price than they had ever imagined.

In almost every age, success has either been celebrated or painted in the darkest of colors, although certain times in history seem to bring its perils into high relief. In the late nineteenth century, when the United States was flexing its industrial muscles, the philosopher William James wrote in a letter to H. G. Wells of "the moral flabbiness of the bitch-goddess SUCCESS. That—with the squalid cash interpretation put on the word success—is our national disease." Another period of splendid excess, the 1920s, produced a definitive American novel, *The Great Gatsby*. Near the end of

Scott Fitzgerald's tale of corrupted innocence and loneliness at the top, the narrator pinpoints the sky's-the-limit attitude that uniquely characterizes the American dream of mythic success: "Gatsby believed in the green light, the orgastic future that year by year recedes before us. It eluded us then, but that's no matter—tomorrow we will run faster, stretch our arms farther . . . and one fine morning—"

We have recently come through another such time: the 1980s, which in retrospect we've labeled the "decade of greed." It had its icons, Trump and Milken; its gospel of supply-side economics; its magic wand, the junk bond; and its countless disciples. Its dominant mind-set was the tendency to measure excellence in one dimension: immediate commercial success. "Management" and "leadership" often degenerated into financial sleight of hand that magically produced results in the short run. The net effect was that a management team could be reaping rewards and recognition while undermining the organization in the long run.

If we could blame these excesses on a single misguided generation or a unique set of historical circumstances, we wouldn't need to worry about falling into the trap again. But the success-at-all-costs myth lives on past the headlines. The factors that allow the myth to run away with us and constrict our vision to short-range goals lie in each of us—in human nature. They surface whenever conditions are right; for example, when hucksters harp on the values of acquisition for its own sake, when the media glorify glitz over substance and worth, and when political leaders equate every form of expansion with moral good, denigrate social generosity, and encourage blind, often destructive egoism in the name of "healthy" competition.

MYTHIC SUCCESS EXAMINED

It is not my aim to analyze why the quest for mythic success dominated the 1980s. Regardless of historical circumstances, choices are made and lives are shaped by individuals. Individuals working together in turn shape corporate cultures and the larger culture. If we are to strive for a deeper excellence, it must begin with an internal recognition that limited, externally measured excellence is not enough.

If we look more closely at some of the assumptions and hallmarks of mythic success, we start to see the shape of its darker side more clearly.

The delusion that success is absolute and final. Once we "make it," we think that our desires will be forever satisfied. This is what all hyperachievers believe on some level, and why we follow their life stories with such fascination. First, we identify with them because the American dream tells us that they could be any of us—with a little luck, of course. When someone succeeds on a larger-than-life scale, he or she must be blessed. So the person is designated to bear the hopes and dreams of millions who aspire to mythic success.

But then it turns out that wealth and power don't guarantee eternal bliss or shield us from all of life's blows. The big winners can't be satisfied with their already massive stock of treasure, but seem to compulsively need more, always more. Or worse, their ambitions lure them into bad judgment and financial overextension, and they are destroyed. The hopes and dreams of millions crash with them; they are resented and reviled for dashing our hopes that bliss awaits if only we can climb high enough.

Money and its buying power are central to the meaning of success. On one level, those who succeed in getting lots of money are truly fortunate. They can be free of anxiety about things which preoccupy most people, and they are able to enjoy whatever pleasures and diversions are available.

However, the problem of identifying success with money is that as a measure of worth, it is purely external. Financially successful people have a quick way to tell the world that they have done something special, that they *are* special. Amassing money has come to serve as a measure of moral worth.

Those who have amassed worldly goods may convince themselves that they are heaven's elect. If they can appreciate their gift for making money on its own terms, for what it's truly worth to themselves and others, that's healthy. But too often possessions substitute for deeper measures of self-worth—whether we perceive ourselves as honest, kind, courageous, humble, loyal, or whatever virtues we decide as adults to prize. When our self-worth is bound to our net worth, we are condemned to living on the surface and can value ourselves only according to how others value our material success.

The craving for more. External measures of success are also relative measures. Wealth and power have meaning only in comparison to what others have; we must be *more* wealthy or *more* powerful than the next guy. So an endless cycle of competitiveness is built into mythic success. As a character in a novel succinctly observes: "It is not enough to succeed. Others must fail."

How often does someone reach a high position, or make a vast amount of money, and declare that he or she is satisfied, that he or she has enough? Rarely. Something in the nature of mythic success—especially if we cling to a particular success for too long—produces an unquenchable need for more. Why would Michael Milken, for example, continue to push the shady boundaries of junk-bond trading after he was already the highest-salaried individual in the country? Megadoses of success can cloud even the most brilliant mind. The inflated ego crowds out perspective and judgment, so we develop a dangerous sense of invulnerability.

The love-hate reaction to success. A familiar contradiction of human nature is that we want both to belong and to stand out from the crowd. In Western societies, the urge to set oneself apart from the masses tends to dominate. The success chase exaggerates these contrary urges; attaining high status, rank, or visibility is gratifying but also threatening.

It feels good to be admired, but it's only a short way from there to envy and resentment. The person who stands out is an easy target for these, or worse. The hyperachiever sometimes deliberately decides that old friends and associates are no longer good enough, especially if their perceptions of new achievements are not always flattering. Or friends may avoid us out of discomfort with the gap in financial fortunes. A dark side of distinguishing oneself is the risk of isolation and alienation.

Envy or resentment cause most people to behave as though the highly successful have somehow been vaccinated against ordinary human pain and suffering. A columnist related such a tale from a woman who wrote, "Do you know what it's like to be written off as a success?" This woman didn't flaunt her success, nor was she undeserving of it. It merely seemed that her good fortune somehow disqualified her from the human race. "I'm talking about the same people who were always my friends—even my relatives. I really do think they're pleased that after all these years, my efforts are being recognized and rewarded. But it's as though I've forfeited my standing among them by being lucky. For example, say a friend complains to me about being tired or overworked. If I sympathize and admit that I'm tired, too, he'll say, 'You? Why, you must be laughing all the way to the bank.'

"If something nice happens to me, the same people who used to jump up and down with glee for me are now bored and ask, 'What did you expect?' If I have a setback, instead of commiserating, they say, 'So what—you can afford it.' "

Leaders may feel the love-hate reaction of others keenly, but are usually so committed to maintaining their position that they see no way to break down the walls. They are likely to feel guilty about their good fortune, given our recent global awareness of misfortune and suffering—and then reject such feelings. All successful people struggle with the tendency of success to isolate them. And they face the challenge of finding where they fit in the larger human scheme.

Success will make you free. Success can bring freedom from repetitive, dehumanizing work, from the boredom or peril of staying in one place, and from many social restrictions. Getting ahead may free us from having to work on an assembly line or live in a slum—but it doesn't necessarily allow us to spend our time as we would like.

I talk to many business leaders and professional people who feel imprisoned inside their business personae. Some feel that essential parts of themselves are bound and gagged by their commitment to the role that led to success. When such feelings build up for too long without any release, the result can be a blow-up that tears relationships and careers apart. A retail industry executive spoke to me about how he felt: "I just want to sweep everything off my desk! I don't want to deal with my past anymore. I want to start freshly. I want that sense of not knowing and mastering and succeeding at something for the first time. It's like wanting to fall in love passionately again. Sometimes when I go to bed, I think: I don't want to wake up in this bed, in this city again. Could I wake up in a tent and hear lions roaring outside? Could I wake up on another planet?"

So many people feeling trapped by circumstances that are supposed to be liberating is part of the paradox of success. Our fevered pursuit of excellence is almost always initially based on healthy drives and good old can-do American values.

Without warning, however, these virtues can be corrupted. Our drives turn on us. We overextend our gifts and commit too much energy to keeping our success going. The initial desire to lead becomes a compulsion to command. A natural yearning to distinguish oneself becomes an obsession to top the other guy. It is as though, without our noticing, something resets our sails so that the wind that powered our early efforts begins to propel us in the wrong direction.

THE PARADOX OF SUCCESS IN ACTION

Calvin was a casualty of the success myth "eighties style" and a prime example of how our natural talents can become perverted. Calvin had the gifts of persuasion and charm. Combining them with a concern for the needy, he embarked on a fast-blooming career as a fund-raiser. When I first met him there was a farm freshness in his Omaha gait. His boyish all-American looks—curly red hair, freckles, and an open smile atop his lean 6'2" frame—gave him an added advantage. People trusted this rangy, friendly young man, and I became one of many who wanted to help him on his way.

Calvin had made an appointment with me weeks ahead and showed up a half hour early. When I went out to greet him, he unfolded promptly from the small chair and shook hands for a long time. Abruptly releasing the grip, he said, "I learned about handshaking from my father, who was a Presbyterian minister. He could hold people or release them by the way he shook their hand. The important people always got the longest shake. I overdo that sometimes." I found his small confession disarming.

He had come to me, he said, for help in learning how to grow as a fund-raiser and public relations expert. Currently the number-two person at a northern California YMCA, he was interested in attending some seminars I was conducting on institutional development and leadership, but his budget couldn't cover it. Would I have time to guide him a little?

I got him scholarships to seminars, introduced him to top pros in fund-raising and public relations, gave him books and other materials. For several years he remained a quick and earnest student, and soon began to move upward, riding a career jet stream. He wrote to me faithfully as he moved from the YMCA to a small college and then on to a large community hospital, where he eventually was named Director of Development. A note announcing the last promotion contained a little bar chart of his salary increases; though done for laughs, it was impressive: six jumps in seven years.

Several years went by during which I didn't hear from him, but I knew that he had joined a major New York consulting firm. Then one day he called and asked to see me. He sounded different—quicker and slicker—or perhaps I imagined so because I knew he was working in New York. When we met, he looked different, too; more sophisticated, certainly, sporting a moustache and a double-breasted pin-stripe suit. He moved with more authority and commented on a painting in a laborious manner that showed no trace of his former ingenuousness.

But he was still charming, and after bringing me up to date, he got down to his subject. "It's gone well, but I'm still learning. And what I'm learning now is how to get more accounts for the firm. We especially need clients on the West Coast. I'm thinking about a high-level seminar series on development leadership. Would you help me design it?"

As he went on, I marveled at his poise and drive, but also felt slightly miffed. Suddenly he had vaulted from student to prospective partner. I was impressed but a tad disturbed. He didn't seem as genuine. The infectious, boyish charm seemed detached from any personal connection with me—clearly it was my Rolodex he wanted. I put him off that day and said no to the idea when he called a few days later. More years passed, bringing the annual just-right note on a tasteful card. He continued to move up and finally opened his own shop in West Los Angeles. Not long ago he called again, wanting to talk.

We had lunch in a downtown club where he had reciprocal privileges. Calvin looked tired inside his Rodeo Drive suit. He inquired perfunctorily about my fortunes and plunged into his purpose, saying that while things had gone well—they had grown to three offices, were doing mostly PR work, and were considering a merger with another PR firm—his troubles had grown also. He referred vaguely to people and organizational problems and asked if I would look things over and give him a reading. Intrigued, I agreed to spend a half day talking to his key people.

I was hardly prepared for the scene he had created in a midrise Santa Monica building overlooking the ocean. Expensive oriental rugs reposed on white floors, and a Hockney painting adorned his office wall. It could have been a set from a movie about corporate power.

My brief interviews with his key staff revealed serious holes in the company fabric and probably just scratched the surface. The place was full of secrets and there was zero trust among the top people. The only woman officer summed it up by saying, "The soul has gone out of here." For my debriefing, Calvin insisted that we go to his house in Bel Air, which looked as if the office decorator had been turned loose there as well: stark, with patches of blaring ostentation.

After Calvin and I got comfortable, I began my customary questioning, sometimes directly based on my observations, sometimes just following clues in his conversation. He may have been hoping for some instant pat analysis of what was wrong with his company, but it wasn't that simple. What was going wrong started with him, and I wanted to help him visit his secrets, get below the surface impression he had worked so hard to create.

I asked him to look at the business he was in and to articulate why he was in it—why he had chosen it at the beginning and what kept him doing it now. We discussed his personal dreams and ambitions, and to what extent he thought his personal development aligned with the needs of the business. I asked, as I always do, what were his biggest secrets, and what he knew of his employees' ambitions and secrets. Finally I asked him to consider what difference it would make if he sold the business.

In an hour or so of grappling with these questions, we dug

down past his smooth persona and some hard truth bubbled up. Once a client realizes that the secrets he reveals are not shocking or his behavior especially abnormal, he usually feels relieved and opens up. Calvin confided that he had become a workaholic, had no friends outside of the business, and trusted no one inside it. His fees were now so high that few charitable clients could afford him anymore. He was in physical pain and had recently spent two weeks in traction for back problems. Married and divorced, he had gone to Mexico at Christmastime with a woman client who stayed drunk the whole time; he felt that summed up his social life. It wasn't a long step from there to admitting that the troublesome business issues were directly related to his missteps in leadership and his floundering personal life.

Fortunately Calvin had reached a flash point of desperation and quickly agreed that he needed a tough consultant for his business as well as a good therapist for himself. I advised him to take a sabbatical from his job and to continue the work of self-discovery that these early questions had prompted. I told him that he was *worth it*. On hearing this, the old Calvin came alive for a moment and shook my hand with the earnest fervor of our first encounter.

In his pursuit of mythic success, what had happened to Calvin's modesty, high ideals, and openness—the sources of his charm? Modesty had been replaced by affectation. Growth and earnings had triumphed over purpose. Curiosity and compassion had lost out to cleverness and conniving. Several of his associates had spoken of his being lost, hard to reach, out of touch. And clearly he was unhappy. He had money, power, and recognition in his field, yet life was sour for him. Was this success? If so, wasn't there something wrong with it?

The paradox of success is that Calvin's abundant talents came with a kind of built-in virus that eventually caused those gifts to turn on him and attack his basically healthy psychic immune system. Paramount in his case—and that of many leaders—was the charisma that drew people to him and made them want to work toward the aims he so eloquently described. Blown off course by the inflating wind of success, Calvin began to abuse his power over other people and to believe that his magic touch in business depended on keeping secrets and making decisions in isolation.

Calvin's case is a common scenario of how the success paradox unfolds. We are all vulnerable to the process whereby our greatest strengths can become our greatest weaknesses. I compare this vulnerability to a latent virus, but a more useful long-range concept is that we all have a shadow side, and any characteristic that we develop strongly also carries a shadow. Looking at the paradox of success in this way has proved to be immensely helpful to my clients and will be the basis of our discussion to come.

FACING THE COST OF SUCCESS

We can understand the idea of a shadow quite literally. The shining grail of achievement has a large, dark, vaguely shaped companion that is inseparable. Its details are hard to distinguish, but it has an ominous look. And if this shadow grows too large and powerful, nothing can thrive in its shade.

In psychology, the shadow has a more specific set of meanings and ways of operating. It is a useful tool for figuring out how the best and brightest go wrong. Successful people struggle with shadows especially in the areas of money, power, relationships, and responsibilities; later we'll look at these areas in detail.

A first step is to notice and recognize the shadows gathering around the edges of your life and endeavors. They may already loom large, evidenced by serious problems at work or at home, or by some stress-related physical condition; or you may merely sense an occasional vaguely disturbing whisper. In any case, the following catalog of symptoms should help you identify where shadows may be operating.

1. *Is your calendar saturated with "important" dates? Do you find less and less time for family and friends? Do you spend little time alone, in fact avoid it? Have you given up some small ritual that refreshed you, like a walk or a quiet cup of tea on the porch?*

Making one's schedule a frantic whirl of commitments is a syndrome familiar to successful people. Its corollary is an inability to recognize and value the uses of solitude. I certainly see the tendency in myself. One day I was grousing to my assistant about my schedule. Finally, she had heard enough and, holding up my calendar, said firmly, "You approved every appointment in here. You must want it that way." She was right, and I began to be much more conscious of what such overscheduling means.

Busy people often have a hard time getting away for a vacation, and even when they do, can't seem to free themselves from their intricate web of responsibilities. Jan Carlson, the president of SAS Scandinavian Airlines, described to me how hard it was to separate himself from his work identity. "I've had to practice getting away. My first attempt after becoming president didn't last a week. The phone rang again and again, and I decided it was easier just to go back. After this had happened enough times, I began to wonder: Why have I set things up so that people can't act without me? What kinds of controls have I unintentionally imposed?"

Being in demand—feeling needed or, better yet, indispensable—satisfies a basic psychological need to connect and belong and feel significant. But chronic overcommitment and avoiding any time alone can signal something less positive. Being alone is uncomfortable if you feel that a dialogue with yourself is wasted time; if disturbing doubts and questions persistently arise about who you are and what you're doing; or if you experience longings that seem improper, immoral, or hopelessly out of reach. All of these are signs that a shadow is stirring and needs attention.

2. *Is competition your primary mode of interacting with others? Is winning central to your sense of self-worth? Are your competitor's losses even more satisfying than your own gains? When your team accomplishes something, do you fret about your share not being large enough or your credit too small? Is your world divided into winners and losers?*

This symptom surfaced at a board meeting of a company of which I was a director. Another director, Peter, began to argue against accepting a major contract from a supplier because he was angry for private reasons at that company's CEO. Cooler minds prevailed, so Peter then changed his tack and began to argue for our firm to acquire the supplier (so that the offending CEO could be fired). It was clear to the rest of us that this move wouldn't have been a good business fit, but he continued to press his case. Finally, he walked out of the meeting, his anger and frustration out of control.

Peter's antipathy toward the supplier's chief stemmed from a business deal some months earlier in which the man had bested him. Apparently Peter had bought a warehouse from him, only to learn that he could have gotten better space elsewhere in the neighborhood for considerably less. One of Peter's partners had ragged him about this.

When he was rising in the real-estate-development field, Peter's competitive fire had served him well, and he seemed to find joy and stimulation in his victories. More lately, though, he seemed to compete out of habit, always needing to have the last word, reacting bitterly toward those he perceived as doing better than himself and dismissively toward others. He couldn't forgive or forget his mistakes and seemed exhausted by the perpetual fight but unable to function any other way.

3. *Have the trappings and symbols of power become crucial to your self-definition? Do you feel upset if people get your title wrong or fail to recognize you? Are you buying things to fit or bolster your image? Are your trophies shielding feelings of inadequacy?*

I know a savings-and-loan executive whose empire recently collapsed. At the height of his success, he had built himself an immense office with two mammoth ornate doors that popped open at the touch of a receptionist's button. At the end of this long room the executive sat on a raised platform. One visitor described the experience as something like visiting a potentate or the Pope. The whole setting was a crude effort to elevate a fragile ego, a symbol of mounting self-inflation and a rapidly growing shadow.

It would be foolish to underestimate the power of material symbols to affect how we feel about ourselves and how others perceive us. The danger lies not in the objects themselves—the limousine, the oriental rugs, the antique desk, the corporate jet—but in their tendency to encourage feelings of infallibility and invulnerability or to create a shell of strength and confidence around a basically weak ego.

4. *Do you overextend or abuse your natural talents? For example, if you are good at relating to people and getting them to confide in you, do you wind up misusing their trust? Or do you use your skill with numbers, words, memory, or whatever to show off, dominate, or humiliate others? Do you neglect developing your latent gifts because you can always count on the old tricks?*

Hope, a deal-making lawyer in Chicago, was well known for her quick mind and tongue and depended heavily on this strong suit. Early in her career people found her very funny, and her quips were passed around town. As her reputation grew, so did her repertoire of one-liners, but they also became more acerbic and barbed. Already busy, she accepted board assignments, commission appointments, and more legal work; the more tired she grew, the more irritability would show up in her language. Old friends were hurt, clients skewered, politicians wounded; her talented tongue became a liability.

If you recognize yourself in the above questions, your development is overbalanced in one direction, narrowing the base of the support for your identity. If the strengths that carried you to success are overworked and other aspects of your personality neglected, those same strengths can turn into liabilities and parts of the self that are left in shadow may break out in inappropriate ways.

5. *When you find yourself stuck, unable to resolve difficulties in your career or relationships, do you invent all sorts of external reasons—bad luck, the economy, other people's weakness or ineptitude—to explain your problem? Do you invariably find your associates or employees flawed and unreliable?*

Favored by fortune and surrounded by evidence that they have made the right moves, successful people are inclined to assign responsibility outside themselves when things don't go right. It's as if the magic that carried them to success will somehow evaporate if they admit to mistakes or acknowledge a side of themselves that isn't so attractive.

Jeffrey was a fast-rising advertising executive, brilliant at the art of taking credit but reluctant to take any part of the responsibility for projects that failed. Co-workers eventually came to feel resentful and tired of accepting blame, and were less willing to work long hours and give an extra measure of themselves. Associates no longer confided in him and even perversely withheld information vital to his decisions. Eventually Jeffrey saw what was happening, but not how he had contributed to the problem. It was always someone else's fault, and by the time I met him, he was listing his enemies.

6. *When you get bad news or criticism, do you brood on it or take more than your just share of blame for it? Do you dwell on critical remarks or slights, imagining what you could have done to avoid them? Do you overlook and downplay compliments or feel unworthy of them?*

Some high achievers, depending on their character and background, are haunted by feelings of guilt or fraudulence about their success. Such people tend to take on too much blame rather than shifting it to others. We might say that their shadows contain a harsh judge that has been given too much power. This inner voice reinforces criticism from outside sources: the parent who challenges, "You think you're better than me" or the friend who belittles your accomplishments.

Women in particular seem to suffer from this "impostor syndrome," although a male entrepreneur spoke of it eloquently. "When people compliment me on the quality of our products," he sighed, "I know it's sincere, but I just can't appreciate it. I used to feel personally involved in every one, but lately it seems like they don't have anything to do with me."

Barbara and Tom run a well-managed and profitable distribution business. Barbara handles customer relations, advertising, and service, and Tom makes the trains run on time—purchasing, warehousing, shipping, and so on. After a few years Barbara's stress level was dangerously high. She had become the lightning rod for customer complaints and instead of spreading the responsibility, took it all on herself. Tom knew something was wrong, but couldn't get her to talk directly about the pressure she was feeling. She recognized that she was behaving like a martyr and knew Tom detested this, but she felt that admitting to it would invite more blame from him. She saw no choice but to keep everything buried. The strain made her suffer from chronic fatigue and mild depression, for which she took medication. The business thrived and lots of credit was showered on Barbara, but it was lost on her because her inner critic had taken over.

7. *Has the need for control and the exercise of power become a desperate and depleting game? Do small irritants and vexing details bother you out of proportion? Are you less tolerant of delays, changes in schedules, slow service?*

The territory of power and control is ground zero for any successful person, the place where psychological quirks and external pressures are bound to show up eventually. If you have a compulsive need for control, unaccepted feelings of powerlessness are part of your shadow. Habits of discipline that once served you can wind up enslaving you. An example shows how such a problem can turn trivial mischief into galloping disaster.

Harry headed an accounting firm that grew very rapidly, so he had to shift from being a hands-on manager to a chief executive. He knew every facet of the business and took great interest in every detail. His passion for control reached an absurd extreme when a document was misplaced because two paper clips stuck together; he reacted with a two-page memo on "affixing and filing documents." His gleeful staff leaked the memo to a local columnist, and that transgression became his next obsession. "Heads will roll," Harry promised when we met at that time.

8. *Are you sometimes flooded with negative emotions that surprise you by their intensity, cripple your effectiveness, and alienate those around you? Does anger boil into rage over trivial events like a car cutting you off or someone pushing ahead of you in line?*

Free-floating anger is a clear sign that emotional needs are deeply buried and yelling for attention. The things that spark your rage may not have anything to do with the deepest source of the trouble. Long-suppressed needs tend to become generalized. Anger is one of the emotions most likely to indicate shadow issues that need to be addressed.

Dr. Meyer Friedman, a pioneer in studying Type A behavior, would not allow his patients to watch sports on TV because many would become so furious over a referee's bad call that they risked a heart attack. His patients were often high-level executives who also might terrorize and oppress those around them while literally killing themselves with their misplaced rage.

Anger may be useful to some successful people in working their way up from a less-than-privileged background or overcoming negative messages from family members. Righteous anger can be used as a rallying point to attract followers to a cause. But unless the deep, often unconscious sources of anger are illuminated, sooner or later they are likely to turn destructive.

9. *Have you become rigid in your views and the way you take in information, in what you consider valuable or acceptable? Are you so committed to what demands attention right now that you can't plan for the future? Are opportunities for change passing you by because you can't see them or can't change gears?*

We tend to stick with what works, but anyone who wants to sustain success over the long haul has to overcome that form of inertia. It's very difficult, because the successful are typically overwhelmed with the urgent demands of running an operation day to day. Opportunities to gain perspective on long-range needs—the company's and your own—don't just arise but must be created. Many executives have a "dream folder," an actual or mental file of scribbled ideas, clippings, inspirational stories, and half-conceived fantasies, but it gets opened too rarely, and the energy in it doesn't get its needed expression.

This tendency to grow rigid, especially as we get older, sometimes becomes evident through its effects on others. An industrial executive confessed to me that his unwillingness to entertain new ideas had driven away more than one creative younger manager. "I didn't like it when they pressed too hard, especially when they questioned what I'd been trained to believe was the prevailing wisdom. I fired one guy who argued against building a new plant without fully automating the production lines—he said it was stupid, and he was right. Two years later, we had to redo the whole thing."

You may not instantly recognize yourself in these thumbnail descriptions of the symptoms of faltering success, though there's a good chance you share at least some of them. Most people are reluctant to own up to the price they are paying for a slice of mythic success. That's not surprising, because a major function of the shadow is to obscure problems. It's a dark place where we can store the things that disturb us, pretend they don't exist. This may be a good way to allow us to continue our pursuit of success, but it's a dangerous one. Like paint-soaked rags left in a dark closet, the flammable materials of emotions and unfulfilled needs can burst into flames when the right spark is applied.

A NEW MYTHOLOGY OF SUCCESS

Mythic success as I've described it still exerts a powerful pull. But its high cost and its paradoxical nature are becoming clearer. As more and more people begin to articulate some alternate images of success and to act on them, there are signs that our concept of excellence may be changing radically. One of the goals of this book is to redefine success in terms that we can better live with.

In Diane Fassel's book about workaholism, *Working Ourselves to Death*, she quotes Tom Peters and Nancy Austin: ". . . the cost of excellence is the giving up of family vacations, Little League games, birthday dinners, evenings, weekends, lunch hours, gardening, reading, movies and most other pastimes. We have a number of friends whose marriages or partnerships crumbled under the weight of their devotion to a dream—we are frequently asked if it is possible to ' have it all '—a fully satisfying personal life and a fully satisfying hard working one. Our answer is *no*."

What kind of excellence is this? Is the kind of success worth having that takes such a high toll on one's health, relationships, and peace of mind? Can someone with an ulcer or heart problems or a series of broken marriages attributable to career pressures consider himself or herself successful? Younger people, beginning their own climb toward mastery in their fields, observe their older superiors with dismay: are burnout or boredom all they can look forward to after a lifetime of devotion to a demanding career?

Today, there is a growing trend toward defining success in terms of a balanced life, in which worldly pursuits share space with "intangibles": rich and mutually supportive relationships and family roles, a healthy body that can cope well with stress, participation in community life, and opportunities to fulfill creative and altruistic urges.

Once the media took note of this shift, it seemed you couldn't open a newspaper without finding the story of some Wall Street warrior who packed it in at thirty-five and bought a ranch in Montana, the fast-track female executive who discovered that motherhood was what really mattered, and so on. *Time* officially blessed the phenomenon with a 1991 cover story on "the simple life," and the trend continues. Today's "man on the go" in an underwear print ad is chasing a crawling baby instead of a commuter train.

Madison Avenue and the mass media have the unfortunate knack of trivializing just about anything they latch on to, yet in the stories of real people we hear authentic longings for a more balanced life. Corrado Federico, the president and chief executive of Esprit de Corp, who won recognition for steering the company through rough waters caused by the feuding of its once-married founders, resigned his post in 1990 to "pursue other interests," as the phrase goes: "Right now I'm going to do the things I haven't had a chance to do for the past decade— go to the zoo with my children and pursue my interest in contemporary art."

Top political consultant Clint Reilly, who grew rich by taking the process of political kingmaking out of the back rooms and into the technological age, announced his temporary retirement in late 1991, saying he planned to "get completely out of the business" and "renew myself intellectually." Reilly, a typically American entrepreneur who sold junk on the San Francisco streets in the 1970s while educating himself in campaign techniques, found himself at forty-four with a brilliant career but limited experience of a wider life. Like most relatively young people who quit successful careers, he did not contemplate a life of leisure but rather a sort of sabbatical "to find a better way to make a living."

The case of Representative William Gray, the black congressman from Pennsylvania who gave up his seat to become head of the United Negro College Fund, is particularly interesting because, though his move was hailed as an example of courage and altruism, press coverage contained an undertone of suspicion and cynicism. The assumption was that Gray's exit from the political arena represented a step down the vertical ladder of success. Altruism is all very well, but anyone who voluntarily chooses what we perceive as a downward move is automatically suspect—such is the immense and ingrained force of the vertical image of success. If we're not always moving upward, we are in some manner failing. As we'll see later, the image of success patterns as a steady upward line or even a staircase is badly flawed.

When successful people contemplate a leap off the ladder, they usually suffer fear and self-doubt. Some who actually make the leap are testimony to the power of other needs and feelings: the fear of stagnation, the sense that life in its fine detail is passing us by, or that the best of oneself is "out there" somewhere, cut off by walls of duty and a carefully constructed image.

Such feelings are rooted in what psychologist Abraham Maslow calls a "hierarchy of needs." Maslow wrote that after people are able to satisfy "maintenance needs"—food, shelter, and clothing—they progress to a higher level of gratification. In his book *The Farthest Reaches of Human Nature*, Maslow writes: "It is true that lower-need gratifications can be bought with money—but when these are already fulfilled, then people are motivated only by higher kinds of 'pay,' e.g. belongingness, affection, dignity, respect, appreciation, honor, as well as opportunities for self actualization and the fostering of higher values—truth, beauty, efficiency, excellence, justice, perfection, order, lawfulness, etc."

These "higher needs" are often fulfilled in a successful working life. They may be stronger motivations for achievement than money and power. When success no longer satisfies those needs, then it truly fails us.

THE LONG-DISTANCE WINNERS' SUSTAINABLE SUCCESS

In the nineties people are becoming more willing to acknowledge family life, self-fulfillment, and service as motivating forces in their lives. Unfortunately, our models of success haven't caught up with this shift yet. Abetted by the media and our own darker drives, we're still fascinated by the likes of Trump and Milken—though perhaps more inclined to cheer their failures than their triumphs.

Clearly, too, there is great interest in the stories of successful people who have opted out of the race, taken time off, cut back, or changed careers. These people have responded to urges that many of us share, taken the first bold or faltering steps toward a more balanced life. But we need to look beyond this stage, to find people whose lives reveal a pattern of sustained success. This pattern is not a seamless and steady rise into the stratosphere, but a complex tapestry of achievement in different areas, interspersed with periods of retreat and re-evaluation.

I've called these models of sustained success "long-distance winners." They are not easy to find. They tend *not* to be leaders whose accomplishments have been attended by a lot of publicity: for example, Lee Iacocca bringing Chrysler back from the brink, Steve Jobs creating the market for personal computers. Nor are they measured by short-term success in a single context. The profiles of excellence in Tom Peters's first book show the dangers of that approach—some leaders whom he identified in 1980 as outstanding were seriously discredited a decade later. Another business writer told me, "I wish I had been more selective in those I called outstanding. Some didn't hold up under fire and others talked a better game than they played."

Authentic long-distance winners are generally less public, less flashy. They recognize that attention is inherently inflating and deliberately avoid it as a conscientious dieter avoids high-fat foods. And their achievements often don't make great copy because many of them can't be conveyed in figures. They prize organizational spirit and community contribution as much as a healthy quarterly profit, for example.

The term "long-distance winner" says much that I intend, but some things that I don't intend, so I will use it along with "success sustainer." "Winner" usually suggests a competition, and therefore a loser as well. The competitive urge is always present to some extent in those gifted to lead and succeed, but in the realm of long-distance winning it is de-emphasized. The idea that there has to be a loser we can simply reject, as does Sandra Kurtzig, the remarkable cofounder of ASK Computer Services, one of the world's ten largest software companies. In her book *CEO*, Kurtzig says: ". . . my value system says I don't have to get everything to win, and I can win without someone else losing."

We'll meet a variety of long-distance winners in this book, both living and historical figures, with varying ways and means of sustaining success. As a general approach, I like the ideas of philosopher C. West Churchman, known as the father of operations research, the field that applies quantitative analysis to the study of how systems (human and otherwise) function. In *The Systems Approach and Its Enemies*, West says that to be healthy and successful, a system must contain ethics (does it have integrity?) and aesthetics (is it pleasing and harmonious?). A good bridge must have an ethic of quality—the right materials, engineering, and construction to make it strong. And a good bridge design must be aesthetically appealing or it will not last; it will be pulled down or allowed to fall down. Churchman argues that these are the most important elements of building any system, but too often the last to be considered.

Long-distance success likewise must incorporate ethics and

aesthetics. The ethic behind much of the striving for mythic success allows one to cut corners, press competitors to the wall, nick a piece of action for oneself. Such ethics are anathema to a healthy, functioning system because they are ultimately damaging to the psyche. Service and altruism are key ingredients in nourishing a resilient psyche.

Aesthetics, too, are often neglected in the frantic timetable of success. Thrashing out big deals leaves no time for a leisurely meal, for gentle courtesies, tender exchanges, or even lovemaking. At its furthest extremes, self-inflation blunts both our senses and sensibilities.

When we put a lock on personal pleasure and turn away from emotion, we have begun to corrupt the "aesthetic" self. At the same time, our system of ethics is damaged because the two are inextricably linked. So when a person forgets how to love, or loses the ability to be emotionally honest, he or she also endangers the inner system of right and wrong, the moral values. He is the architect who will compromise design for profit because he has ceased taking pleasure in designing— because it doesn't matter anymore. She is the broker who will cheat or ignore the rules to advance in her career because she has forgotten the pleasure of doing it right—because she now believes the "right" way is for saps. He is the scientist who cuts corners on research to land the big grant; she is the CEO who, as she grows more powerful, fails to acknowledge the contributions of the "little people."

A narrow view of winning that attends only to extrahuman goals is no way to sustain long-term health either for an organization or its leaders. The excesses of the 1980s indicate that we need a vastly expanded concept of excellence in business. We can get some clues about how to frame that concept from a multifaceted study of 191 executives conducted by the team of McCall, Lombardo and Morrison in 1988. Researchers investigating how these people got to the top were given reasons ranging from technical and managerial to social and personal. But when asked to compress their hard-won wisdom for the next generation of managers, the executives boiled it down to: "Take advantage of opportunities, aggressively search for meaning, and know yourself."

Significantly, these principles deal mainly with personal growth and the inner life. The study suggests that career success doesn't result from one kind of behavior and a happy life from a different kind. However, the study did not imply that successful people can easily "have it all." In fact, the subjects believed that conflicts and dilemmas, losses as well as gains, were all valuable in their development. They agreed that it was important not to shy away from conflicts and to sniff out problems in the organization before they become institutionalized. This could as easily apply to problems, or shadows, in the individual.

The long-distance success sought by many is a harmonious, synergistic fit between the tangible, measurable aspects of work and achievement and the intangibles of health, family, community, friendship, creativity, and altruistic service. This harmony is so hard to achieve because measurable goals are often easier to define and attain. It is simpler to satisfy externally imposed standards than to articulate and live up to our own internal ones. We are trained to judge ourselves by the applause and criticism of others—and in an era when spiritual values no longer guide most lives, approval is most likely to be sought and found in worldly realms. Even though we know the intangibles are worthwhile, they are more easily dismissed or their absence rationalized away. Thus gradually we become victims of an incomplete or corrupted version of success.

Measures of authentic self-worth come from many sources: valuable work, health, a good family life, creative expression, friendship, and help given and received. When we depend too heavily on any one source for our sense of self-worth, the ego becomes easily threatened and defends itself even more aggressively. It was this shrinking base of support that left my friends Morgan and Calvin teetering perilously on a knife edge. Long-distance winners are determined to work effectively in a world of numerical measurement and yet not measure themselves by that world.

BEYOND THE LOCKED DOOR

It's difficult for us to recognize that our success may be hurting us. The paradox of success is something we don't want to see. Yet breaking through denial is the essential first step in building a deeper, more sustainable excellence. Too often when I meet with leaders they are unwilling to look, and they claim that their actions are all out in the light, with no shadowy motives. I hear statements like: "There are no secrets here"; "We are just one big family"; "We get our problems on top of the table in this organization." An organization that pretends to have no secrets has grown preoccupied with image over substance and doesn't know itself.

Perhaps the single greatest danger of success is that it encourages us to overlook or discount the darker sides of ourselves. At bottom, this failure to confront what we don't like to see is responsible for why so many high achievers fail in a deep way. As we begin to identify our areas of vulnerability, they become less threatening, and new ways of looking at things will appear where we had run up against blank walls. For example:

- Hypercompetitive leaders can discover new and different goals, larger and more satisfying games to play. Finite games can be seen for what they are and still played, but within a broader context.
- Those caught in time-and-control obsessions can learn practices that loosen time's grip, diminish the fears that promote hypercontrolling behavior, and help us explore new dimensions outside of linear time. We will introduce the concept of seasonal planning. Time management can become more meaningful as purpose management.
- Trophy collectors can find an exciting aesthetic of clear

wall space, achieved by re-examining our values and identifying new pursuits.

- The gifted can discover how to protect and nurture their talents, while avoiding the temptation to overextend and manipulate them for external approval.
- Those pounded by a harsh internal critic can learn to locate the source of that powerful voice that commands them from the shadow and to quiet it down.
- Victims of self-defeating behavior and attitudes can develop many techniques for uncovering emotions and experiences buried in the shadow so that they need not be acted out in disturbing ways.
- Change seekers reluctant to let go of an obsolete learning curve, for fear of losing their identity and worth, can explore how to gently plant the seeds of new prospects in a frightened mind.

In the next chapter we will examine more closely how the qualities that produce excellence can be corrupted by the shadow. And we will discover why Jung referred to the shadow as "pure gold," by seeing how long-distance winners mine this psychic resource for high-grade energy and guidance. By sharing their wisdom and learning their arts, each of us can pursue our version of a deeper excellence and minimize the chances of having our success turn on us.

CHAPTER 2

The Hidden Assets of the Shadow: Mining for Gold

I N A 1991 *TIME* ESSAY about Senator Edward Kennedy, writer Lance Morrow referred to the "shadow that hovers over Kennedy's life," a "dark presence" that has changed the course of contemporary American history.

It is easy to grasp the idea of Ted Kennedy and his celebrated family being dogged by a kind of shadow. The image is almost unavoidable. Here is a family that lived mythic success, was at the pinnacle of wealth, power, and celebrity, and which had risen from an immigrant background to the highest offices in the land. Yet President John Kennedy has been pursued by a shadow far beyond the grave, in a seemingly endless parade of revisionist exposés of his private life. Brother Robert Kennedy's life was cut short while he was at the top. And Ted's career stalled in the Senate as scandals piled up one after the other.

The shining image that the Kennedys presented—that patriarch Joe and matriarch Rose apparently were determined to present—did not allow for human weakness or failure. Nor does the perfect image that we demand of our high-profile public servants. Ted Kennedy clearly has his weaknesses. But the pressure on him to keep his failings hidden is greater than most of us have to bear, because the fate of his clan has been mythically identified with that of the nation.

As Morrow points out, however, "The only shadow that he is responsible for . . . is the one inside himself." We cannot know everything that lies buried in Ted Kennedy's shadow, but we know a lot about how shadows work. We know, for example, that when character weaknesses or traits that we have been taught to view as undesirable, such as a quick temper or alcoholism, are kept in hiding for too long, they will almost surely break out sooner or later in behavior that is at odds with our public image. The Kennedy shadow, or parts of it, is visible by now, thanks to the public's relentless fascination with America's royal family. But for decades Ted Kennedy struggled to keep his demons private—only to have them rise up and attack in unguarded moments, from the waters of Chappaquiddick or the sands of Palm Beach.

The paradox of success has its genesis in the shadow. Everything that comes with achievement—money, power, attention—tends to feed a shadow that obscures much of the true self. And when the shadow is stuffed too full, success and its benefits are imperiled. While highly prominent figures most dramatically illustrate the workings of the shadow, anyone who has enjoyed even modest success is vulnerable to this phenomenon.

I have already spoken about how successful people can come to feel dissatisfied, trapped, burned out, or arrogant and isolated; how their strengths can gradually turn into handicaps; and how they can eventually self-destruct. I've described some of the ways we can recognize shadows operating in our lives and growing in power. I have suggested that the shadow's defining principle is secrecy, covering up what we don't want ourselves and others to see.

In psychology, the idea of the shadow has been described by various thinkers, beginning with Carl Jung, who wrote, "Everyone carries a shadow, and the less it is embodied in the individual's conscious life, the blacker and denser it is. At all counts, it forms an unconscious snag, thwarting our most well-meant intentions." Every life is affected by the shadow to some extent, but I've found it an especially useful way to look at what happens to high achievers who falter or get lost in success. We need not go into therapy or become Jungian scholars to understand more about the shadow and how it operates—and anyone who is serious about becoming a success sustainer will benefit from such understanding.

As we learn how forces arising from the shadow can work against us, threatening what we have achieved, we also will see how they can help us in our search for the kind of success we can live with over a lifetime. Jung called the shadow "pure gold" for good reason, for in it lie hidden the passions and gifts that are the raw materials of personal growth.

WHAT GOES INTO THE SHADOW

The shadow is our hidden self, the aspects of our personality that we don't like to acknowledge or that we have been discouraged from showing. It is part of what makes us human. In an anthology of writing on this subject, *Meeting the Shadow*, editors Connie Zweig and Jeremiah Abrams note that the shadow goes by many names.★ It is known as "the disowned self, the lower self, the dark twin or brother in bible and myth, the double, repressed self, alter ego, id." Jung first used the term "shadow side of the psyche" around 1912, in further developing Freud's ideas about the "repressed" sides of people.

It is a natural human tendency to dwell on our virtues—intelligence, perseverance, kindness—and avoid seeing their opposites in our character. We know these darker elements are present—our capacity for cruelty, laziness, greed, or cowardice—but we'd rather keep them out of sight, down below our surface awareness. So the chief characteristic of shadow contents is that they are part of our unconscious, that

★ The following discussion draws heavily on *Meeting the Shadow*, and many of the sources cited here are found there.

vast collection of experiences, emotions, and drives that is not available to us in conscious awareness.

What resides in the unconscious, however, still has great power in our life. Our unconscious drives and feelings account for much of what Jungian analyst Marie-Louise von Franz calls "the real biography of the human being."

We begin putting parts of ourselves in the shadow very early, and its contents accumulate over an entire lifetime. When a small child exhibits wildness or unconstrained emotions (especially "negative" expressions of anger or fear), adults ask the child to put away such behavior or feelings. After a while, children learn to repress those authentic but socially unacceptable parts of themselves without prompting. As the poet Robert Bly expresses it, everything that our parents, our teachers, and later our peers disapprove of, we put into "the long bag we drag behind us."

In the process of growing up, we hide many things in the shadow to avoid suffering, ridicule, or shame: dreams that others disparage, truthful perceptions they would rather not hear, fantastic ideas and grand aspirations, all get shoved into the shadow. I can recall a small child who had just seen the movie *Mary Poppins*, standing at the curb, umbrella in hand, getting ready to fly. Naturally her siblings and her dad (me) teased her for such foolishness, shaming her fantasy of flight and in some way curtailing both her imagination and her joy in life.

By the time we reach "well-adjusted" adulthood, we have formed a public persona that is acceptable to the world and to family and friends. The wild side generally has vanished, except in the case of social outlaws and many artists (both of whom fascinate the rest of us for similar reasons). Dreams and fantasies are not revealed to teachers, who look for performance in line with prescribed curricula, or to employers, who demand sober, reliable employees. But these rich, emotional parts of us—in some ways our most authentically personal qualities—don't disappear. They are just stashed away in the shadow and they occasionally rise up to surprise us.

The shadow contains much more than our "negative" traits such as anger or jealousy. What we put into the shadow is directly related to who we are and the values held by our family and culture. Thus in some cultures weeping in public goes into the shadow, and in others, sexual feelings or their expression. Conversely, our shadow may contain qualities that society usually regards as positive, but we see as inferior or unworthy. Often this happens with traits that are thought of as gender-linked: women traditionally have been taught to hide the same competitiveness or urge for power that is encouraged in males, and men to devalue the nurturing qualities prized in females.

Today, healthy sexuality is starting to be seen as a positive trait, but until recently sexuality was one of the first things children were made to put in the shadow. In many societies, artistic, creative impulses, too, are consigned to the shadow, not considered useful parts of the well-adjusted personality.

Our shadow is already well formed by the time we leave our teens, and the powerful lessons of childhood stay with us all our life. However, we continue adding to the shadow as adults. Jung came to believe that our current actions are at least as important as early influences. So whenever we shy away from dealing with a difficult personal situation, ignore some warning signal in our business, or adamantly deny expression to some deep-seated urge, we are adding fuel to the shadow.

How we live our adult lives can change the shape and content of our shadow for better and for worse—an important and hopeful thought for anyone who fears being irrevocably handicapped by his or her early programming. It is a simple, observable fact that people who open up and confront their shadows, whether in therapy or by other means, are doing their psychic health a great favor.

Up to this point we have been mainly referring to the *personal shadow*, but looking further we can also identify different kinds of *group shadows*: the family shadow, the collective or cultural shadow, and the organizational or corporate shadow.

The family shadow contains shared secrets and denied emotions that powerfully affect family dynamics; any family that colludes to cover up secrets such as alcoholism, incest, or a history of mental problems is carrying a heavy shadow. Collective and cultural shadows are the repositories of fear, hatred, and misunderstanding on a mass level. Typically this results in other groups being made into enemies or scapegoats: racism, the Third Reich, and the Cold War are all manifestations of the collective shadow.

MEET THE SHADOW

Since the shadow is by nature concealed, we most often are not aware of being under its influence. Yet there are many times when it intrudes on our daily life, and we can discover much about ourselves by learning to notice when this happens.

There are the times when our conscious guard is down, in sleep or daydreaming states. Dreams are messages from the unconscious, though their meaning can be hard to interpret. Waking fantasies often contain more explicit information from the shadow. As you drive on the freeway, ride the train, or doze during a boring meeting, you may be startled by thoughts that seem to bubble up from nowhere. That guy in the next car: doesn't he look like Charles Manson? The train derails, and you rescue the women across the aisle. . . .

The shadow often is humorous, appearing in jokes that play on social taboos, sex, our hidden fears of others, or in the delight that the misfortunes of others brings us. What strikes us as funny can tell us a lot about what's in our shadow. Our moods, too, can reflect the influence of our shadow. Depression can be seen as a close encounter with our dark side, and as such it can offer useful information to us. Too often, though, we try to mask or blunt the edge of despair with overwork, distractions, or substances that act on us physically, including food.

We can also uncover elements of our personal shadow in the

feedback we get from others. This is hard to do, especially when the feedback is negative; we try to convey only a positive image of ourselves and resist admitting that our shadow side may be showing through. We may even be amazed that some-one perceives us as being arrogant or distant, because it is not what we intended. To test the validity of the feedback we are getting, therapists advise soliciting more than one opinion.

Our slips of the tongue and social gaffes are another way the shadow appears in daily life. When we "accidentally" insult someone whom we mean to compliment, some suppressed feeling is usually speaking from the shadow. Or when we do something whacky, which is as surprising to us as it is to those who know us—like missing an appointment. Also in this category is "misperceived behavior." This is when we convey an impression other than what we intended: a speaker may intend to present herself quite congenially to her audience, only to be informed after her presentation that she came across very sarcastically.

In addition to daily brushes with the shadow, major life crises are almost always responses to shadow forces. Quitting or getting fired (except in the case of "downsizing" or layoffs), a financial catastrophe, the breakup of a long-standing mar-riage or relationship, the predictable midlife crisis—in all these situations, something in our shadow can no longer be kept in hiding, and its eruption buckles the smooth surface of our life. Or the crisis may be a product of our shadow interacting with that of our spouse or boss.

THE MAGIC ARROW OF PROJECTION

Because we are reluctant to see and acknowledge what is in our shadow—especially the negative traits we despise and fear—they emerge most often in our relationships with others. *Projection* is the primary mechanism by which the shadow oper-ates, and it is crucial to understanding how the shadow guides our lives. We "project" when we notice and react to some trait in another person that is really an unrecognized part of ourselves. Marie-Louise von Franz came up with the vivid image of a projection as a "magic arrow" that finds its target somewhere outside ourselves.

Projections can be negative or positive. Negative projection involves some undesirable aspect of our personality that catches our attention in someone else. To understand what is in our shadow, we should take careful note of qualities in others that evoke strong reactions in us. For example, a consultant named Carol found that in her interaction with a particular client, she would become infuriated by his slowness at grasping her points. Her reaction seemed out of scale to any real difficulty this caused—until she realized how highly she prized quickness and feared being accused of being slow herself.

As a way to identify the qualities we are most likely to project onto others, therapist and author William Miller suggests listing "all the qualities we do not like in other people: for instance, conceit, short temper, selfishness, bad manners, greed, and others. When the list is finally complete (and it will probably be quite lengthy), we must extract those that we not only dislike . . . but hate, loathe, and despise. This shorter final list will be a fairly accurate picture of our personal shadow."

The tipoff to knowing when we are projecting is the strength of our reaction. If our response is exaggerated, our perception of the other person carries a powerful emotional charge. Our projections usually have some basis in the reality of the other person; he or she may indeed have the quality of arrogance or insensitivity we perceive, and this makes it even harder to sort out how much of the reaction is coming from inside us.

The greatest danger of projection is that it blurs our view of the other person. Even if he does happen to possess the trait we project, our refusal to see that quality in ourself causes a kind of blindness that "interferes with our capacity to see objectively and relate humanly," according to analyst Edward C. Whitmont. We cannot distinguish the reality of the other person in the confusing darkness of our own shadow.

Transferring blame, or scapegoating, is perhaps the most common form of projection. It happens when one spouse accuses the other of indifference because he or she can't admit having lost interest in the marriage. It happens when we curse the driver in front of us, instead of our own lack of planning, for making us late. It happens when a racial group attributes its poverty to immigrants. In business, it happens when partners blame each other for failures or when a manager can't see past the personal, shadow-based antipathy for employees to make effective use of their talents. Or when leaders complain, "This group just can't get going," when they are secretly afraid that they are losing their edge.

Successful people often suffer the effects of other people's projections, as when employees resent a supervisor because they have put their own ambition or power needs into their shadow. The successful may be pigeonholed as the "lucky ones" and deprived of true humanity.

In *A Little Book on the Human Shadow*, Robert Bly talks of a time in his life when he projected certain shadow qualities—his own "stiffness" or need for tight control—onto business-men as a group. He even wrote a series of poems called *Poems for the Ascension of J. P. Morgan*, part of which went like this:

> *. . . now the darkness is falling*
> *In which we sleep and awake—a darkness in which*
> *Thieves shudder, and the insane have a hunger for snow,*
> *In which bankers dream of being buried by black stones,*
> *And businessmen fall on their knees in the dungeons of sleep.*

Later, he says, he became suspicious of his own motives in singling out bankers and businessmen. If he were to rewrite those lines acknowledging what was in his own shadow, they would read:

> *. . . In which good planners dream of being buried by black stones,*
> *And men with stiff faces like me fall on their knees in the dungeons of sleep.*

Through his art, he was able to look into his shadow projections and take ownership of what was there.

Projection is not in itself a bad thing, Bly reminds us. There are positive projections, in which we are attracted to people because they demonstrate qualities hidden in our shadow. The socially timid person feels drawn to someone who is at ease in any situation; the high-flying creative type sends her projection arrow into someone who seems grounded and stable. Projection is a necessary step in making a connection with the world, often the only way we can get our shadow sides out where they can be seen. But we have to take the next step of making the effort to see them and admitting we own them. "Recalling" the projection back to ourselves is not easy and takes courage—yet it is essential to our personal development, to understanding the traps we set for ourselves.

HOW SUCCESS FEEDS THE DARK SIDE

We can propose a law of the psyche—the more visible the person, the more likely she or he is to carry a big shadow. The combination of wealth, power, and celebrity is the most fertile ground for the mythic shadow to operate in, an atmosphere that promotes denial and self-inflation and can make us the target of projections. We are all familiar with this in politics, where absolute power corrupts absolutely; we see it in the tabloid follies of entertainers, sports figures, business moguls, and other People-with-a-capital-P.

To be psychically healthy—to know ourselves fully, to enjoy meaningful relationships, to feel ourselves members of the human community—we must acknowledge and come to terms with our imperfections. But being in a position of success works against such self-knowledge. Leaders are constantly bombarded with messages that they should show no signs of weakness or impropriety. When victims of success explode in the media, the public crucifies them as traitors to the image of how winners should behave. They, of all people, shouldn't need to resort to philandering, substance abuse, or unbridled greed—give me that money and power; *I* wouldn't make those mistakes!

Nowhere more than in politics is the pressure so great to present a cheerful, well-scrubbed image to the world, so it isn't surprising that political leaders regularly disappoint us. Jung accurately describes the temptation faced by someone in public life "to jump over his own shadow in order to hurl himself avidly on some idealistic program that offers him a welcome alibi. How much respectability and apparent moral-ity is there, cloaking in deceptive colors a very different inner world of darkness?"

But fame is only the most obvious stage on which the shadow performs. Anyone who attains worldly success and some visibility will have a strong partner in the shadow. The hidden contents of people's shadows often prod them to excel. Fears born of childhood poverty may feed a fierce determina-tion to be financially secure; the child who was mocked for being "different" resolves to attain a position safe from scorn. Generations of Americans were brought up on the story of Charles Atlas, the original skinny kid who got sand kicked in his face and went on to found a bodybuilding empire.

In general, successful people possess gifts of intelligence, organization, wit, or charisma that enable them to attract, inspire and manage others and produce results. They have used their strengths well, thus forging a strong ego. This positive self-image, while a great advantage, also means that few nega-tive thoughts are allowed close to the surface: feelings of lazi-ness, indifference, rage, or envy.

The process of attaining success also usually involves over-coming our weaknesses, an achievement of which we can rightfully be proud. But those weaknesses—shyness or lack of social graces or bad health—may also be ruthlessly denied, and our overcompensation measures come back to haunt us.

Usually, too, the energies of successful people in business have been tightly channeled. Most high achievers have climbed the ladder because they were good at following the dicta of family and society, doing things the way their parents, teachers, and employers thought they should be done. If such a person had a longing to become a teacher, a ballplayer, or a poet, but these goals were not encouraged, the frustrated desire would surely end up in the shadow.

Both attaining success and guarding it raise the ante for keeping our personal shadow hidden. We want to maintain a positive image at all costs, to say "It's okay," when it really isn't.

It is wishful thinking to believe that negative emotions, and whatever else is in your shadow, can be willed away. What success-purveyors are really saying is "pretend they're not there." This can work—up to a point. Putting things in the shadow is a necessary part of human development and socialization; only criminals and other social outcasts normally wear their shadows on the outside: working from your strengths is the best way to get where you want to go.

But denying your dark side, or imagining that you can do away with it, poses hazards to your psychic health.

How One Man Met His Shadow

My first call from Harlan, the CEO of a fast-growing Silicon Valley company, revealed his ambivalence about the need to talk at all. Suggesting no hint of urgency, he said that he wanted to talk over some "personnel issues" and "new corporate directions." But then he added, "I've got to meet you within the next two days."

He began our meeting by saying that his call had been prompted by a highly confrontational exit interview with a key corporate officer named Bob. It turned out that Bob was the third "star" to quit that year and that Bob, during a heated exchange, had urged him to call me. Although he expressed concern over losing the company's next generation of leaders, Harlan's face was impassive as he began speaking, his tone as bland as my breakfast oatmeal. Describing the interview, Harlan said, "Bob had this big offer waved at him, not for the first time. When he came to tell me, I assumed that he wanted me to match it, so I said I would. And that set him off. He got mad as hell and said something like, 'You don't get it. When Marilyn and Charlie left, you did the same thing. It's not the damn money.' Before I could respond, he leveled me again. He said they had all joined the company because of me, but I had changed—and not for the better."

By the end of this story, Harlan's hand holding his cup of coffee was shaking in anger. His voice had risen, but his face was sad, disappointed, confused. Then he changed the subject, asking me to interview his top people and review the strategic plan. I instead suggested that we meet again to determine what he really needed, and he went along.

Toward the end of our second meeting, the shadows began to part a little, revealing a few secrets. Apparently Harlan's success was in large part due to his knack for picking exceptional people and building strong, aggressive teams. His firm was known for marketing smarts and solid service that held customer loyalty. In recent years, however, competition and price cutting had eroded profits. Harlan admitted that he was running scared, and had changed from being a patient coach to an irritable boss, second-guessing and blaming the talented people he had hired. He was pushing them harder, and some had complained that their personal lives were "limited" or "messy," and the work less satisfying.

He had driven himself harder too, claiming nothing was wrong that a few new customers wouldn't fix. The stress had invaded his home life; he described it as "turbulent." He avoided the tensions at home by absenting himself through more work, traveling more to help the business.

Harlan's denial, his macho tendency to brush off bad news, had allowed the shadow to make trouble in his company and personal life. Trying to keep the problems under seal had only made them worse. Although Harlan was strong, wily, and

engaging, he was clearly losing ground. Bob's blunt asser-
tions, together with his caring attitude, had jarred Harlan into
seeing the futility of his current course.

Harlan recently sent me a poem about Sisyphus, the greedy
king doomed perpetually to roll a large stone up a hill in
Hades, only to have it roll down again. His accompanying
note talked about the unsettled but exciting feeling of learning
a new role and all of the false starts he was "enjoying." On the
business side, Bob ultimately decided to stay, taking over large
chunks of responsibility that Harlan has cautiously relin-
quished. On the personal side, Harlan is taking more time to
be alone and with his family. He also talks regularly with a
firm but supportive counselor.

As so often happens, Harlan's troubles stemmed from the
very traits that made him a winner. It was his talent for picking
good people, motivating them, and building effective teams
that made the company prosper. But this knack for motivating
turned into a compulsive pressure that led to resistance and
resentment.

Harlan's symptoms and reactions are shared by most of us
when we are under fire. It is practically a law, a psychological
first principle, that under stress, when behaviors that once
worked are failing us, we will reach for the wrong wrench to
fix our problems. Then we apply more torque, putting ourselves and those around us under ever greater strain.

THE FLIP SIDE OF THE COIN

Every positive, success-producing trait has its shadow side,
revealed under certain conditions. Just as every admirable human quality can be used badly, the gifts and habits of mind that
lead to achievement can become counterproductive. When we
keep problems and inconvenient desires in the shadow, when
our goals remain too narrowly focused for too long, when the
rarefied air of winning seems to set us apart from ordinary
mortals, our natural gifts may be exhausted or perverted. Even

the strong, healthy ego can become overinflated, leading to personal or organizational disasters if not diagnosed and checked early enough.

Examining these success traits and their flip sides illustrates the paradox of success in detail. Here is a quick reference list. We will look at some of them more closely.

Confidence	Sense of infallibility
Quickness	Overhastiness
Sharp wit	Abrasiveness
Alertness	Narrow focus
Dedication	Workaholism
Control	Inflexibility
Courage	Foolhardiness
Perseverance	Resistance to change
Charm	Manipulation
Thriftiness	False economy
Commitment	Blind faith

For example, success demands *confidence*. A positive self-image is an immeasurable asset, but even a normally healthy ego can easily become inflated on a diet of mythic success. If all we hear are messages of praise and flattery, the swollen ego comes to need ever more applause, more good news, and shuts out any hint of things that may be wrong. If we become convinced that we have nothing more to learn, errors that could provide valuable lessons are ignored or covered up instead. So confidence gradually turns into a dangerous *sense of infallibility*. (Think of the leaders of America's auto industry dismissing those "funny little cars" from Germany and Japan.)

Robert, a middle-aged Chicago neurosurgeon, was lured into this trap by his success with a new procedure for removing calcium deposits that affect nerve endings. Problems had cropped up in a couple of cases, but he dismissed them as aberrant and didn't slow down to investigate them. He performed the procedure as often as possible to perfect his technique, and finally made a major mistake that resulted in permanent paralysis to the left side of a young woman's face. Still he failed to see that his overconfidence was responsible; his reaction remained mainly one of concern for his own career. When later told of her depression, he responded, "*She's* depressed! Imagine how *I* feel!"

Success is aided by *speed*—an admirable quickness of mind, the sense of urgency that spurs productivity. But when we press too hard, speed can blur into a *blind rush*. Quick thinking and snap decision-making can degenerate into a tendency to deal with superficial, short-term issues and ignore deeper, long-range concerns.

A closely related trait is *sharpness of wit*, which in its shadow version comes out as *abrasiveness*, cutting like a razor's edge. Adam, at forty a partner in a large Los Angeles accounting firm, had the gifts of high-speed mental processing and verbal agility, which hastened his rise to a partnership. Problems became apparent, though, when several assistants quit after being lacerated by his angry and often demeaning wit. On being warned by the managing partner, Adam grew cautious at work but even more biting at home. Only after his twelve-year-old son ran away did he finally seek help. His son told Adam in the therapist's office that he had run away to avoid "the dragon's mouth."

Success requires *alertness*—the capacity to scan widely, to spot both opportunities and trouble from a distance. But full-spectrum alertness can gradually degenerate into a *narrow focus* on what looks good at the moment. This is encouraged by opportunities that promise quick profit, and by the filtering of information as it ascends the corporate pyramid. To truly serve success, alertness must operate on a broad band, picking up danger signals as well as attractive ones.

Helen worked her way up through residential and commercial real estate sales and then turned to development. Alert to good locations, she first built small apartment units, which filled quickly. But, flushed with success and urged on by an optimistic lender, she began to put up bigger and more highly leveraged projects. Although still alert to opportunities, she grew blind to increasing market softness; the information she needed to exercise restraint was discarded in her denial of changing circumstances. Her last four projects went sour.

Success calls for *dedication*—sacrifices of leisure time, recreation, energy for family and friends. Such sacrifices are understood to be temporary; one day there will be enough success to pay loved ones back, get back into shape, devote time to a cherished activity. But an appropriate level of dedication can easily be subverted into *workaholism*, leaving you hopelessly stuck in a quagmire of obligations, compulsions, and prideful stubbornness.

Lloyd, at thirty-five the branch manager of a building-materials company, had the right stuff: a strong Midwestern work ethic, boundless energy, and controlled ambition. Early in his career he had a mentor who provided a model of a life in balance. But after the older man died, Lloyd's hitherto contained ambition and dedication went amok. His work days and weeks spilled over into his personal life. Sundays became golf days with important clients. Not until his wife filed for divorce (and his own parents sided with her) did he grasp how seriously out of kilter his life had become.

Typically, successful people value *control*—over both externals and themselves. Hands-on management, decisiveness, attention to detail, and a comprehensive understanding of one's business are all useful tools with which to build success. Yet the drive to maintain success can turn control into *inflexibility*, a compulsive grip that chokes off initiative and adaptation. In large organizations, sound principles of uniformity and risk management can turn into mindless regulations filling massive policy manuals.

Even entrepreneurs with small firms can become control freaks. Nadine, the thirty-five-year-old owner of a small, highly profitable clothing chain, had a reputation for excellent customer service and minding the store. She set up computerized inventory controls to track where every garment was located at any moment. Problems began to surface, however, when her printouts didn't match the physical inventory. Committed to the software, she refused to believe her employees' counts and began checking on certain people she thought might be stealing, installed expensive video monitoring equipment, and challenged employees to "come clean." Morale plummeted and good salespeople left, their customers not far behind.

Success needs *courage* for risk-taking—the willingness to buck conventional wisdom and trust your instincts. But when the shadow takes over—when we feel invulnerable or compelled to act out some hidden impulse, or are no longer truly challenged—it can drive courage over the brink into *foolhardiness*. In certain contexts, the all-out last run down an icy ski slope, for instance, recklessness can be a calculated risk that imperils only the daredevil. But elsewhere, heedless risk-taking can be catastrophic.

A sixty-two-year-old bond dealer, aptly named Sterling, persuaded his friends to form a partnership to buy so-called high-grade junk bonds. He called it his retirement plan. But in his rush to sell the concept, he played fast and loose with the offering statements and sales pitches. Although there were no overt legal errors or omissions, the deal tap-danced near the edge of ethics. When the bonds' value dropped, the limited partners asked him to cut his fees. He refused, precipitating a suit for fraud, and may end up losing much more than his fees.

Other success traits and their paradoxical sides include *perseverance*, which can pull one through adversity but also harden into a rigid *resistance to change; charm*, so easily sliding into *manipulation; thriftiness* that becomes *false economy*; and *commitment* to a personal vision, which sometimes leads into a dead end of *blind faith*.

Examine your own strengths. List those qualities you feel have been most responsible for your success and then ask yourself what their shadow side is or might become. You might look at key people on your staff in the same way (and probably find out some things about your own projections in the process). Or suggest that they try this self-test themselves, perhaps in the context of a corporate retreat.

THE ORGANIZATIONAL SHADOW

When I consult with a company or organization, I often interview each director or member of the leadership team in private. I ask them, under a promise of confidentiality, to tell me what they think are the company's biggest secrets. Sometimes it takes a little coaxing, but some startling information usually emerges—things people would never dare say out loud in a group setting. Then I meet with the whole board and play back what seemed to me the most significant of these secrets, without attribution.

The effect is remarkable: a wave of nervous relief seems to sweep over the group, and each point becomes a springboard for fruitful discussion. Even if they had ostensibly wanted to consult about more superficial issues, such as marketplace strategy or management turnover, this technique of cutting straight to the core issues—shadow issues—saves time and provides unexpected insights.

Just as individuals have their personal shadows which rarely come to light, every group of individuals—whether a government bureau, a nonprofit organization, or a corporation— develops a collective shadow. This is inevitable, since organizations are only gatherings of human beings, yet in some ways group shadows are more elusive than private ones. We may admit that as individuals we have flaws and secrets, but a group can be seen as depersonalized, abstract, neutral, and thus somehow immune to shadows. This is probably one reason why we like to belong to groups: they provide an illusion of safety. Identifying with a larger entity shifts the burden of responsibility. If things are not going well, another group—the competition—can be blamed. But despite denial, the shadows are still there. Each member of the group brings his or her own, and, merged, they form a sort of synergistic shadow that can be very powerful—especially since it's easier to deny a group shadow than a personal one. The group shadow embraces a variety of secrets, taboos, unquestioned assumptions, and unbalanced values. If these are not dragged into the light for scrutiny on a regular basis, they can turn highly toxic.

Organizational secrets are usually the closely guarded property of a few, "the bosses." This generates fear, uncertainty, resentment, and loss of a sense of power and self-esteem among the remaining staff. Often such corporate secrets have to do with how well the company is really doing, as opposed to the smiling face it shows to the world. When employees know from firsthand observation that all is not as rosy as the higher-ups are painting it, the effect is similar to a dysfunctional family with an alcoholic parent: the "children" lose faith in their own ability to perceive reality. While this is not as devastating to a group of adults as it is to children, trust certainly suffers, and people's belief in their own ability to get the job done falters.

Taboos are an organization's deepest, darkest secrets—unwritten laws that are never discussed even among the top people. Sex among co-workers is often a taboo subject, as is the existence of special privileges reserved for the powerful or evidence of wrongdoing by a leader.

For example, in one family-run company I worked with, the founder had expropriated (stolen, that is) some government land, which became the cornerstone of the firm's wealth. No one ever mentioned this detail of corporate history. The heirs who now ran the company were constantly applying a white-wash of legitimacy to conceal the corruption, but doubt and guilt lingered and surfaced from time to time: in an intrafamily lawsuit, one sibling accused another of being "no better than Grandfather."

An organization that does not communicate well is usually full of unquestioned assumptions that may be in conflict with its actual goals. In conducting a consultation with a company proud of its leadership program, I learned that only six of thirty people interviewed understood the firm's much-touted current mission statement and only ten could even recall the goals of the next year's plan. The self-inflation of top managers was leading them to spend more energy seeking approbation from their business peers than keeping in touch with their own people. The organizational shadow was filled with denial about the effectiveness of their communication.

Unbalanced values characterize a company that views and treats its employees as something less than complete human beings and subtly encourages a style of behavior that is in conflict with publicly stated positions. Perhaps the most common shadow of this kind is seen in enterprises that promote an aggressively competitive "masculine" style, driving its employees' more creative and nurturing instincts into the shadow. We can recognize such places by the kind of language used there, largely derived from warfare and sports. In his book *Liar's Poker*, ex–bond trader Michael Lewis described the atmosphere at Salomon Brothers as one in which competition was encouraged to run amuck, reflected in abusive language. He quotes a Wall Street analyst as saying, "The best producers are cutthroat, competitive, and often neurotic and paranoid. You turn these people into managers and they go after one another. . . . That is why there are cycles on Wall Street . . . because the ruthless people are bad for the business but can only be washed out by proven failure."

My task as a consultant is to air out organizational shadows before they create a big smell. In this effort, no subject can be off-limits, though it is important to make no individual vulnerable in revealing secrets. Confidentiality is critical to getting the maximum information on the table—the point is not to focus on anyone's private shadow but rather to get at the unspoken consensus. A well-disguised actual case demonstrates many issues that typically emerge.

SECRETS, INC.

Atoz Conglomerate, a high-tech and communications services firm, had just completed a three-year downsizing plan, which disgruntled employees described as "shrink till it clinks." Six divisions had been sold or cannibalized (management's own word). Sales were up in eight remaining divisions, down in two; profitability was up but the stock price hovered at near book level. Morale was low all around, not surprising under the circumstances. The president and chairman, both brought in to manage the downsizing, were relatively new to the scene, and Atoz's policy-making groups—its board and executive council—were split between old-timers and new blood.

My consulting brief was fairly broad and vague: look into the morale problems and the lack of unity on board and council; dig up clues as to why the downsizing hadn't resulted in the expected jump in stock value; come up with ideas for an action plan.

I started with the president, Brad. A tall, affable, hawk-faced man of fifty-two with a great shock of white hair, he looked genetically selected for a leader's role. I'd been a bit surprised that my opening interview wasn't with both him and the chairman, Sydney; I'd put it down to scheduling problems, but that wasn't the case. I had also assumed they made a good team: bad assumption. Within the first fifteen minutes, I learned that Brad had never been given enough power to "really shape things up," and that Sydney "was not a power sharer." My attempt to probe the relationship more deeply brought up selected facts but no feelings.

One of the facts was that Sydney had been elected chairman only weeks before Brad's hiring. In my first conversation with Sydney, this came up right away. "Brad and I came in about the same time, and though technically I hired him, it was a done deal. He has never been my man." When I asked diffidently whether this had been a source of any stress or confusion, Sydney shoved deeper into his mammoth black-calfskin chair and denied it: "Not really."

From his bulging portfolio of secrets, Sydney carefully offered a few. The directors apparently didn't know each other well, and Sydney liked it that way. Earlier there had been a power bloc, a "gang of six" that he viewed as having retarded progress. The remaining older directors and senior officers had never reached out to him; they were "friendly but distant." Brad, however, worked closely and even socialized with the division heads. Sydney was worried that the board's leash was too short on financial matters; its finance committee operated in a constant spirit of impatience about lagging earnings and stock prices. His reaction to the work of previous consultants was negative; he used the words "a bunch of overpaid young eggheads."

A good deal of nuts-and-bolts work already had been accomplished by the earlier consultants; I had their statistics to draw on. It was agreed that, after my team finished interviewing and analyzing, we would present our findings in an oral presentation and brief written reports (neither Brad nor Sydney wanted to wade through long reports). I told them I would look for stress points and critical unresolved dilemmas at Atoz, try to identify any serious blocks to communications and planning. Part of my agenda was to uncover the company's deepest, most draining secrets. If I start out speaking in terms of secrets and shadows, I find that people clam up and defeat the process. But when the secrets they collectively reveal are fed back to them, they experience great relief and new energy enters the discussions.

We began mapping the shadow territory by conferring with the past consultants, specialists who had provided formulas and decision-making tools for the downsizing process. They explained, however, that their techniques had been used by

Atoz management to make decisions that were abruptly announced, top-down, cold. This had resulted in fear, distrust,
defections, second-guessing, the formation of cabals, and elaborate survival games.

People opened up to us in the staff interviews. Some were
encouraged by our promises of anonymity and a blunt, honest
report; others figured it couldn't get worse. Survivors of the
downsizing described how people burned up time and energy
speculating, fantasizing, trading cheap overheated rumors and
bogus information. Within days we had the outlines roughed
in: a pattern of secrets and denial and rituals of shifting blame.

Our preliminary report presented the following general
conclusions:

1. Atoz Corp. was in a new business: rumors and secret-
   keeping, and it was draining energy, time, and talent.
2. Splits among leaders over future directions and time-
   tables were causing uneasiness and reluctance to take
   action among those below.
3. Blaming or scapegoating was a frequent method of addressing problems.
4. The company needed a clear new road map of where it
   was headed, agreed upon by leadership and communi-
   cated effectively to all 20,000 employees. This was reflected in the figures quoted earlier about few people
   knowing the company's mission statements and goals.

The oral report to the Executive Council was more specific
and shocking. Secret after secret was listed on easel pages, and
the most vexing dilemmas described. The room grew quiet,
and I asked if anyone challenged these findings. Aside from a
question about semantics, no one did. After a short break, we
began working on methods for resolving the dilemmas and
using the emerging resolutions as cornerstones in a new strategic plan. The emphasis would be on creating communications
links at all levels and keeping them open.

The energy level in the room began to climb; people got engaged in discussing these new prospects. Brad and Sydney had a short, sharp, out-in-the-open dispute, which I mediated. After assignments for various planning tasks were made, I turned the meeting over to Brad and Sydney, telling them that they had taken a big step in prying the lid off the shadow. Now, they must work hard to keep it off.

The lack of detail in this account may make the consultation seem glib or simplistic, but too much detail would obscure the general points that apply widely to organizational shadows. Also, this case represents a certain type of brief strategic consulting that works best when there is a deeply ingrained pattern of organizational secret-keeping. It is striking how often it has the same effect: initial shock and dismay, disorientation and pain, followed by a general feeling of relief and an influx of new energy.

SHADOW-SPOTTING IN ORGANIZATIONS

Here is a partial list of symptoms that leaders can use to analyze how the shadow operates in their own organizations:

- Certain topics are never discussed. Aspects of organizational life become taboo and employees are discouraged from asking questions about how things work.
- Information is a carefully guarded commodity, its flow blocked by rules and bureaucratic procedures. It is traded in power games. Rumors replace information; rumor brokers become powerful.
- Rituals serve to exclude rather than bring people together in activities such as eating, playing, and bestowing honors.
- Relationships are characterized largely by game-playing and elitist, sexist, racist, or ageist attitudes.
- "Politically correct" propaganda dominates the culture; dissent is uncomfortable or even painful. Some people possess "revealed truth" and others don't.

- Language is characterized by deliberate obfuscation, lazy or imprecise expression, or vulgarity, so it is less rich and useful; or it panders to short attention spans—the sound-bite style of communication.
- Leaders openly or covertly scrap for power and turf, waste time and energy in personal aggrandizement. Power is held tightly in the hands of a few instead of being shared downward and outward.
- Those who dare to call things as they see them are shunted off into backwaters, where they cannot damage the organization's image.
- Real dilemmas go unstated and unresolved, and un-acknowledged competing factions form on both sides. Decisions are made with heavy fists or chronically postponed; planning is reactive and diluted by politics, rather than proactive and courageous. The leadership arts of consensus-building and dilemma-resolving are not highly valued.
- Ethics and aesthetics are not protected and promoted as important institutional values. Matters of beauty, quality, appropriateness, scale, and social or environmental impact are treated with indifference or as mere afterthoughts to quarterly earnings. Ethics are very elastic, and people are treated as parts; leaders fail to set a clear and ethical tone in their words and conduct.

Once leaders learn to become more skilled at spotting and lighting shadows, the organization's regular processes of planning and evaluation can become occasions for teaching others how to be good shadow managers.

DISOWNING THE SHADOW

Our resistance to seeing shadows clearly, in ourselves or our organizations, is perfectly natural. They contain everything we believe that we are not supposed to be, or do. The means of disowning are many and varied, but these are among the most common:

• We disown the shadow when we deny or hide from the truth. Denial is a subtle activity for most of us. Only young children or the truly pathological deny willingly, in full awareness of the act, and feel fine doing it. Because of our conscience, most of us are uncomfortable denying if we are aware of the truth. If we persist, it can consume vast amounts of energy. Often, though, denial is simply a matter of failing to notice, a reflex of the mind that occurs whenever an unacceptable thought begins to intrude.

• We disown the shadow when we project our failings onto others. When we are not performing well, or feel threatened and insecure, it is natural to redirect those painful emotions, to blame a scapegoat. In modern society our scapegoats may be people from other cultures, the head of the organization, the competition, or "the government."

• We disown the shadow when we keep secrets and allow them to become embedded in the organizational or family culture. When I hear, "We don't have any secrets here," I know the opposite is true. There are always secrets, even in the most open and nurturing organizations. A key job of leadership is to create an environment where candid input is okay, indeed, highly valued. Many organizations can barely function because so much stress is built up and energy wasted by creating, swapping, and burying secrets.

• We disown the shadow when we dismiss deep-rooted problems as mere "communications failures"—one of countless euphemisms people resort to in trying to dress up bad news. "Spin doctors" are hired by politicians and corporations to whip out phrases that mask, diminish, or distract our attention from unpleasant realities. Good executives need and demand accurate information, delivered in clear and straightforward language. A telling contrast is presented, for example, between Johnson & Johnson's forthright handling of the

Tylenol poisoning crisis and Exxon's squirmy behavior after the *Valdez* oil spill.

The longer we persist in disowning the shadow, the darker it becomes and the more we fear to see what is in there. If we have never allowed ourselves to show anger, for example, when we do catch a glimpse of it in some situation, it scares us by how dangerous it feels.

Disowning the shadow doesn't make it go away. As Jungian analyst Edward Whitmont notes, "We merely relegate this energy to the unconscious, and from there it exerts its power in a negative, compulsive, projected form. Then our projections will transform our surrounding world into a setting which shows us our own faces, though we do not recognize them as our own. . . . We relate to the world not as it is but to the 'evil, wicked world' " that doesn't understand us or is hostile to us.

Sometimes we fear that by simply allowing ourselves to notice a shadow trait, it will possess us. Denying it seems safer. If we allow ourselves to express a fantasy of violence or lust, or of abandoning career and family to become a beachcomber, we may feel that we must act it out, inviting disaster. But as difficult as it is to confront and wrestle with shadow feelings, it is far more dangerous to ignore them, for then we may act them out in some way without understanding why.

Everything in our shadow is part of us and therefore worthy of our attention. As von Franz says, "The shadow is not necessarily always an opponent. In fact, he is exactly like any human being with whom one has to get along, sometimes by giving in, sometimes by resisting, sometimes by giving love— whatever the situation requires. The shadow becomes hostile only when he is ignored or misunderstood." This thought is echoed by Robert Bly, who says, "Every part of our personality that we do not love will become hostile to us."

The ultimate effect of burying pieces of ourselves in the

shadow is that, even if we become successful, we are using only a small part of ourselves—the part that is acceptable and adaptable to the needs of success. Sooner or later those needs will change, and the strengths we have banked on will no longer serve us.

GOLD IN DARK PLACES

I think that every successful person sooner or later feels cut off by the demands of success from some inner treasure—something inside that could provide fulfillment and make a unique contribution to the world, if only we could get at it. The place where we are likely to find this treasure is our shadow. That is why Jung said there was "gold" in the shadow, and why becoming better acquainted with ours is a necessary part of continuing to grow and evolve.

Jung's journeys into the dark, buried parts of his psyche persuaded him that investigating the shadow's contents is essential to personal development and adaptation: "The material brought to light from the unconscious had, almost literally, struck me dumb. I could neither understand it nor give it form—I knew that something great was happening to me—I knew that it would fill my life, and for the sake of that goal I was ready to take any kind of risk."

Later, he is a little more explicit, saying that the shadow "contains childish or primitive qualities which would . . . vitalize and embellish human existence, but convention forbids." British psychiatrist and author Anthony Storr contrasts Jung's view of the shadow with Freud's: "Freud thought of the unconscious as chiefly derived from repression: a kind of dungheap of the personally unacceptable. Jung thought that, while the unconscious certainly contained elements of personality which the individual might repudiate, it also contained the germs of new possibilities, the seeds of future, and possibly better, adaptation."

In *Meeting the Shadow*, Connie Zweig notes that "A right relationship with the shadow offers us a great gift: to lead us back to our buried potentials." She offers the following list of the benefits of "shadow-work," which can enable us to

- achieve a more genuine self-acceptance, based on a more complete knowledge of who we are;
- defuse the negative emotions that erupt unexpectedly in our lives;
- feel more free of the guilt and shame associated with our negative feelings and actions;
- recognize the projections that color our opinions of others;
- heal our relationships through a more honest self-examination and direct communication; and
- learn to use the creative imagination via dreams, drawing, writing, and rituals to integrate the disowned self.

The primal energy latent in the shadow is hard to access when we have been narrowly pursuing success all our lives. Our public image and need for control become a straitjacket that inhibits the spontaneous expression of joy and other emotions. Men especially have denied themselves play, tears, joyous, giddy laughter, and natural, loving sex. To avoid the pain of such denial, people may become addicted to work, drugs, or alcohol. Anne Wilson Shaef, author of *The Addictive Organization*, writes, "Love and nurturing are necessary for individuals to become fully functional. Addictive behavior is an effort to deny the painful reality of their absence."

We can recognize the energy of the shadow in the excitement that accompanies new learning and mastering fresh challenges. The most common complaint of successful people at a certain point in their lives is that the thrill has gone from what they are doing, and of course this applies to relationships as well.

We remember the early days of mastering a career field or learning to love someone, and we long to recapture that sense of expanding possibilities, but we cannot do so by continuing to depend on the strengths that brought us success. We must look inside to see what other gifts and longings are languishing in the shadow; only by giving them room to operate can we re-experience the surge of energy that makes our work a play-ground rather than a prison.

The idea of reclaiming our inner child is widely known today because of the widespread use of that concept in recovery groups and the books that have popularized the concept. This is an important part of shadow-work. Along with other childlike attributes, many of us have bottled up our playful and creative capacities in the shadow because we did not see them as helpful in the march toward success.

Finding the playful, anarchic child in the shadow enhances our prospects for creative thinking and problem-solving. Science-fiction writer Ray Bradbury credits his amazing productivity to his capacity for play. In their book *Science, Order, Creativity*, "serious" scientists David Bohm and F. David Peat note, "Thought is generally considered to be a sober and weighty business. But—creative play is an essential element in forming new hypotheses and ideas. Play, it appears, is the very essence of thought."

To be whole is the definition of health. Jung came to believe that adult development is a lifelong effort to integrate various aspects of the personality. When we deny parts of ourselves, we are not whole. Many people achieve worldly success at the sacrifice of wholeness, and everyone can benefit from doing a little archeological work in the shadow to discover aspects of self that might be usefully revived—a nurturer, a scholar, an artist, a performer?

Brought into the light and encouraged to grow, our hidden selves can balance the dominant side of our personality and re-energize our working lives by lighting new directions. The gold in the shadow has been discovered and mined by all long-distance winners.

THE GHOST TRAP

So the task of learning to acknowledge our shadows, even to love them, and eventually to use their power, is vital to personal growth and sustaining success. But it isn't easy. We are afraid of what we will find if we peer too closely into the dark side of our selves or our endeavors—some vast, generalized evil, perhaps, awaits us there. Our culture teaches us to think in terms of a single monolithic source of Good or Evil, whereas other cultures recognize a wide variety of demons specific to every situation and incorporate these images into daily life.

In a collection of remembrances of Jung, one writer recalls showing the great man a Tibetan ghost trap, of which there were a great variety made to contain specific ills. One of these traps, which greatly interested Jung, "was used to counteract the evil consequences of great success." It might help us to have such a talisman—a physical or a mental reminder that the contents of the shadow need not be overwhelming, but can be managed if kept out in plain sight and inspected often.

We will examine in the next chapter the more specific ways that shadows operate in working relationships and organizational life, and the consequences of letting this happen unconsciously and unchecked. Later, we'll see how some long-distance winners have learned the benefits of lighting their personal shadows, as well as principles and techniques that minimize the chance of shadows damaging the enterprises they lead.

CHAPTER 3

Money, Power, People, and Performance: The Rise of Hubris

I N THIS CHAPTER we will see how shadows function in the lives of successful people, especially in the workplace, and how our personal shadows interact with group shadows in business and professional life. We begin by identifying four key areas in which shadows thrive: *power, money, relationships,* and *performance.*

We all have issues that fall into the four categories stashed in the shadow. We might exercise to an excessive degree our need for power, or, conversely, rein it in—afraid to assert it because of negative conditioning. Money casts a broad shadow for many successful persons because it is deeply bound up with family dynamics and blinds outsiders to the wealthy person's unique identity. Working relationships, as we all know, are hardly the tidy, linear links pictured on organizational flow charts; instead, they are enriched and burdened with all the messy baggage of our personal shadows. Finally, performance covers how well we do and how much we take on at work; here we deal with drives from the shadow that cause some people to work themselves into breakdown.

The problems that grow in these shadowed areas will not cease to exist just because we know more about them.

Bringing them to light, however, is critical to keeping them manageable. The alternative is that we may act out of shadow motives without realizing it, leading to rampant ego inflation or *hubris*.

The idea of hubris—excessive pride or self-inflation—has deep roots. The myths and historical accounts of heroes who fell because they reached too high resonate through time. In Greek mythology, someone suffering from hubris aspired to be like the gods, an affront to those deities usually punishable by death. In classical Greek drama, hubris was the hero's fatal flaw.

The ascent into hubris can happen to any individual or organization. Even if people do not fall prey to full-blown hubris, if they deny shadows at work, they inhibit their ability to perform at their best, promote consistent avoidance of problems, and drain creative energy.

POWER NEEDS

Generally, successful people don't have much trouble expressing their power drives. The strong, healthy ego finds satisfaction in molding circumstances, in creating a new product or service, managing and directing the energies of a group, making an impact in a field or the larger society. Any process fueled by positive energy, whether in business, academics, or entertainment or public service, is an expression of basic human power needs; so is any worthy accomplishment.

But when the wielding of power itself becomes more important than its goal, something is speaking from the shadow. A disproportionate need for power may stem from a sense of helplessness in one's personal life, when we feel thwarted in a relationship. Some people who were made to feel powerless and extremely vulnerable in childhood overcompensate in their careers by getting caught up in power. Sometimes the perks of power are so seductive that they become the primary motivation for continuing to exercise it. But unlike the real nourishment of doing and producing, status and luxuries are like sugar or cocaine, leaving the consumer ever hungrier for more.

For many successful people, power needs hide in the shadow when the passion has gone out of what they are doing. This is often a natural and inevitable effect of doing the same thing for too long—clinging to a particular learning track long past mastery—especially if inner changes have begun to urge us in a different direction.

Often, too, leaders become indifferent because they are isolated from the real action, promoted past the opportunity to use their inherent skills. This is part of what happened to Calvin. Starting his career with a commitment to social causes that launched his rise, he eventually lost touch with the hands-on satisfactions of service and became engulfed by the external trappings of power.

Power and control needs are nearly synonymous; people seek power because they feel a need to control their own fate. A strong individual's need to control his or her own working life can result in products or services that stand out from the competition—the classic story of the successful entrepreneur. As long as that control remains focused on the needs of the business, it is healthy.

What often happens, however, is that control becomes the end rather than the means. If an entrepreneur becomes too closely identified with the product, for example, she may continue to refine and redesign the prototype, preventing the other functions from being performed well or creating tremendous scheduling pressures. The greatest challenge for successful entrepreneurs is knowing *when to let go*, not allowing justifiable pride in their accomplishments to become a stranglehold on growth—theirs and their organization's.

Manfred Kets de Vries, in a *Harvard Business Review* article titled "The Dark Side of Entrepreneurship," says that entrepreneurs typically have an exaggerated need for control. Some he has studied "have serious difficulty addressing issues of dominance and submission and are suspicious about authority." This characteristic is probably what leads them to strike out on their own; however, it can create problems in the evolving enterprise, especially if the business is acquired by a larger company: "Many of the entrepreneurs . . . are preoccupied with the threat of subjection to some external control or infringement on their will. When such people are suddenly placed in a subordinate position, power conflicts are inevitable."

De Vries also points out that "people who are overly concerned about being in control also have little tolerance of subordinates who think for themselves. In organizations, this can lead to extreme behavior; for instance, an owner-manager needing to be informed about even the most minute operation of the company."

While de Vries focuses on entrepreneurs, many of the shadow traits he observes could apply to executives functioning in larger companies, leaders in government, or other high achievers.

When power is exercised from the shadow, when it becomes important for its own sake, all problems are seen as power problems. In the graduate school I administer, I saw one manager transform a simple morale problem into a power struggle. When one of her people, who had had difficulty working with her, asked to be transferred to another department, the manager could see the request only as a threat. Instead of tracking down the source of the trouble, she became even more rigid and reliant on the "structure." The prospect of losing someone from her organizational chart made her act irrationally.

People whose power need lurks in the shadow often project it onto a stronger figure. This can sometimes result in a good working partnership, where one person latches onto a more powerful leader, performing loyal service and getting a sort of vicarious power fix in return. But it's a dangerous dynamic, for sooner or later everyone has a need to experience an authentic, individual sense of power. Kept under wraps too long, it can lead to apathy, avoidance, resentment, even betrayal.

Bruce Shackleton tells the following story in *Meeting the Shadow*: Harold, a middle-aged vice-president of finance in a small high-tech firm, had inherited a sense of inadequacy from his family, a classic case of low self-esteem.

> Harold's current boss, a hard-driving man, was often arrogant and insensitive, running the company with a bottom-line management style. To the CEO's aggressiveness, Harold responded with an accommodating and often anxious willingness to be subordinate. He had found a boss onto whom he could project his shadowy feelings of power, arrogance, and competence, and around whom he felt ill at ease and insecure, reinforcing his family's image of him.
>
> For a while it was a perfect fit. Harold put on a good front of getting the job done, but did nothing more. . . . But beneath this façade of roles, Harold was withholding his creative energy and enthusiasm, thereby avoiding any confrontation that might bring risk. . . . Soon the dam began to leak. Although he was generally an ethical and religious man, Harold began to resort to petty embezzlement and passive-aggressive behavior in an indirect effort to discharge his sense of anger, frustration, and belittlement.

The kind of symbiotic partnership in which one member contains the other's shadow qualities is all too common.

Teams that cannot reconcile the varying power needs of their members often come apart. A committee can waste valuable time or even fail in its mission if the extroverted power urge of one or a few is allowed to run rampant and disempower others. Or the work may be distorted into fruitless games by members who do not acknowledge their power needs.

How power shadows operate in the workplace is partly a reflection of how they operate in society. Most cases of political and racial repression, of conquest and colonization, are rooted in power needs. Jungian analyst Anthony Stevens calls power "the shadow problem of our time" (pointing out that another dangerous shadow issue, sexuality, has been better integrated into the personality since the work of Freud). The unconscious and debilitating exercise of power has become a "universal anxiety," compelling us to come to grips with it everywhere. The workplace is a good place to start. A key task of leadership is to monitor the overt, as well as the unconscious, distribution of power, and turn those needs toward healthy purposes.

MONEY TABOOS

The mother of a friend once said to him, "I'd rather you saw me sitting on the toilet than have you ask me about money." From such remarks, and more subtle signals by which parents convey discomfort with the subject, many of us learn early to put money in the shadow. There is a striking double standard where money is concerned: it's all right, indeed laudable, to get or have plenty of it, but talking about it is usually frowned on.

Money is a loaded topic in part because it's the most direct, visible, unambiguous symbol of mythic success; the easiest way to measure how far a person has come. When someone asks, "What's he worth?" they are hardly ever inquiring about the person's moral ledger or his value as a friend or a parent.

People who are most aware of the shadow side of money are those who have it in abundance. A wealthy friend told me, "Money is the great accentuator. If you are inclined to be brash, money will make you a boor. If you like power, it can make you a tyrant."

There have always been those who obsessively or crudely flaunt their wealth; in recent times we have marveled at Donald Trump's unabashed excesses and Ivan Boesky's proclamation that "Greed is okay." But they are the exception. Most wealthy and many moderately well-off people find it difficult even to be frank—much less boastful—about how much money they have. Often they are especially reticent with those most likely to be injured by deceit and mistrust: their own children.

John Levy, a skilled counselor to individuals and families on issues of inherited wealth, claims that this reluctance to talk openly about money is a cultural taboo—that is, a prohibition marked by an irrational intensity not justified by the reasons given for it. According to his research, these reasons include good taste ("It's just not done"), fear of manipulation by others ("It will give them power over me"), concern for their children's welfare ("If they know how much we've got, they'll never make anything of themselves"), embarrassment or shame ("I don't deserve to be so much better off than most people"), and fear of being judged on this basis ("All they can see is my money").

All these reasons can be used as a smokescreen to create distance from other people, to avoid the work of forging more meaningful friendships and associations, to mask parents' real aims for their children or fears that the kids are just waiting for them to die (a reminder of the shadow of mortality).

Ducking the issue by not talking about it is no solution. Silence on this topic is why many people grow up with the ingrained belief that it is verboten, that they cannot be trusted with information about money or with its management. This can be a handicap even for people who have done well in their careers, leading them to avoid financial negotiations, skim over important reports, leave money management to others.

Many women are still raised to believe that they are neither capable of managing money nor obliged to learn how. This is changing, but nonetheless a woman who is forced, especially on short notice, to be assertive in financial matters can experience a lot of anxiety and resentment based on early messages regarding her self-worth and competence. Widows with little or no money-management experience are still patronized by friends and advisers and often victimized. Money, especially vast sums, brings many shadows heavy with secrets, doubts about self-worth, and guilt.

WORKPLACE RELATIONSHIPS

We have all heard someone say, "It's just business" to characterize unethical actions in a sticky negotiation or a touchy personnel situation. We are fascinated by books that probe the backstage machinations of corporate takeovers because they rip off the "just business" mask to show us the shadows of powerful people running rampant.

In a *New York Times* article about the battle between Time Warner chairman Steve Ross and then-majority shareholder Herb Siegel, writer Deirdre Fanning notes: "Despite the size of the businesses and the egos involved, executive feuds tend not to be about money. Most are about more intangible issues: points of honor, integrity, loyalty and truthfulness. 'I think after a certain point, having made enough money, the markers become different,' said Dee Soder, a New York psychologist. 'Losing a million dollars isn't as important as if someone lies to them. Some of the most successful executives have the deepest-rooted insecurities.' "

Relationships are routinely tested in the workplace, since choices frequently arise in which self-advancement comes at someone else's expense. Most of us have faced some kind of ethical dilemma at work: for example, if a friend reveals information from a confidential talk with the boss about percentage wage increases, should you use that information in your own salary negotiations? What if in doing so you risk harming the friend? You might have chosen to deny the possibility of such harm, thereby feeding your shadow.

The shadow acts up when such interpersonal issues are not acknowledged, when it's "just business." The ruthless atmosphere of some working environments serves to further obscure the emotional needs and reactions going on beneath the surface: for someone who cannot admit to being hurt by a partner's defection or disloyalty, the only acceptable option may be revenge. People who have devoted most of their lives to survival and success in such environments often reach a point where the lack of personal relationships becomes painful. They simply have not developed the communications skills to sustain them.

One of the great dangers of success is the tendency to ignore or discount negative information about ourselves or our business. Real friendship—sharing the self that lies below the pleasant surface and trusting someone with sensitive information—becomes impossible. It's a too common scenario that, as the achiever rises, old friends are gradually dropped and only sycophants and bringers of good news are allowed in. As honest information needed to sustain success becomes scarce, the leader, who now gets only carefully filtered feedback, is operating in partial darkness, missing important signals that should be heeded.

Projection, shifting onto others the qualities we reject in ourselves, flourishes in the workplace. When you conceive an instinctive, irrational dislike for a colleague or simply cannot relate to your superior, projection is often at work. When it seems that a co-worker is unbearably impatient, stubborn, dense, or flippant, you are usually revealing something in your own shadow. Fortunately, many leaders can understand this and smooth out kinks in a working team or move people around if the issues can't be resolved.

Projection often appears in working life as scapegoating. During the struggle for control of Eastern Airlines, Frank Lorenzo and the unions found in each other perfect foils and repositories of guilt. So they joined in a corporate dance of death rather than analyze their own motives, mistakes, and culpability. White House chief of staff John Sununu tried to blame the press and other top Bush advisers for getting him into trouble on his transportation improprieties. In Sununu's view, "everybody's doing it to him," one source told *The Los Angeles Times*.

Projections attract as well as repel us in relation to others. As in the example of Harold, many of us are attracted to those who exercise power because their own power needs exist in the shadow. If you can recognize this projection, you may be able to take positive action rather than let the shadow poison your work.

Many effective working relationships and partnerships are based on the attraction of opposites. Daryl Sharp, in *Meeting the Shadow*, describes a friend whom he found infuriating. Sharp was organized, methodical, and punctual; Arnold was free-spirited, messy, and unstable. One morning Sharp flew into a rage when he found a pot boiled empty on the stove— until Arnold reminded him that it was Sharp who had cooked dinner the night before. This led Sharp to realize that they were "shadow brothers," secretly attracted by qualities in each other that they had repressed or not developed in themselves. As the friendship ripened, he noticed Arnold becoming tidier and himself loosening up.

Sex in the office is an area of dangerous shadow potential. Tinged with exploitation possibilities and shrouded in secrecy, office sex is usually governed by an unwritten taboo. There is far more awareness today of sexual harassment, but we haven't progressed very far toward a healthy acknowledgment of co-workers as sexual beings or a sensible set of ethics for dealing with harassment. To the extent that we learn to integrate sexuality into our personal lives, it should become less troublesome in the workplace.

PERFORMANCE ADDICTION

Perform well and you will be rewarded: we learn this as children, perhaps before learning to walk. A good part of our drive to succeed during adulthood originates in the expectations of our parents (or parent), expectations later reinforced by teachers, professors, employers, and by our work-oriented society.

But, as the growing literature devoted to stress and burnout shows, high performance has its shadow side. Workaholism is now seen as an addiction, a pattern of compulsive behavior—a good thing pushed to the point of abuse. There are a number of factors in our personal histories that can cause us to over-value productivity. Among them are the obligation to succeed taught to the children of impoverished immigrants and the fears transmitted by parents who were ruined during the Great Depression. You may have inherited a compulsive need to perform well in order to measure up to high-achieving parents or siblings, or from your parents, who want their children to take full advantage of opportunities denied to them.

Workaholism is deeply involved with our sense of respon-sibility: to our families, ourselves, the group we associate with, and in the case of leaders, the employees to whom they are examples. I have heard many harried executives say they would get out tomorrow if so many people weren't depending on them. Those who work to better society are especially prone to overextending themselves.

Whatever the source, a performance compulsion is not easy to control, because productivity is so highly valued and be-cause it truly can bring sweet rewards. But workaholism can eventually become the end rather than the means: sheer volume of output may substitute for creative quality; exhaustion numbs our dissatisfaction with performing a task that has lost its original excitement.

Workaholism also flourishes when the office or factory be-comes a refuge from other situations in which relationships and performance are less clearly defined. Many workplaces are surrogate homes for men and women who distance themselves from family or friends whom they can't cope with. In our increasingly mobile society, in which the role of the family is diminishing, the workplace can be a primary source of social relationships, adding untraditional strains to the work envi-ronment. When the workplace is burdened with such a large share of people's emotional life, countless hopes, desires, and expectations must languish in the shadow.

Persons possessed by performance needs constantly battle time. With no down-time, it is impossible to stay in touch with the inner self. Our early adult lives are guided largely by what others wanted and expected of us; but, as we grow older, an inner voice begins speaking more insistently, leading us to re-examine our values and directions. Hearing that voice through the din of external demands is critical to our continued self-development—it is the *sine qua non* of sustaining success.

If you remain a prisoner of the forces that drive you to work and excel, you are in danger of short-circuiting this internal guidance system. If enough people are telling you that you are indispensable, it's tempting to go along; the result is a life seriously out of balance.

HUBRIS: WHEN THE SHADOW RULES

Michael Lewis, in *Liar's Poker*, chronicles his experiences as a trader at Salomon Brothers in the fevered days of the 1980s boom, when he found himself swimming in a sea of money, borne along on a powerful tide of hubris. He tells this story: "I'm yelling at the top of my lungs at the bellhop at the Bristol Hotel in Paris: 'What do you mean there is no bathrobe in my suite?' He's backing toward the door shrugging his shoulders, as if he can't do anything about it, the little shit. Then I notice. The fruit bowl. Where's that bowl of apples and bananas that's supposed to come with the suite? And, hey, wait a minute. They've forgotten to fold the first tissue of the roll of toilet paper into a little triangle. I mean, can you believe this crap! 'Goddammit,' I shout. 'Get me the manager now. Do you know what I'm paying to stay here? Do you?' "

Here we see the darkest aspects of mythic success. This scene, it turns out, only happened in a dream—perhaps a foretaste of the person Lewis might have turned into had he stayed at Salomon. He left the company a few years before a trading scandal erupted that led to a *Wall Street Journal* headline that read: HOW SALOMON'S HUBRIS . . . LED TO LEADERS' DOWNFALL.

THE EGO, THE COMPASS, AND THE SHADOW

Hubris can be understood as the ego becoming swollen with success, a sort of psychological blindness. Signs of this blindness may be a tendency to reject information that doesn't fit a cherished self-image, an attitude that implies, "I have nothing more to learn," or an inability to perceive the needs of others, to behave as if they existed only to serve our own needs.

I use the term ego in the usual way, meaning the conscious self, the part of us that is shaped by external feedback, the acceptable persona we have created to deal with the world. The parts left in the shadow have a hard time getting attention, and when success swells the ego, they are crowded out still more ruthlessly. Fear of being dominated, or losing control, or not performing well, have no place in the public portrait of someone who needs to be seen as invulnerable. But those disowned fragments of self in the shadow can put your success at risk.

Imagine your ego being guided by an internal compass as you proceed toward your goals. Like a magnetic compass approaching the poles, your ego's compass can be pulled off course by the magnetic force of success. This can happen so gradually and imperceptibly that you may founder on the rocks of hubris before you notice that you have gone astray.

At the furthest extremes of hubris, we may "fall into the shadow," simply letting loose the dark impulses that we have tried so hard to suppress. If we do not regularly bring our shadow urges into the light and work with them, integrate them into our daily life, we may abandon all hope of controlling what we fear in ourselves and simply act it out. This is seen in literature, in the stories of Dr. Jekyll and Mr. Hyde, or of Faust allowing himself to be possessed by the devil. Unable to admit the shadow, these archetypal characters were eventually overtaken by it.

HUBRIS COUNTRY

Shadows exist in any working environment; but they flourish in particular kinds. Working landscapes in which shadows tend to gather quickly include the offices of Washington, D.C., lawyers, New York investment bankers, Paris and Milan designers, Hollywood actors and power brokers, and Harvard professors—but the location can be almost anywhere. Recently we have seen flash floods of hubris wreak havoc among Phoenix savings and loan tycoons, Denver office-builders, and Texas oil barons. Where the dominant values are power, status, and money, we are in Hubris Country.

High-risk environments for hubris can be identified by the rare few who manage to inhabit them and still escape hubris. Steve Allen comes to mind when considering the entertainment business. Hubris Country can be the downfall of someone who seems immune to the shadow but finally succumbs. A case in point is Clark Clifford, who thrived in the murky waters of Washington politics for decades without being tainted. Near the end of his illustrious career as an adviser to presidents, however, hubris overtook him. Perhaps because the White House was no longer calling, he listened to the shadowy figures at BCCI who wanted his prestige associated with their dubious banking empire, and a puffed ego sabotaged his alertness.

There is no hard and fast rule that pursuing a certain profession leads to hubris. Individual factors are equally important in the equation; we have seen our share of corrupt figures in the clergy, the helping professions, and other altruistic fields. But when a working environment has the following characteristics, its inhabitants are probably at high risk.

• When success comes early and fast, and those who share in it presume that it comes because they are special, a breed apart. The youthful traders at Salomon Brothers and other brokerage houses, portrayed by Lewis in *Liar's Poker* and Tom Wolfe in *The Bonfire of the Vanities*, are in this category.

• When vast amounts of money move around, and there is minimal connection between the efforts and skills employed and the rewards harvested. Again, the financial markets are a prime example.

• When the pace is so dizzying that you depend almost exclusively on instinct for decision-making. The atmosphere at Apple Computer in its early days was sweetly chaotic in just this way, and the founders almost let it crash.

• When power is thrust into untested hands and account-ability is either fuzzy or absent. Many third-generation heirs are ill-prepared to take on the management of a family business or estate.

• When success is mythologized and secrets institu-tionalized so that no one may speak ill of the enterprise or its leaders. The auto industry in the 1950s and IBM in the 1980s were such citadels of corporate culture, impervious to criti-cism.

NO-LIMITS THINKING

"You can do anything." This simple phrase may be the best clue to why contemporary American success figures seem to be so prone to self-inflation. "You can do anything" is the basic American credo. Most of us learned it as children, especially if we grew up in the post–World War II boom. The first corollary to the message said: "You've got everything it takes to make it—economic security, education, an egalitarian tradition." The second said: "You can overcome whatever inner barriers are holding you back." Both of these upbeat messages ignore many shadow problems. The first leaves out the role of family and personal history in shaping lives, and the power of the unconscious. Neither acknowledges economic and social inequ-ities, the breakdown of family and community values, and the painful and costly emergence from blissful isolation that Americans have experienced since the First World War.

If we look more closely, what are the shadow implications of "I can do anything"? Does it mean: "I can have anything I want"? Or: "I can do whatever it takes to get where I want to be, at whatever cost to anyone else"? Does it mean: "I can rise above any character weakness or negative experience, bury it so deeply that it will never trouble me again"?

As individuals and as a society, we have attempted time and again to leap over these moral and psychological obstacles, only to wind up enmeshed in the consequences. Certain inescapable realities such as a deteriorating environment and a newly configured world economy have forced us to re-examine the American "I can do anything" mentality—but it doesn't come easily to us. It may be the largest attitude adjustment we will ever have to make as a nation.

THE CONSCIOUSNESS-STRETCHING PROPERTIES OF THE LIMOUSINE

Don't discount the delights of power that lubricate the slide into hubris. The excesses of tyrants may belong to the past, but we can hear their echoes in Michael Lewis's dream tirade in a Paris hotel, and in the dictates of rock stars who insist that their dressing rooms be stocked with only certain brands of mineral water and champagne.

Even remarkably self-aware leaders are not immune to the sweet enticements of hubris. One such executive tells this story:

> By chance I had the opportunity to use an enormous stretch limousine for a trip from Atlantic City to New York instead of the usual town car with driver. I got in back, set my briefcase on the seat, and away we went up the highway.
>
> I was feeling pretty good. I'm in the back of this incredible car, being taken all by myself to an important meeting in New

York City. Suddenly the thought comes over me that I must be a wonderful person, worthy of great deeds and rewards, to be transported around in this way. I begin thinking about my work problems—not in the usual confined way, but, I imagine, as if I were Donald Trump on his best day, thinking about his problems. I have new ideas, I formulate plans that are appropriate for a limousine but not for a Greyhound bus. When we pull up in front of the hotel in Manhattan, I believe I notice the doorman treats me differently than when I get out of a taxi.

By the end of the trip I began to understand the inflation of the guru who gets into his Rolls-Royce every day and connects this material circumstance with his spiritual development. I even understand why five, or ten, Rolls-Royces would add to one's sense of the certainty of one's virtues and make one feel even larger. The Rolls altered my consciousness in an exciting way. I seemed divinely blessed. The universe spoke and said: "Hey, you're a limousine rider. Other people should do your bidding because they're only taking the subway home."

THE MANY FACES OF HUBRIS

The signs of hubris can seem trivial or harmless at first. Here are some of the forms in which it most often appears.

"SPECIAL GIFTS"

Top-echelon men and women often fall prey to this type of self-delusion. A world-famous concert pianist *does* have an extraordinary talent, as does a first-rate architect; a corporate leader heads the pack because she is blessed with a sense of grand-scale strategy. It would be hypocritical to deny such gifts; they are rightfully a source of pride.

But a person whose work frustrates his or her genuine talents—for example a frustrated research scientist who finds himself tied to administrative duties—may invent "special gifts"—fantasies that compensate for loss of job satisfaction and give him an illusory edge over his co-workers and competition. Blind faith in intuition as the basis of decision-making is a common form of believing in special gifts, as is excessive reliance on sheer willpower, instead of judgment and analysis, to make things happen.

A senior editor at a big New York publisher, Jeanie was devoted to books and got to the top because she had a canny literary intelligence and finesse in negotiating. Bestsellers seemed to blossom under her cultivation. But as she moved up the ladder in her prestigious firm, she moved away from a hands-on relationship with her books. Her company valued her reputation more than her literary skill; acquisitions became more important than "quibbling over commas," as one of her colleagues put it.

Outwardly accepting this situation, Jeanie made the best of it by endowing herself with a "magical nose." "I can smell a bad manuscript through the envelope," she assured me. Neglecting her talent, however, left her on shaky ground. Privately she knew that her real ego strength came from helping to make good books, not from publishing sorcery.

Former British prime minister Margaret Thatcher boasted, "I make up my mind about people in the first ten seconds and I rarely change it." Her arrogance, it is said, caused her own party to vote her out of office. I have heard colleagues judge a new client or associate by a handshake, how they dress, or what kind of car they drive, and in one case by how they seasoned their food.

Carriers of such hubris believe that, like Midas, their mere touch can turn dross into gold. A merchant or designer may justify her outrageously expensive life-style to creditors on the basis that she is magical: that her personal presence, her aura, bring in business. In show business, this may be true to some extent. But trusting in charisma as a recipe for success is inviting shadows to rise like yeasty dough.

Belief in special gifts may lead us to think that we have all the answers, even outside our area of special competence. "If

I'm this successful," so goes the reasoning, "then I am wise in all areas of life."

The media encourage this form of self-inflation, elevating achievers in one or two fields to the role of all-around expert. A writer of historical romances is pressured to comment on international events; a TV personality is expected to offer sage advice on complex social or economic issues.

The notion of magical powers that enable a person to pass judgment on an unread manuscript, let alone on a human being, sounds preposterous to anyone except the person making the claims. The compulsion to invent unreal gifts is an expression of irrational impulses from the shadow: fear that we really do not deserve our success; anger that we feel trapped and victimized by the goals that we worked so hard to attain. Dependence on illusory gifts weakens our vital critical capacity for perception, analysis, and communication, and promotes a dangerous sense of invulnerability to consequences and immunity to criticism. We may need to believe in magic because for some reason we have been blocked from exercising our innate talents or perhaps because we have lost faith in them. But irrational magical thinking will merely make things worse by further distancing us from the real roots of our success.

By contrast, success sustainers have learned to identify, appreciate, and nurture their true gifts by making sure they have opportunities to use them. They are always alert to the perils of basing decisions on the "magical me." If they find themselves thinking: "If it's not in the first paragraph, I don't need to read it," or, "I can glance at a balance sheet and tell you what the business is worth," they are crossing the boundary into Hubris Country.

NEEDING TO RUN THE SHOW

Knowing who approves what and for how much is at the core of good management. Control of a healthy kind and degree helps ensure clear communications and accountability. But control can exceed its healthy limits when hubris takes over, or can degenerate into a need to run the show—to wield power for its own sake.

An appropriate exercise of control means taking decisive action after consultation and due consideration. An inflated need to command comes from the shadow, from an irrational fear of losing control. It can result in arrogant, cruel, wasteful, and paranoid behavior. It tends to go hand in hand with other signs of hubris: the leader who must dominate the conversation at a meeting is not only hyperextending command, but also blocking out unwelcome information and engaging in magical thinking, such as quick-fix strategies.

Many so-called spiritual leaders take the need for control to ritualistic extremes. A religious leader and well-known teacher invited me and two other men to lunch. We sat on huge pillows in a beautifully furnished room. Lunch was served by women who bowed to us after each course and then backed out of the room. As the meal proceeded, I became more and more un-comfortable; when our host invited me to join his advisory board, I declined. Surprised, he wanted to know why. I said that besides being too busy, I couldn't let myself be waited on in his fashion. He laughed and winked. "They don't mind. They know that it is good for their souls to serve me."

While serving on a corporate board, I was asked to intro-duce the chair and president to a prospective client. When they arrived to pick me up in a white stretch limo, I cautioned that this style would offend the conservative client. I was assured with a patronizing smile that my advice was appreciated, and that was that. Not only did we fail to land the client, but word spread that the company was run by city slickers who couldn't possibly understand their customers.

Some people's egos react to challenges by flaunting their power, often in unpleasantly petty ways. Stories used to float around Washington about how President Kennedy took plea-sure in requiring high government officials, including Cabinet heads, to run errands such as fetching him clean shirts. This bizarre need to make people jump speaks loudly of an endangered ego, and it can be seen in organizations ranging from corporations to churches to restaurants.

Running the show often takes the form of a compulsion to control information that is made public, or one's public image. The concern for image is most obvious in politics or show business, but it affects the business world too. I counseled one young man who was trying to extricate himself from a partnership gone bad. He had called me in to help construct an equitable strategy for his separation that would cause his firm the least possible harm and be financially fair to all parties. It soon became clear, however, that his story about why he was leaving was as important to him as the breakup of the business, or its impact on the employees he would leave behind, or how much he would be compensated. In his effort to "keep the record straight," he was considering disclosures that would have been personally and professionally devastating to everyone involved. He finally resisted those impulses, but not before he wrote out his version of events and gave copies to me and his lawyer—just in case his ex-partner tried to go public with a different story. He saw the rage toward his partner that was in the shadow could be managed without causing others harm.

The need to be in control usually originates from a basically commendable vigilance. Lurking in the shadow is the fear that if we take our eyes off the ball for one second, everything will fall apart. Unless admitted and dealt with, this feeling leads to hypervigilance, an extraordinary level of effort that no one can maintain without danger to himself and others. It is possible, though, to change an eagle-eyed glare into a kind of gentle gazing, a more benign position from which you work to share the responsibility for control, toward a whole culture of vigilance.

For the hubris victim, letting go of control is akin to fighting nature. Surrendering power in a corporate structure feels like a loss of personal power. Yet, in the quest for sustained success, the opposite is true. Long-distance winners understand that true power lies in being able to let it go; they have learned how to do this, and when. For such men and women, the act of letting go provides a positive charge, enhancing their personal as well as professional strengths. Success sustainers also know that the exercise of control contains inherent risks of self-inflation, and must be carefully monitored, directed to specific goals beyond personal gratification.

GAINING STATUS BY ASSOCIATION

A particular form of ego inflation occurs around power social events, especially in Washington, D.C. Such events are judged by how much they cost, the famous people they attract, and the reviews they garner. The event is frequently a party but can be anything that qualifies as "the most fabulous," like opening night at the opera.

Publisher Malcolm Forbes' seventieth birthday bash, heavily covered by the media, was staged on his yacht. It was intended as the party to end all parties, with its glittering cast of celebrities and its stupendous budget. Truman Capote, in the stage play *Tru*, pegs his black-and-white ball as the highlight of his life, "the top of my form." "They all came," he says poignantly, reciting the names of the celebrities in attendance. The main purpose of such events is to impress as many people as possible. Elaborate charity affairs and fund-raisers provide a moral justification for otherwise outrageous displays of power and excess.

Putting on an Event is perhaps the surest way to stroke your ego and guarantee the spotlight, but it can signal ego inflation when you care too much whether you received an invitation to someone else's Event; when seating arrangements become a measure of worth; when you need to know who else will be there before deciding about attending. Other common symptoms of status hunger include dominating conversations or telling stories about yourself, name-dropping (of people, places, or things), feeling and showing annoyance when you are not deferred to, and even avoiding places like restaurants where you risk not being recognized and stroked.

The pursuit of the rich and powerful can be a way of trying to determine where you belong in the social scheme of things. By participating in power events, or, better yet, by being in charge of them, you could be striving for self-definition. I can't deny that these bashes are fun—who is immune to the thrill of rubbing shoulders with celebrities?—but common sense should warn us not to get swept away. When power socializing becomes an identity crunch, something unhealthy is going on.

Long-distance winners, who have forged a firm sense of their essential selves and values, tend to excuse themselves from events that are primarily status displays. They consider small talk in excessive quantities to be a waste of time and abhor being seen as an end in itself. They want their life stories to be based on achievement and service rather than on their ability to make some Cabinet officer or socialite jump at the crack of their whip.

CLAIMING THE MORAL HIGH GROUND

This symptom of hubris is an early stage of a process that can end in the corruption of moral values, a profound confusion that can cast deep shadows on your personal and professional life. One of the devilish things about how the shadow operates is that the early symptoms of hubris feel so good. Winning is euphoric. Clients of mine have described getting a physical high, an adrenaline rush, from making a big sale or winning at negotiation. Studies of the language of deal-making show that its metaphors are drawn from the gratifying pastimes of games, sex, and occasionally war (whether we like it or not, aggression can be energizing).

The early stages of self-inflation do not feel like ego weakness because the ego's effort to block out any threat to the self is functioning, enabling us to feel confident and in charge. And when we feel strong, it is also easy to feel righteous—to claim the moral high ground. Don't you agree that it feels great to believe that you are right and that the others are wrong?

When a group claims the moral high ground, an infallible ideology, or the one true faith, it can justify anything. Individuals who suffer from the delusion of moral superiority endanger themselves and others. In extreme cases they imagine themselves to be avenging angels or monarchs bestowing grace and mercy on their obedient and grateful vassals.

In one organization I worked with, an evangelical consultant had trained small groups within the company to take pride in their unity of purpose, their vision of how things should be, and their capacity to "cut through the crap" to get there. These CTTC (Cut Through The Crap) groups were punishing employees outside their cabal for various crimes and misdemeanors, mostly for not "getting it"—"it" being the enlightened behavior and beliefs of the chosen few. The bad feelings that ensued were threatening the company's future.

The assumption of moral superiority is an occupational hazard among religious leaders and spiritual teachers and is especially prevalent among cults and cult leaders. The late Indian guru Rajneesh and the Reverend Jim Jones are examples. But the moralistic form of self-inflation is not limited to cults and their leaders and does not always result in the excesses committed by prophets such as Rajneesh and Jones. More often it appears in the form of pious advice and counsel—insights supposedly derived from the perspective of a clear view from the high ground. Wisdom emanating from "on high" is just another "special gift," and is usually a signal that the adviser is fresh out of new ideas. (I am particularly aware of my own potential for imparting dubious wisdom because my position as a consultant and author gives me a convenient forum from which to do so.)

When people dwell too long on their good intentions, there is frequently trouble in the offing. I know a would–be business leader who is well known for preaching "enlightened" human values in dealing with staff and customers, yet his vicious and underhanded battles with his partners are also well known. He has undermined his pious stance.

The moral high ground appeals to the part of us that seeks easy answers, clear distinctions between good and bad. Healthy people recognize ambiguity and allow themselves to experience doubts. But if we have convinced ourselves that we are the guardians of moral certainty, we can keep those questions in the shadow, act on impulse, and make decisions without painful inner debate. Like the other forms of hubris, the moral high ground is the refuge of an insecure ego.

TUNING OUT THE INNER VOICE

Each of us has an inner voice that speaks of the gold in our shadow. It is the voice of our secret, hidden self—our most authentic self in many ways—the parts of us that have lain dormant because they were ignored or denigrated by our parents or by society—not considered to be useful in making our way in the world. If we listen, this voice can give us information essential to our continued growth and sustained success. Too often it is drowned out by the clamor of an overly busy life.

Many people look at an overfull schedule as a badge of importance or popularity. For them, a heavily annotated calendar says, *Look at how important I am! How in demand! How many people and events depend on me!* An inflated ego is speaking. Self-inflation turns a busy life into a frantic one, testing our stamina, creating a lopsided set of priorities and values. Private time becomes a commodity so precious that we "save" it like something bankable. A man I know boasts that he needs fewer bathroom breaks during long meetings than any of his associates. Meyer Friedman, coauthor of *Type A Behavior and Your Heart*, tells of a patient who made his meals in a blender so that he could save the time it takes to chew. An industrialist I know scheduled a fifteen-minute visit to his son's birthday party.

In order to hear your inner voice, slow down and allow room for quiet, unstructured time. In his book *Solitude*, British psychiatrist Anthony Storr concludes: "It appears . . . that some development of the capacity to be alone is necessary if the brain is to function at its best and if the individual is to fulfill his highest potential. Human beings easily become alienated from their deepest needs and feelings. Learning, thinking, innovating and maintaining contact with one's inner world are all facilitated by solitude."

Solitude means more than simply being alone. It is the condition necessary for the psyche to replenish itself. The time, conditions, setting, and purpose served vary from person to person: my quiet walk may be equivalent to your extended retreat.

Hubris in the form of disdaining solitude is a tactic to deny the shadow's request for an audience. We hope that we can hold off the shadow as long as we stay busy, but this evasion works only for a while. Eventually the shadow refuses to be ignored. And when its suppressed longings and fears are suddenly unleashed on a person whose strength is all external, without the inner resources that solitude nurtures, even a formidably structured life may come apart with a crash.

TUNING OUT THE OUTER VOICES

Hubris results from vigorously and consistently denying the shadow, so it's not surprising that one of its chief symptoms is the tendency to reject negative input—to screen out information that does not agree with a carefully constructed self-image or corporate plan, and to send the messenger packing. A person in the grip of self-inflation dismisses the bearer of unwelcome news as cranky, envious, or too dumb to grasp the big picture. Therapists report that very wealthy and powerful men and women frequently (in the words of a well-known California psychiatrist) "disregard insights that conflict with their perceived needs. . . . They often break off therapy by firing the therapist as they might a disagreeable servant." Friendship, too, often falls victim, as truth-bearing friends aren't welcome in Hubris Country.

Healthy egos need honest information, so we must trust our closest friends and colleagues to communicate honestly with us. Such trust is not arrived at quickly but accumulates over time. But many people on the fast track don't devote the necessary time to establishing intimate associations, and few of their relationships develop to the point of trust. As a result, they are not fed honest information. Their complaint goes: "Nobody around here understands what I'm up against."

A few years ago I helped design a survival strategy for an old, "establishment" educational institution in serious financial trouble. I met the president of this prestigious school in his office at the end of his business day. The room was enormous, with cathedral ceilings and vaulted windows, appointed with antiques and paintings of obvious value—a place of power. The man himself was quite young for such major responsibilities, but he looked drawn and worn in the fading light. During his first martini, we looked over the current financial statements. As he poured his second, I asked him to describe his administration and how it functioned.

A horror story unfolded, with a cast of characters apparently devoted to their personal betterment at the expense of the school, the president, and sometimes one another. There were cabals among the faculty, he confided, cutthroat competition among department heads. He admitted that he enjoyed engaging in divisive tactics that further split and weakened this unscrupulous pack.

Loosening his rep tie, he poured a third martini and began to dissect the board of trustees, using surprisingly vulgar language to describe these exemplary citizens, leaders of industry and community. According to the president, they were all cowards, liars, or fools. I interrupted him to ask about his friends and close associates. He paused, staring into his half-empty glass, and muttered, "I haven't any."

"Then who do you trust for honest information?" I asked. His secretary, his driver, and his wife were the sources he trusted. When I pointed out how unreliable such informants might be (paid employees usually want to please the employer; his wife didn't work at the school and knew only a few of the players socially), I could see him bite back anger. "You simply don't understand how cunning and dangerous my colleagues are," he insisted. "I can't trust any of them." But that wasn't the problem, in his view, and he didn't see why I was "harping" on it. He trusted his own instincts; they were why he was in charge, right?

It was becoming clear to me that I was also being labeled an outsider who didn't understand him. Instead of seeing me as his advocate, a source of new information or alternative solutions, I had quickly become another critic to be bested. His capacity for trust was so stunted that I knew I could not help.

Long-distance winners cultivate honest informants and suspect those who flatter them and sugar-coat reality. You can offer candid input even if the warmth of a personal relationship is lacking. But where friendships among colleagues are possible, they provide an additional motive of caring to prompt the flow of viable information. A leader who is both respected and liked can unify staff to the advantage of the organization.

Smart leaders look for associates who care about the organization. They seek information from sources both personally warm and cool to themselves. And they become experts at spotting where self-interest or friendship might be coloring the data.

GOODBYE TO LIFE'S SMALL PLEASURES . . .

A few years ago I sat in on some negotiations over the acquisition of a friend's business. The final mediation took place in the offices of a large New York investment banking firm, and was set for eight P.M. on a midweek night.

In the harshly lit workspace, dozens of suspended,

stressed-looking young men stood at computer monitors, phones in hand or wearing headsets, moving money and making deals around the globe. People came and went, ordered coffee and food in fancy white boxes that didn't get opened, made obscure references to other deals, waited for the meeting to take form. It was a ritual dance of power, eighties style.

Most of them were still there when I left at one in the morning. I shared a car out of the city with a young lawyer who asked if I minded making a quick stop at his soon-to-be-finished condominium. We walked through the large rehab project while he made some notes for his decorator about paint colors and carpets, and were back on the road in less than twenty minutes.

"Beautiful place," I remarked. "You must be looking forward to moving in."

He laughed shortly. "I rarely think about it at all," he said. "For what it's costing, all I think about is how long it's going to take to work it off." This young man had arranged his life to exclude the possibility of any time off, at least for the immediate future, and even the possibility of enjoying what his work produced.

When hubris reaches its extreme form, it erodes away the gentle, small savories of life. At the climax of Shakespeare's drama, King Lear is stumbling around naked, covered with branches and leaves, blind, tormented, and out of touch with reality. For a tragic figure drawn from real life, look at Howard Hughes, a man of charm and accomplishment, by the end of his life obsessed with privacy and cleanliness, living on drugs and unable to enjoy company, food, or friends.

When we hear that people have it all, we should be concerned for them. In most cases what they have is in firm control of their life. The price paid for having it all is incalculable: no walks in the park, no spontaneous plans to catch a movie or a Chinese dinner, no time to bounce a child or play a quick set of tennis with a friend. Ultimately, the question must arise: What is really worth doing?

I once helped conduct a seminar for a group of high-level corporate leaders on the theme of bridging the inner life and external demands. It included, for those who wanted to try it, an hour-long guided meditation using standard techniques of sitting or lying on the floor, with music to encourage a state of deep relaxation. The reactions, from people encountering meditation for the first time, were positive. One man, a CEO in the banking industry, experienced an unaccustomed state of peacefulness in which he thought of his dead father and had a loving reunion with him.

Several weeks later I ran into this same man, who reaffirmed how much the seminar had meant to him and then related an incident that took place afterward. He had flown to the Midwest for a meeting with his board chairman, who had noticed something different about him, commenting that he looked "positively rejuvenated." Enthusiastically, the CEO described the seminar and its purpose, its participants, and alas, the meditation session. This was too much: the chairman interrupted in midsentence, admonishing him to "keep the part about the meditation to yourself."

When I asked the CEO about this reaction, he answered without hesitation: "It was the idea of lying on the floor with other people." He outlined the barren landscape of the chairman's life—that of a man who shared no intimacies, was frozen into a position of Victorian propriety, and felt threatened simply hearing about someone else's emotions, pleasures, or intimacies.

Long-distance winners I've met all know that the pleasures that come with success, as well as those that don't depend on it, are as valuable as the success itself.

DEFLATING HUBRIS THROUGH RENEWAL

Almost any successful person will catch a glimpse of him- or herself in our catalog of hubris. Ego-inflation is so much a part of the territory of success, and so insidious in its operation, that long-distance winners develop techniques for early detection. They treasure truth-telling friends and listen to them, whether they bear good news or bad. They look for mentors and teachers who challenge them, even at times make them stumble, recognizing that this helps them grow. They tackle learning projects that tax them and deny them the use of their old bag of tricks. And they reflect on what is worth doing instead of doing what yields easy results.

One way to understand hubris is to recognize that the ego has swelled to the point at which inner growth is stifled and new learning is impossible. When you run out of answers, it is time to look into the shadow to learn what you need. If you are a true lifelong learner, falling into hubris is impossible, for in the excitement, humility, and gratitude of continuous learning, hubris has no room to grow.

Learning is the fuel that will enable you to sustain success in your personal life and in your organization. In the following pages we will describe a "cycle of renewal," which begins with an evaluation of your present self and your situation, proceeds through retreats that enable you to explore your shadows in depth, and leads to a greater integration of your hidden self into your daily life. Long-distance winners will share their wisdom at every stage in this process, which is a tool you can use over and over to renew your capacity for healthy success.

CHAPTER 4

The Promise of Renewal: Begin by Stepping Back

YOU MAY HAVE RECOGNIZED some part of yourself in the picture I have drawn of success under a shadow. Successful people come to this recognition by many routes—a financial catastrophe, a physical breakdown, a broken relationship, or negative feedback that accumulates past the point of denial. For some it may be a purely internal revelation. Though they may push it away for a long time, sooner or later it usually catches up with them, like a reflection in the mirror of a self we weren't prepared to see.

We'll start this chapter by looking at how people react to this confrontation with the shadows of their success—often by making things worse. Then we will outline a comprehensive, long-range approach based on the experience of long-distance winners: a path toward self-renewal that can enable us to avoid hubris, use wisely what we find in the shadow, and build a framework for sustained success.

I am not addressing only those who are in crisis, like Morgan. Most of you are not in that situation. But let's say that you have felt some early tinge of dissatisfaction souring the taste of your achievements. Perhaps you briefly glimpsed your potential for hubris in the way you reacted to a challenge. Or you were surprised to find yourself scheming to keep a corporate secret.

Men and women confronting shadows have described themselves to me as hungry for change, disillusioned with what they do, or buried alive in work. They may feel bored, ashamed, undeserving, or scared by their success. Or they may feel that they've lost their edge. One man told me, "I'm running on fumes and don't know where the next gas station is." A woman said, "I'm in a kind of spiritual bankruptcy and need a Chapter Eleven. I know I have great personal assets, but right now they can't keep up with the demands on me. I need some time to reorganize, regroup, and redeploy my assets."

Some feel the need of a counselor but don't know where to look. Some may be in transition between careers; many are fully committed to their career path but want to enrich their working experience. Some are facing an upheaval in the marketplace that dictates adaptation for survival. Others sense the pressure to change coming from somewhere deep within.

Among those who come to talk to me, the most common early reaction is simply to admit that they are in trouble. Usually they haven't thought about what might come next, but I try to encourage them for having taken the first step of simply recognizing the existence of problems.

A typical case was a mid-fifties CEO, well known in his service field, who opened our meeting by saying, "This week has been a bastard. Actually, the past several months have been bruising. I'm tired all the time, drinking too much."

I asked him when was the last time he had taken some real time off to engage in personal reflection. He thought hard and said, "Does it count if you take work along and call in every day?" No, it doesn't.

A young minister, not yet forty, tells me he feels he must make a major change in his working life, perhaps in his vocation. "My contract is up," he said. "I'm finished with what I set out to do at this parish. I've got to start thinking about what to do next." It was interesting that he had used the excuse of an expired contract to nudge himself toward change, when he could easily have renewed his agreement. When I asked if he had a new direction in mind, or had been training for another field, he said no, he needed help for that. "I have no idea what I might be able to do."

An attractive woman in her late thirties complained that parts of her personal life felt atrophied. Her career was solid and she was still learning her craft as a marketing executive, but she was unhappy about her home life. "My husband and child aren't getting anywhere near what they deserve and what I want to give them. Besides, there are other parts of me that need attention."

I heard something similar from a corporate VP in his early fifties, describing how much time he had to give to the firm: "There is practically no discretionary time in my life. I draw some lines around my family, but the rest is flat-out scheduled. This isn't a time management problem. I just oversold my hours about 110 percent." He too didn't have much idea of his next move, except to speculate that "maybe it would be different if I ran my own show."

CHANGE STRATEGIES THAT FAIL

So far, so good, I would say to all those above. Facing shadows is the essential prelude to dealing with them. The next step is where people often falter. When successful people notice that all is not well in their world, when they finally acknowledge the need for change, they do not always respond constructively. Because the shadow does not want to be seen, and because success encourages its denial, people get scared when they meet it face to face. Shaken by the encounter, they may misidentify what they're really looking for—a younger lover, a new town, a different job. They may leap just for the sake of leaping, from the frying pan into the fire.

People in this situation often dream up strategies that look good in the short run but don't really get at deeper issues or match up with their current stage of personal development.

Among strategies that usually fail, the most common are the following.

READY . . . FIRE . . . AIM

If early signs of discontent have provoked excessive anxiety, or if you have let your situation deteriorate to the point where you're desperate, you may opt for a major life change that isn't well considered. People who feel compelled to make a dramatic move often focus on the wrong target. These all-or-nothing types sometimes break up their marriages or leave town to avoid facing serious shadows in another area of life. The mechanism of projection makes it appear that all the problems are located in a spouse or an unfulfilling environment rather than in themselves.

One sixty-plus former CEO of a Fortune 500 corporation came to see me, looking very tired. "After years in corporate life I knew I needed a change," he said. "So I took on a brand-new challenge, and it turned out to be a mistake." He had undertaken a rescue mission to turn around a smaller company, but underestimated the problems and how sweaty the work would be.

"This is a job for a younger person," he admitted in frustration. "I could imagine succeeding at it twenty years ago." Rather than presenting an exciting challenge, the new job forced him to perform on a nose-to-the-grindstone level that belonged to a past stage of his development.

"How much time did you take between assignments?" I inquired.

"Not much at all," he replied. "Not enough, evidently."

The Big Leap is a case of firing before the gun is ready and aimed, without fully exploring our shadows, examining which deeply buried influences are propelling us away from one thing and toward another. Instead of reacting reflexively, take a more patient approach. Being in a hurry may well be how you got to the top, but figuring out what's wrong with your lofty perch and what to do about it will take some time . . . and time used in ways that you may not be used to.

Living with a certain amount of doubt and discomfort is essential to getting deep inside the shadow. If you are feeling pressured toward change by some force you can't quite identify, serious research is in order before you make a move. Perhaps a small adjustment or rebalancing is all that's needed.

THE ALL-OR-NOTHING APPROACH

Like the Big Leaper, someone who takes this approach believes that only a profound, life-shaking change can fix things. But such people usually can't actually bring themselves to take the leap. They set up an all-or-nothing scenario in which "nothing" invariably wins out. These people's sense of self and values is not very strong. They are terrified by the prospect of losing a shred of their carefully constructed personas.

A celebrated media figure came to talk over his choices in the wake of a diagnosis of hypertension. His affable, composed manner belied the medical evidence, and I could only guess at what cost. He acknowledged that his life was stressed and "out of balance," but claimed that the only obvious choice was to get out of broadcasting.

This wasn't going to happen—the fragrance of success was too intoxicating to him, and his ego relied heavily on praise and attention. Yet he had to take his medical problem seriously, and eventually he began to see choices he had been blind to, possibilities for modifying his work habits and spending less time in the spotlight. Even doing that much was scary for him, but fortunately his life wish triumphed.

THE MAKE-BELIEVE LEAP

People often move from one situation into another that is only superficially different. The actors may change, but the roles and relationships are comfortable, familiar—and ultimately stifling. Truly renewing changes stretch and use new parts of us, but nothing is being stretched here except credibility.

A successful fortyish woman with no children "escaped" from her big public relations job in Chicago to seek a better-balanced life with her husband in the Bay Area. "It seemed easy enough. We still had enough money to live well, so it was just a matter of shifting gears—or so I thought." Soon she began accepting freelance assignments to supplement their income, and "now I find myself still working crazy hours on my so-called smaller deals." She also found that she disliked working alone and missed being part of a team.

The basic problem was that she had undergone no inner journey in relation to her work to match the outer move across the country. The shadow pressures that drove her to over-schedule had not been addressed; she was merely living them out in a more soothing physical environment.

In a similar form of taking action, changes are made, but in such a cautious, incremental fashion that they don't produce any real growth.

A friend remembers his father saying over and over that he wanted to get out from under the advertising agency he had spent his life building. At one point he sold off part of the business, then another part; eventually he merged with another firm. But apparently he never became free of the sense that the business was an intolerable burden. He spent a lifetime hunting for small escape valves whenever the pressure became too great, but avoided searching his shadow for the inspiration that would bring joy back to his work.

Incremental change is not necessarily bad; in fact, it is often the healthiest way to work toward long-range renewal. It is a failed strategy only when the increments are too small to make an impact or not deeply rooted in the understanding of both your outer and your hidden self.

THE RENEWAL IMPERATIVE

When people first try to describe what they feel, they are usually vague: "a change, something new, a feeling like I used to have about my work, some fresh energy, a sense that what I'm doing means something," and so on. It is impossible to formulate the secret compound each person requires. The unique formula for life development that suits your needs will emerge only over time and through conscious effort devoted to self-understanding. However, we can sum up what we're seeking in the idea of *renewal*.

At some point in the life of every individual and organization, the need for renewal becomes paramount. We need only look at nature to see that every living system, down to the most primitive cell, requires periodic renewal to survive. And we need only look at human history for countless examples of societies that clung to a winning formula in the face of pressures to change, and perished as a result: from the Mayan tribes who lived and died by exploiting their forest environment, to the empires of Victorian England and Communist Russia.

John Gardner, who has written eloquently about self-renewal, asks, "Suppose one tried to imagine a society that would be relatively immune to decay—an ever-renewing society? What would it be like? What would be the ingredients that provide the immunity?" We can and should ask the same questions about sustaining success in our lives.

Some people seem immune to stagnation and hubris. They have a bottomless reservoir of energy and enthusiasm, an instinct that tells them when to dig in and when to move on to something new. These are the long–distance winners or success sustainers. But there is nothing inborn about what they know. All have had their personal encounters with the dark side of excellence and have learned not to shun them but to find in them clues to guide their journeys.

The processes and practices that lead to self-renewal *are* learnable. We will identify them, show how they fit together in an ever-repeating cycle, and describe many approaches for incorporating them into your life. Long-distance winners provide inspiring examples and usable wisdom. While the focus is on individual development, we will also see how the same principles can foster self-renewing organizations.

The renewal imperative does not apply only to people in trouble. You may be deeply engaged and excited by your work, trying consciously to live a balanced life, aware of shadows, free of any symptoms of hubris. Perhaps you see the costs of success only in others around you. In this case, you are in an ideal position to benefit from learning the arts of self-renewal, *before* shadows grow dark and threatening, and hubris gets its hooks deep in you.

THE CYCLE OF RENEWAL

We can best understand the entire cycle of renewal by seeing it in three stages. We'll call them *stepping back, deep learning through retreat*, and *matching action to insight*.

Unsuccessful strategies of renewal show us that the changes and choices that lead to renewal cannot be rushed. The cycle should begin with *stepping back* for a clearer view of your life and endeavors, disengaging from the immediate action to enter a mode of observation and evaluation.

Observation is a key skill of self-renewal, and one that many successful people must work to develop. If we categorize people as observers or doers, most high achievers would fall into the latter camp. But we have seen that hubris appears when observation fails. If you are racing full-tilt toward a goal, the blinders that focus your gaze on the prize also cut off important signs in your peripheral vision: changes in the marketplace, discontent among employees, restless stirrings in yourself. Balancing decisive action with observation and introspection is essential to long-distance winning.

Becoming a keen observer begins with getting an accurate fix on your external situation: where you are in relation to your work, your personal relationships, your place in the world. This kind of self-inventory is a central feature of the stepping-back stage.

But we can't stop there. We must also go deep inside and learn to be keen observers of our hidden selves, our unarticulated values, our suppressed shadows. That is the second-stage work of *deep learning through retreat*. It is the heart of the process, though it will probably (and should) begin as soon as you start to step back. This deeper exploration of the hidden self—the fears, doubts, desires, needs, and gifts that lie beneath your everyday awareness—usually involves retreat time.

The eventual goal of deep learning is to take the insights you have gained in retreat and reapply them when you return to the world, even though you may choose a different world in which to put them to use. In phase three of the renewal cycle, *matching action to insight*, the goal is that what you do fits your evolving self. Sustaining excellence in your life and work calls for sustained practice of self-renewal skills.

Deep learning goes beyond our established professional competence, our managerial skills, cognitive capacities, or social adeptness. It is not simply absorbing information; it is learning *redefined* as the process of discovering our hidden needs, nascent talents, shunted aspirations, and denied prospects. Will a promotion at work, inevitably calling for some new task learning, satisfy our craving for a more congruent and satisfying life? Probably not. But there are ways to care for our deeper needs, and they begin with deeper self-awareness.

These stages of the renewal cycle proceed more or less in order, though the boundaries between them are not sharp. (You may learn to step back only in the course of retreat, for example; and the practice of retreat should continue while re-engagement is taking place.) Success sustainers will go through the entire cycle more than once in the course of a lifetime.

Individual factors aside, however, continuous renewal is a universal imperative. The fuel to sustain success is ignited by the spark of learning. And learning of any kind does not proceed on an unchanging level path, but follows a traceable curve. To understand why shadows gather around people in high places, and why they need to make self-renewal a lifelong pursuit, let's chart the curve of learning and see how it operates in our lives.

LEARNING CURVES: BEHIND THE RENEWAL IMPERATIVE

Every effort at mastery, whether learning how to ride a two-wheeler or how to run a major corporation, follows the classic pattern of the S-shaped or sigmoid curve (see illustration). Rising from a valley, it arcs upward slowly and then more sharply to a peak, where it begins gradually to curve back down.

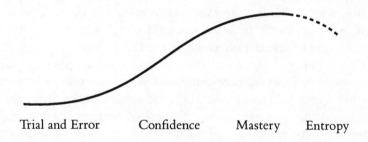

Trial and Error   Confidence   Mastery   Entropy

Depictions of this elegant yet commonplace form are found in some of the earliest decorative art, as a repeating border on Greek vases, for example, and its wavelike shape has fascinated artists, scientists, engineers, and learning theorists. Biologist Jonas Salk, a noted success sustainer, began thinking about sigmoid curves while researching the propagation patterns of fruit flies in a closed colony. Salk noticed that the flies would breed rapidly until they reached the limits that their environment could sustain, and then learned to change their breeding patterns, thus curtailing population growth and prolonging survival.

Plotting the rates of propagation produced an S-shaped curve, which eventually led Salk to propose a learning theory that applied to human development as well as nature. Other learning theorists, such as George Land, have used the curve to plot patterns of task, career, and even organizational learning.

TRACING THE LEARNING CURVE

The lowest point on the curve corresponds to the earliest stage of learning, where the aspirant must deal with the chaos of getting started, the confusion and frustration of an unfamiliar environment.

The curve ascends as we begin to replace the unknown with the known. Confidence builds as chaos yields to discernible patterns. Our grades tell us that we are on track; other rewards may come in the form of positive feedback, promotions, or more money. The greatest motivator is usually the excitement of learning itself, that wonderful feeling when frustration gives way to fascination as we figure things out.

In the next phase, the curve bends upward more steeply as the pace of learning accelerates and positive feedback comes more quickly. This is the stage of enhanced performance, culminating in rapture—the feeling of getting it right and knowing you can do it again. More than a sense of power, it's a feeling of being in harmony with the experience, shared by athletes performing at their peak, by the attorney who can hold a courtroom in her spell, and by the sales executive who knows how to keep his team humming, grease the corporate wheels, and show outstanding results.

Near the very top of the curve, the slope starts to level off as we approach our peak of success. The pace of learning slows, and we often begin to lean back and trail our oars, coasting effortlessly. This moment at the top is usually well-earned and publicly recognized. It's the moment when the actress brandishes her Oscar, when Muhammad Ali exults, "I'm the greatest!", when the newspaper's business section writes up a company leader. Such moments feel great, and everyone who has worked hard to attain mastery deserves to revel briefly in the acclaim it can bring.

But the peak of the curve is also the place where it begins to descend, where the energy of the wave dissipates, the pace of learning slows, and stagnation begins. It is when, after the rapture of winning has worn off, we may secretly start to wonder, "Is this all there is?" Or when we realize how exhausted we are from scrambling to hold our edge. In this place, external voices of warning and internal voices of need may go unheard amid the din of congratulations or the cocoon of a leader's isolation. Paradoxically, the summit of success is fertile ground for the shadow to grow in. It is where we are most vulnerable to hubris, and thus a dangerous place to linger too long.

It's natural to want to sustain the good feelings of rapturous learning and peak success. But it's a mistake to think that staying in the same groove will automatically keep those feelings coming. Circumstances change—economic conditions, social trends, staffing, corporate goals, personal needs, rising expectations ("What have you done for me lately?"). The brilliant young executive reaches middle age and no longer appears to be a wonder child. Any or all of these can be factors in determining where a learning curve peaks and begins to decline.

ANTICIPATING ENTROPY: THE EPIC B CURVE

The term *entropy* can be loosely but conveniently applied to the loss of energy that occurs past the top of the learning curve. The slide into entropy is inevitable unless we consciously fight it—or anticipate it. In describing his ideas about learning, Jonas Salk showed how knowledge grows rapidly around certain new insights (scientific paradigms, for example), until entropy sets in, pulling the curve down. But new theories are always arising, apparently out of chaos. Salk portrayed this phenomenon as a new learning curve growing out of the old one, calling these curves Epic A and Epic B:

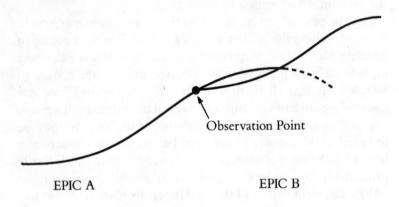

Salk proposed that when an organism (or an individual or society) reaches the top of the Epic A curve, it is inefficient to spend more time there. So, at some point before the curve begins to bend down, we should begin the search for a new learning curve—or work against entropy by other means if it's important to sustain the Epic A curve.

That point on the curve where learning starts to slow was identified by Land as the "observation point." It is in many ways the optimum time to step back, evaluate our progress along the current learning curve, and perhaps contemplate launching a new one. This is shown in the illustration, with the Epic B curve intersecting the Epic A curve at the observation point. To imagine this, you might think of a surfer who senses the dynamic of the wave beneath him, and compare the observation point to the instant when he knows it is time to abandon the sinking or breaking wave and catch a new one that is building.

Salk is a salutary example of Step 3, matching action to insight in his own life, a heroic adventurer in nonstop learning. Nobel prize–winners notoriously have found it hard to top that high point in their careers, but he is the exception. A

Nobel laureate for his discovery of the poliomyelitis vaccine, he could be spending his later years at ease in his seaside home in Southern California. Instead, he is risking his reputation and his life by trying to develop a vaccine for AIDS. When I last ran into him, he was sitting on the beach near his home with a dictating machine. Asked what he was doing, he replied with a mischievous grin, "Solving this AIDS business." A few weeks later, I read that he might inject himself with a virus to demonstrate whether his approach was valid. He was proceeding full gallop on an Epic B chase.

THE OBSERVATION POINT

Self-observation is essential to the process of renewal. Too often in our struggle for success we fail to probe into our deeper selves and to rigorously assess our progress in learning. I'm doing well, so why bother? When the pressure's on, who's got time? Yet the time for self-observation is before the learning curve has peaked and begun to lose momentum, while you are still in the rapturous state of enhanced performance— George Land's observation point. From this excellent vantage, you can see the summit of your success and take stock of where you have been.

To become a skilled and unflinching self-observer takes practice. Try to step aside and note where you are, even when it is premature and the exercise yields minimal information. Think of this process as a trek up a winding mountain trail. Veteran trekkers periodically step off the trail to size up the work done and the task ahead. During the respite, they explore certain questions. Is the rate of energy being expended appropriate for this point on the trek? Are sustaining satisfactions being derived or has the venture lost meaning? Is the summit still ahead or have they strayed from the right path?

The advantages of stepping aside for a clear appraisal of progress seem obvious. Why is it so hard for many to do? Why do people press on mindlessly, Sisyphus-like pushing their rocks up the hill only to have them roll down again? We may fear losing out. What if by stepping aside a competitor passes us? We may fear that it will be painful. Too often our experiences of self-observations are harsh judgments when benign, forgiving eyes are appropriate.

The toughest barrier to becoming a good self-observer is not knowing how the knowledge gained is to be put to use. How does self-knowledge, awareness of learning needs, get transformed into new goals and plans? Proper self-observations should result in goals and plans anchored to deep, personal learning requirements that, once achieved, will result in great satisfaction. The primary reason for stepping aside from your present trail is to determine what current efforts are delivering in the way of learning satisfaction compared to the needs you uncover. If you have reached the place on your present learning curve where increased effort results in diminished returns, it is time to change curves.

We come to many observation points over a lifespan, arriving there at different times for different learning curves. Your career may be moving upward on the steep part of the curve, while your primary relationship is approaching a downturn in intensity. Or personal growth and development may be beginning to rise out of chaos while family demands are peaking.

Over the years I have seen many people go whizzing by observation points without pausing to step aside. Though it may seem unnatural to slow down when the summit is in sight, it is much easier to deal with life changes and spot growing shadows before the learning curve begins to deteriorate. Many a mountaineer, eyes fixed on the summit, has failed to notice the stormclouds gathering and has never been sighted again. You may not be dealing with such life-and-death matters, but a pause at the observation point can profoundly affect your future.

If you glance back at the learning-curve illustration, you'll note that the observation point is where, ideally, a new learning curve intersects with the old one. Those who make the most graceful transitions are those who know where they are, anticipate change, and prepare early.

LOCATING THE OBSERVATION POINT

A farmer in rural Ireland directed a traveler: "Well, you go down that road awhile and when you come to an old, tired-out brick hospital, you know you have gone about twice as far as your turnoff." So it is with spotting our observation points: We may not know where we are until we sense we have gone too far. As a forty-four-year-old banker told me, "I thought I knew where I was until I developed ulcers and lost my marriage. It was a big wake-up call and I realized that I had not been paying attention to any of the more subtle warnings. But they were there." This bright fast-trekker is now on extended leave, asking herself the questions that she neglected to review earlier. Unfortunately, all too often the overdue stock-taking is forced upon us.

Determining when you have reached an observation point is rarely obvious, but if you pay attention, you can pick up signals. Making early assessments is bolstering to the spirits. You learn that you are still enjoying the benefits of your trek. Once past the observation point, however, the feedback is different. You could experience a mild slowdown, diminished enthusiasm for work, sex, life in general. You could spot a growing impatience or irritability, find yourself wishing to escape and vegetate, or drive yourself even harder to mask the symptoms of unrest. You could notice (or a friend could point out) that the virtues of success—mental agility, confidence, alertness, dedication, control, and courage—are being turned inside out.

Spotting an observation point and preparing for new learning ventures means taking some time away from your normal routines and asking yourself pertinent questions.

• Have your days become more routine, and your tasks and responses mind-numbing? A forty-two-year-old partner in a major accounting firm told me that 80 percent of her time was spent working on an "assembly line" of boilerplate forms, reports, and standard letters. "I can do most of it without much thought at all." She was clearly ripe for renewal.

• Are you missing the feelings of thrills and breakthroughs in your work or other endeavors? A fifty-year-old physician complains, "The scientist part of me is totally wasted, and since I work alone most of the time, I don't even know how much I may be missing. My wife says I'm almost always cross when I get home from work. Something is causing that." He is considering returning to school for another degree that will enable him to combine research with his clinical practice.

• Are you living more cautiously, cutting down your exposure to new challenges? A forty-nine-year-old corporate executive acknowledged that he reacts differently to risks since he began to think about retirement. "I know I need to plan ahead for when I'm not working. I feel too young to stop, but I'm beginning to wonder what will keep me going in the 'third act' of my life. I've grown more cautious but don't like the feeling of just treading water." Spoken like a man who needs to seek out, not avoid, new challenges.

• How much of what you do really stretches you? A thirty-six-year-old professional woman answered promptly: "My hobby, playing guitar, is the only thing I do where I'm constantly striving for mastery and always looking forward to the next session. Even my primary relationship has become more of a comfort zone." This is a woman at the observation point of two curves: work and love.

• What difference would it make to those around you or the world if you kept on with what you are doing or made a change? A high-ranking midfifties executive grew to hate the disparity between his beliefs and values and the work he produced. "I should have made a change long ago. Now I feel stuck. I can't let go of my paycheck, and I can't find another position with more personal meaning that comes close to paying me what I need." He is struggling to find a good job that meets his altruistic and financial needs.

• Are you engaging in denial? From a man highly positioned in a multinational corporation, I consistently heard reports that everything was just fine. One day I opened the paper to find a headline story about a scandal involving his company. When I called him to see how he felt, he tried to laugh it off. Everything was still "just fine." His belated recognition will hurt him and his company.

• Are you sweating more and getting less satisfaction? The owner of a successful media firm put it this way: "I'm in a coffin with a glass top, and I can see more dirt being shoveled on top each day." He certainly came to the observation point late, but at least he now has a view and is looking for a new partner to take on aspects of the business that are weighing him down.

• Can you see your part in failures? A very bright venture capitalist had suffered a string of sour deals. He saw the problem as bad luck in picking partners. "I guess I don't know how to read people well enough. I have a degree in business, not psychology. Perhaps I'm too trusting." By keeping the problem projected onto others and by twisting failure into a sort of virtue—being overly trusting—he was avoiding observing what was really going on.

• Have you developed obsessive behavior patterns? A manager in the service industries, in her late thirties, reported that she hadn't had a real vacation in years. Seeming unconcerned about the consequences at first, she finally admitted, "It's not that I don't need the time, but I just can't let go."

• Has hubris taken hold? Virtually all the symptoms of hubris are good indicators that you have rushed past at least one observation point. A dramatic example is the fifty-something entrepreneur who came for counseling after firing his first two therapists. "This year I bought two houses and a new yacht, but my girlfriend just walked. My sister is furious because I won't back her in some dumb business. I bought my parents a new co-op in Florida, but they still hassle me about helping my sister." Now he's looking for a new therapist and a new relationship.

Using the observation point to step back is never easy. Even if holding on to a weakening success curve has become wasteful and inefficient, your pride is at stake; you feel you've earned that place at the top. More important, your identity may be so bound up in your success that the idea of abandoning it is like losing your life. When you consider stepping back from your current structure, you may see only a fearsome void instead of the potential for new learning.

For all these reasons, the observation point should be a place to slow down. I compared it to the moment when a surfer senses a loss of momentum in the wave he is riding and looks for a new one to catch. But while the surfer's moves happen in the blink of an eye, life decisions have a much more gradual rhythm. Most often, they call for getting out of the water entirely and spending some time on the beach, silently watching the larger patterns of the waves and looking inside to learn why you're riding them in the first place.

TAKING STOCK

For highly driven people, one of the hardest things about stepping back is feeling comfortable with unstructured time. At some point in your renewal journey this will be important, but my experience is that people are more comfortable at first with a structured task such as taking a detailed self-inventory, noting the parts of yourself and your situation that are no longer of service to future growth.

A useful preamble to this inventory, in terms of tracking your changing vision of who you are and want to be, is to periodically draft a personal "mission statement," along the lines of a corporate mission statement. A mission statement will vary in its content, intensity, and timetable depending on where you are in your life-span and what values you hold dear. Young people have mission statements that are often quite concrete: "I want to have a solid career and a family under way by the time I reach forty." Or, "I will pursue graduate work and work with the psychological problems of refugees over the next ten years." The rare individual writes a mission statement that covers the whole of a life or a boldly ambitious one at the age of sixty.

A mission statement often contains multiple goals. However, the goals need not be hard-and-fast; a life is not a business.

Long-distance winners often have disarmingly simple mission statements. When the question was put to Jonas Salk, he replied: "To reduce human suffering." But one can have parallel missions, too, as Winston Churchill did at times. During World War II, his mission was to save the world from totalitarianism. His other mission, which spanned the same time and beyond, was to record the history of the English-speaking peoples.

When you step back and begin to inventory, you are trying to see your situation through the eyes of an objective, kindly observer: what you have tried to accomplish, the results shown in your working and personal lives, and the personal consequences of your achievements in the professional or business world. You are checking up on your goals.

Write down whatever responses and issues the following questions provoke. Doing this could lead you deeper into yourself and your shadow territory than you expected, but that is all right. If it becomes clear that you need more time to dig into the questions, consider scheduling some retreat time.

1. *In what way is your work consistent with your self-image and in what way inconsistent?* Are you comfortable with the balance? What could you do to get greater consistency?
2. *Are you actively learning, feeling stretched and positively challenged in some endeavor you care deeply about?* When

was a time that you felt most stimulated and stretched? What did it feel like? How close to that are you now?

3. *What is the current status of your work and personal relationships?* Whom do you blame for what is wrong in your life? Whom do you need to forgive or make peace with? Whom should you teach or mentor?

4. *What are your secrets?* Secrets contain bound-up energy which, when released, can often bring freedom from shame and a sense of renewal.

5. *What are your deepest regrets?* Shadows gather quickly around regrets and resentments. When they are aired out, they become less oppressive. Try to look beyond obvious financial and professional mistakes that resulted in the loss of money or prestige so that you can discern the deeper regrets about losses to your personal capital.

6. *What are you most afraid of?* The mere act of articulating fears in black and white can exorcise some of their effect. An acquaintance tells me: "I ask myself what is the worst thing that could happen to me if I make some changes in my life. I write down each disaster that comes to mind. I carry the list around, check some of them out with friends. I play with the worst fears, even dream about them. By the time I have finished the examination I usually wonder what frightened me in the first place."

7. *What kinds of troublesome behavior do you engage in? What deeper issues might they be connected with?* Many people are too quick to apply surface remedies to deeply rooted behavioral problems. This includes many psychosomatic problems such as obesity, insomnia, addictions, and mood swings. Large problems are often signaled by small, self-destructive behaviors. If you have some, it's important to look them in the eye before they grow beyond their current size.

A regional sales manager named Ted managed to

ignore his ballooning weight, despite his family's not-so-subtle hints, until his company's board chairman humiliated him in a meeting. Enraged, Ted put himself on a semistarvation diet that soon produced a new problem: outbursts of foul temper.

His family unconsciously conspired to restore him to his old, jolly self. The weight came back and life returned to normal—on the surface. But Ted never got around to finding out why his eating habits were out of order in the first place. If he had looked more closely, he might have discovered a connection between his obesity and where he stood in his life, what the extra girth might be protecting.

8. *How have your goals changed?* The purpose of reflecting on the history of your goals is to determine if they suit your needs at the present time.

9. *How bad is your time crunch and what are its primary causes?* What are the implications and costs of spreading yourself too thin or of cramming every waking moment with business? From time to time I look at the number of organizations I belong to and the amount of work and time it takes to keep up with these affiliations. It's often a shock to discover what the aggregate costs are and how few real benefits are derived and bestowed. Leaders who stretch their resources over too much territory often do likewise with those of their organizations.

A glance at your weekly calendar may reveal how much of your time is eaten up by the pursuit of success and how little is left over for personal growth. Have meetings become habitual rather than essential? Once-productive routines merely spinning the wheels? What can you drop? What would you like to add?

10. *Which aspects of your character need strengthening? Which talents do you feel you are ignoring?* This is an instance of mining for gold in your shadow, and past experiences and daydreaming can help you do this.

11. *What are you contributing?* What are you returning to your children, your younger associates, your community? What personal satisfaction do you derive from your contributions?

You can follow up this inventory with a "personal cost-benefit analysis" to determine what degree and type of changes are called for. Factor in your obligations, real and perceived, your strengths and weaknesses, and of course whatever buried treasure you come back with from your explorations of the shadow. Don't overlook family and personal history, and don't fail to find and use excellent guides, teachers, and mentors. Your life is a story shaped by many influences, and the more sense you can make of it, the better equipped you will be to write the next chapter in a way that works best for you.

FIRST STEPS

This chapter dealt with the components of self-renewal—what John Gardner called "the elements that provide immunity to decay"—and showed how they operate out of the need for continuous, lifelong learning. Long-distance winners know that sustaining a life of excellence is not a linear progression like the myth of vertical success. It has a much more complex dynamic, with wins and losses forming waves in an ever-shifting sea of learning ventures. Both the crests and troughs give us perspectives on how the waves form and what lies ahead.

As dancers and martial artists literally step back to gather energy for the next movement, so regenerative down-time is essential to refueling our energy and focusing our sense of direction throughout a full and demanding life. In some ways, this first stage is the hardest part of renewal. It requires breaking through denial. Insofar as renewal is a kind of rebirth, it must begin with a symbolic death, a readiness to let go of an old learning curve, a psychic security blanket, perhaps a mask of satisfaction and contentment.

It is hard to step back from a successful but diminishing learning curve. Where does the motivation to move on come from? Where do you find the courage and impetus to abandon the wave that is losing its momentum and heading for entropy? In the next chapter we will delve further into the reasons why successful people often cannot let go of a failing learning curve, and suggest a variety of approaches for easing the difficulty of stepping back. We will look at myths and metaphors for letting go, examine a range of attitudes and practices that promote renewal, and offer help and inspiration from the lives of deep learners.

A word of reassurance: Most of you are already familiar with the cycle of renewal. And since you are reading this book, you are a likely prospect to become a lifelong deep learner. If success has hurt you, you can recover. If you have escaped damage so far, you can learn to avoid its traps and hazards. There's no such thing as a quickie course in self-renewal, but the skills and attitudes described in the next chapter can set you on the track.

CHAPTER 5

Promoting Renewal: Getting Past the Fear of Letting Go

W HEN CLIENTS COME IN to see me about changes they want to make in their lives or organizations, I begin the visit on a congratulatory note. Most of these men and women are doing well, accustomed to "charging the hill," and stepping back often feels uncomfortable—even like an admission of defeat. Many of them have attached themselves like barnacles to the hull of a ship, and cling even though all the warning lights are blazing. Many of them were enduring isolation, destructive relationships in the workplace, stress, and boredom, and refused to see how stultified they had become, even when friends and spouses hinted that all was not well. Inertia, habit, the need for security, and fear of identity loss kept them in line.

Likewise, I have encountered and read of organizations that have ignored obvious danger signals until they were sunk by competitors or by their own leaders. The larger and more powerful the organization, the harder it is to evade hubris. Also, we as Americans tend to associate the success or failure of our monster corporations with that of our nation—one reason for the costly bailout of Chrysler and the S & Ls.

In his book *The Reckoning*, David Halberstam shows how the lords of Detroit lost their edge in the automotive world through their own arrogance. They rejected warning after warning, smugly dismissing petroleum experts who foresaw the end of cheap fuel and suggestions that their foreign competitors' cars were more in tune with consumers' tastes. Times Mirror chairman Franklin Murphy, a member of Ford's board of directors during the 1970s, was scorned for noting how popular Japanese cars were in California. Lee Iacocca, then at Ford, told a friend not to take a Toyota dealership "because we are going to kick their asses back into the Pacific Ocean."

For individuals too, a variety of barriers keep us from stepping back when we should. As the sign warns visitors embarking on a muddy back road in rural Canada: *Pick your rut carefully—you may be in it a long time!*

OBSTACLES TO STEPPING BACK

In the discussion of finding observation points in Chapter 3, several obstacles were mentioned: pride, insecurity, and fear of lost identity were listed as factors that work against stepping back. Of course, many unconscious factors may be at work, keeping us in our grooves. In my experience, certain of these factors seem to create a particularly firm adhesive. Perhaps it is because they are once-positive virtues that have deteriorated into psychological deficits.

• *The Drive for Perfection*. The obsessional parts of our nature are especially hard to grapple with since they have often paid off for us. Take the story of Edwin Land, the founder of Polaroid. His perfectionistic genius produced the innovations that created a powerful company, and yet these same tendencies put Polaroid in jeopardy. At one point Land became obsessed with developing a so-called revolutionary SX-70 model. Millions of dollars were lost before he was moved aside. We too can find ourselves in the perfection groove and, once there, unable to step aside and see how our path has become our prison.

• *Clocks That Tell Us What to Do*. Our necessary and useful linear schedule can become a tyrannical clock, telling us when we should pursue which parts of our personal and career lives. Take the case of an attractive go-getting woman in her early fifties who was suddenly laid off due to a merger: "My first reaction was panic. I wasn't financially or emotionally ready to retire. After the panic subsided and I had some good counseling, I began to realize how hemmed in I had felt in my old job. It was a dead end with a pretty good paycheck." This same energetic woman is now a partner in a professional services firm and cannot imagine why she had been hanging on to her old job waiting to retire.

• *Pride and Other False Mirrors.* Well-meaning encouragement from friends and family members can often turn into unspoken expectations that grip us like a vise, blocking any changes we may be considering. It can also prevent us from stepping back and seeing ourselves clearly. A Hispanic woman in a new career relates the following story: "My family never encouraged me to seek a career, so each step I made felt like I was violating some unspoken value that my parents could not say out loud. I realized that for many years I was looking in a mirror that my parents had constructed. I was trying to be the person who matched their image, and yet something inside told me it was wrong. I finally had to break their mirror and find my own. I love my new job and have given up hoping to please them with my career moves."

Whether our self-image is fashioned by parents, friends, or co-workers, we are unconsciously aware of their approbation or disapproval. Ever so gently, often lovingly, they weave a soft cocoon around us, working to keep us in a niche that is comfortable—for them!

• *Risk Aversion.* Financial demands or the perceived need to protect or increase wealth often glue successful people to failing learning curves. Risk aversion for the sake of financial security is perhaps most pronounced in those of us molded by the Great Depression, but few are free from it. Here are the words of a baby-boomer: "I had no idea how trapped I was by financial insecurity until my significant other lost his job. Our upwardly oriented path was suddenly a slippery slide. I began to clamp down firmly on all of the safety apparatus that a steady job offers. Our discussions of future dreams have stopped—just when we really need to review and analyze our aspirations, values, and hopes."

If you are clinging to material security, you still may be more adaptable than you realize, but it might take a jolt to shake you loose unless you realize the amount of risk aversion that you are experiencing.

FINDING THE MOTIVATION TO CHANGE

There are many obstacles to overcome when you try to step back and examine your situation, but there are also ways to evade the hold of old habits.

One method is to understand how motivation operates.

Motivation can be seen as a "push-pull" dynamic. The unsatisfactory aspects of your life are the "push" that could get you moving: the negative motivation. You could be pushed toward change by an unfulfilling personal relationship, a failing business, a hostile board of directors, or health problems. Or you could experience a positive "pull" from the promise of a better life, a job that allows more free time, a restructuring that requires a more hands-on role, the opportunity to pursue a long-delayed dream of travel, or contact with the arts.

Healthy change is usually based on responding to an attraction, something that pulls you forward. You may respond to a negative push reflexively and make an ill-considered move just to escape discomfort. Decisions that turn out badly often result from the painful need to escape an unsatisfactory situation. Simply being aware of this can help you avoid similar errors in the future. But if you take the time to figure out what really pulls you, and make decisions that nurture it, you are likely to discover a learning curve with "legs."

Change is usually less daunting if approached indirectly rather than head-on. Winston Churchill, a world-class success sustainer, was a compulsive learner. He would pursue an endeavor long after it played out. Overextending his political and military projects caused him to suffer ego-crunching defeats. He discovered that the way he could step back and gain a better perspective was to distract himself with learning about a totally unfamiliar subject, or involvement with some creative, hands-on project. This comment from an unnamed American psychologist caught Churchill's attention because he felt it applied to him: "Worry is a spasm of the emotion; the mind catches hold of something and will not let it go. It is useless to argue with the mind in this condition. The stronger the will, the more futile the task. One can only gently insinuate something else into its convulsive grip. And if this something else is rightly chosen, gradually, and often quite swiftly, the old undue grip relaxes and the processes of recuperation and repair begin."

"Gently insinuating" a healthy distraction is a good way for vigilant achievers to move toward renewal. Rather than thinking you must set out on an epic journey, take a few steps down a path that beckons and see where it leads.

HANDY'S "LUBRICANTS OF CHANGE"

We all know that growth means survival, but we are also prone to inertia and fearful of change. In *The Age of Unreason*, management expert Charles Handy offers a theory of learning in which he describes the typical barriers to continuous learning and some valuable "lubricants of change."

Handy notes that "because most people do not like change, change is forced upon them by crisis and discontinuity." While this kind of change can be productive, he urges that we initiate and manage change rather than merely reacting to it. Such readiness to learn and evolve will be an advantage in a world more and more characterized by discontinuity.

Like the process of renewal, learning proceeds in cyclical fashion, Handy asserts. It is a wheel that begins with a *question*—the problem to be solved or challenge to be met—and proceeds through *theory, testing*, and *reflection*, leading always to further questions. The question is "a problem to be solved, a dilemma to be resolved." And it must be *your* question, one in which the outcome really matters to you. Or, he says, you will not "push the wheel around to the final stage of reflection. . . . Discovery doesn't happen unless you are looking."

By theories, Handy simply means possible answers to our questions, "a stage of speculation, of free-thinking, of reframing, of looking for clues." Our theories must then be tested in the real world to see which ones work and which don't. Finally, we must learn *why* they do or do not work: the stage of reflection. "Change only sticks when we understand why it happened."

Barriers to learning proliferate with age, which brings specialization in our skills. "Mankind, I am sure, is born to learn," says Handy. "One has only to look at little children to see that wheel turning furiously. Why, we must wonder, does it slow down for most of us as we get older?" The problem is that most adults engage only one segment of the wheel—the dominant side of their personality leading them to get stuck in speculation, or action, or philosophizing. Or their progress may be blocked by external factors.

Handy's lubricants of change are useful tools that can help us get unstuck when our learning is blocked. What is necessary is "responsible selfishness," which includes (a) assuming responsibility for yourself and your future, (b) having an accurate view of what you want that future to be, and (c) having the desire to make your vision come true and the confidence that you can do so.

I believe that I was exercising responsible selfishness when I left the world of business for higher education, a new learning ground where I started from scratch with new language, customs, and relationships. This move was not part of some long-range master plan; it was an attempt to answer a question that had assumed great importance: How could I find in my working life the compelling excitement it had once had? Finding the new path was a matter of staying open to a wide range of possible answers to that question.

The change called for some adjustment by my family and friends, but I was lucky in having their support. What makes this kind of selfishness "responsible" is that it is really about developing a self that you as well as others can live with. The reward for acting responsibly selfish extends well beyond the individual.

A way of reframing. This is "the ability to see things, problems, situations, or people in other ways . . . to put them in another perspective or context; to think of them as opportunities, not problems." Talking with others, one-to-one or in groups, is an aid to reframing. Using metaphors and analogies to describe your situation also helps.

Here, too, I'll use an example from personal experience. Part of my leadership role with the California School of Professional Psychology is working with associates to reframe our educational mission. The traditional academic view is that higher education benefits society by articulating ideas that slowly filter down from the ivory tower. We have tried to expand this mission, to reframe it, by blending the principles of commerce with those of nonprofit education. Our training of clinical psychologists produces a variety of marketable "products" such as assessment tools and research results; for example, research on handling children with early-onset diabetes. Via a marketing approach developed by business, these products can be distributed to many more people more quickly.

A negative capability. Handy borrows this phrase from Keats, who defined it as the ability to live with uncertainty and doubt. He extends it to include living with our mistakes and failures as well: "Getting it wrong is part of getting it right."

Handy illustrates the idea by recounting the story of an appointment that his university was considering. "Richard, the person in question, was well known to us, a brilliant lecturer, an authority in his field. . . . Why then were there so many unspoken reservations in the faces around the table? Someone then captured it for us: 'The trouble is,' he said, 'Richard has no decent doubt.' Without that, there was no questioning, no learning, no deliberate change." Without doubt, without a negative, there could be no growth.

Handy's lubricants of change are also lubricants of renewal. Later in this chapter, I have added to his list a set of attitudes and skills that promote deep learning and lead to renewal.

LETTING GO: THE LEAP OF FAITH

Another way to think about stepping back is to imagine letting go. If you are having trouble getting some distance and perspective on your situation, you probably need to let go of something—it may be a career path that has run its course or something less obvious and drastic. Perhaps you need to let go of an attitude toward yourself or your work, a kind of hypervigilance that shuts out other possibilities. Perhaps you simply need to let go of the belief that "I don't do that sort of thing."

From the experience of long-distance winners come three ground rules for letting go:

- *Don't delay.* Most of the gains of any learning venture are realized before the curve tops out.
- *It's never risk-free.* Without risks, no new learning is possible. However, the risk of change and the chaos it brings are far less than the danger of lingering too long in an established niche.
- *You* can *take it with you.* You don't really begin a new learning venture from scratch; you can transfer the skills and wisdom you have gained from any endeavor.

Letting go of anything involves risk, a certain amount of faith that you can survive and even be better off without the prop you have been clinging to. It's risky because the outcome will not be clear at first. Usually you must commit yourself to a new learning venture before you know the payoff. Offsetting the risks, though, are the inherent, substantive advantages of self-renewal. Any change that brings new learning is revitalizing. In psychology as in biology, the rule of "stretch it or lose it" holds: all of our systems benefit by being challenged and utilized.

A favorite character of mine is Tarzan. Tarzan was a hero of his times, the product of Victorian fascination with humanity's newly discovered ascent from lower primates. He became "king of the jungle"—an arrogant and imperialistic notion, surely—but like any mythic king, he took seriously his responsibility to protect his domain from invaders and exploiters.

To do this, Tarzan had to abandon the arrogant security of being *homo sapiens*, the lord of creation, and nurture his animal side (I would call it a shadow side). The ape's gifts of agility and timing became Tarzan's strengths. He became a creature who literally knew how to let go—swinging from vine to vine without hesitation, as at ease in his environment as one of his primate pals. Imagine Tarzan failing to let go of the first vine when he reached out to grab the next one—he would get nowhere. He knew that his success lay in movement, not in finding a safe place to hide.

In a different way, the tale of Odysseus demonstrates the need to let go in order to move forward in life; he is an object lesson in the consequences of clinging to old success. One of the heroes of the Trojan War, Odysseus decides to do some roaming and raiding on the return voyage to Greece. Twenty years and a multitude of disasters later, he finally limps home to find his kingdom in chaos and his embattled wife, Penelope, using all her wits to fend off would-be usurpers.

The Odyssey can be seen as a kind of extended midlife crisis, the story of a man who fiercely resists making a transition from the youthful role of a wandering warrior to a more settled, responsible, domestically oriented king. Odysseus thought that the way to maintain his power was to continue fighting with the boys and winning battles. He could have quit while he was ahead many times, taken home some trophies, dealt with the problems there, and so retained the respect of his people. But he lost his way literally and figuratively, growing ever more reckless in the course of a rapidly deteriorating learning journey. Like other victims of hubris, he also closed his ears to wise advice. When a whirlpool sucked down his last ship, he was forced to creep home alone, in rags.

Superficially, it might seem that Odysseus had no problem letting go, drifting as he did from one adventure to the next. But like many another restless personality, he sought new experiences as distractions from the real business of life, substituting external change for deep learning. Though he gained wisdom at last, hitting bottom is a rather hard way to let go.

We can find plenty of tales of the hero's fall among people of our own era. It happens again and again that bright, ambitious people lose their bearings and drive their ship of success onto the rocks of disgrace or failure. In business, corporate raiders Robert Campeau, of the Campeau department store consortium, and Frank Lorenzo, of Eastern Airlines, gripped their successes too tightly and couldn't swing away. In politics, Alan Cranston and John Sununu couldn't resist stretching their power until it snapped.

Power is one winner's quicksand; money serves for many others. A friend, retired from the manufacturing business he started, invested a chunk of his retirement money in a hedge fund. At first the returns were incredible: 20, 30, 40 percent. After a while he grew worried because the firm's reports were vague and there were rumors of problems. Based on sound advice, he got out of the fund. Months later, the firm crashed and its top people were indicted. But I learned that my friend had reinvested in the meantime. "I was hooked on those returns," he confessed when we next met. He was unable to let go.

LIVES OF DEEP LEARNING

My work brings me into contact with many people like those mentioned above, who learned to step back the hard way. I have also encountered remarkable individuals who responded to the renewal imperative in their lives, finding ways to let go and thereby survive near-lethal success.

One such example is Phillip Moffitt, a young man who came from a discouraging childhood in east Tennessee to achieve major business success in the flush eighties and navigate New York's publishing maelstrom, all before he turned thirty-five.

In 1979 he and his partners bought *Esquire*, a decaying magazine with a grand tradition. They cared for their patient around the clock and achieved a remarkable recovery; soon the business grew far beyond the magazine itself. Around that time, Moffitt reached an observation point. He didn't like what he saw.

I met Phillip while he was prowling around northern California in search of promising writers and stories. Since his advance billing led me to expect a larger-than-life character, I was pleasantly surprised to encounter a soft-spoken, modest man. As we got better acquainted, he talked about how hard it was to keep part of himself separate from his career, to avoid being devoured by his work. He seemed to have a natural wariness that is unusual in someone so young, as if some aspects of his thinking and personality had matured early.

Out of our early talks came a column he wrote for *Esquire* called "The Dark Side of Excellence." It stimulated a huge volume of mail from readers who identified with the symptoms of success sufferers. After this, Phillip became even more interested in the shadows lurking behind high performance, and devoted more time to retreat and self-observation in his own life, while remaining very active in the publishing company.

Phillip has always had the advantage of being a keen observer. He recognizes that good observation springs from being able to see oneself clearly. As he said once, "You must keep telling your own life story accurately to others, but, most importantly, to yourself. Your integrity is rooted there."

He was one of those fortunate people who loved to read and could learn from other people's stories: "Books were my teachers. It was tough growing up in the Appalachians, but the inspiration that was missing in my community I was able to find in my reading. Early on I started to tell the story of my life to myself; in retrospect I was amazingly honest about it. Having to do this was not always a good or happy situation, but it served me well later on. I had few illusions about the outcomes of success—certainly that financial success was an end in itself. For me, the deepest meaning in life is living out my story such that it honestly expresses my beliefs; it would be tragic to sacrifice that for success."

The acquisition of *Esquire*, with its tradition of fine fiction (especially concerning the aspirations and frustrations of men), was an outgrowth of his hunger for information and insights. His observational skills were enhanced by proximity to writers and editors, and by learning more about the arts of fiction and reportage. Well-expressed ideas and observations can shift consciousness and change life's prospects. The best writers aid us in observing what we miss; with a deft metaphor they can help us to feel, taste, see, and intuit what they experience.

In his role as publisher, Phillip became a professional observer of his time, and what he saw of his own generation in the eighties troubled him and evoked his compassion. He saw yuppie strivers as rootless, overextended, reactive, and fearful. He came to feel that a larger sense of purpose was the most fundamental void in their lives. Toward the end of the decade he wrote in his column: "My wish for America as a country is that it finds a greater dream, to create the new, not just to somehow hold on to what it has. . . . I would wish that each and every one [of us] would feel more compassion toward others, and that they should feel united, in community, through that compassion. If we could reach that point, it would almost make the eighties worth it."

Phillip's skill as an observer allowed him to see where he was on his learning curve, to recognize an imbalance favoring work, and to hear what the shadow suggested about his future prospects. In retreat, he could begin to ask the hard questions: Was his work as satisfying as it had been? If not, which parts were debilitating and which represented new growth? Could he keep growing under the circumstances and responsibilities he had chosen? Was it possible and practical to renew his passion for work by restructuring his position, or was real growth possible only in a new setting?

It became clear to Phillip that selling the Esquire Magazine Group and putting distance between himself and New York was a necessary step out of inflation's reach. He did so and entered a new phase of learning chaos, choosing guides and teachers from a wide array of dedicated people. He was seeking wisdom about the process of change itself, and needed the advice of those who were familiar with the territory. He deliberately chose to study certain practices which were particularly difficult for him; temporarily abandoning all the proven skills he had acquired in twenty years in publishing. This was a process that proved difficult for Phillip and baffled many friends and colleagues. Recently married and a cofounder of an exciting new software company, Light Source Computer Imaging, Phillip is also active in The Social Venture Network, using his skills to address a broad social and environmental agenda for business. He is achieving a balance in his life that meets his needs and conforms to his larger sense of life's purpose.

Another successful executive, Susie Tompkins, of the Esprit clothing empire, found that social activism was a key element in renewing her entrepreneurial energy after a well-publicized and exhausting struggle with her ex-husband for control of the company.

Esprit shot to prominence in the retail world during the 1970s. In the late 1980s, it was rocked by plunging sales and the Tompkinses' marital strife. But Susie persevered, took some time away from the job ("I spent two years trying to learn what I wanted to do"), and then entered a rebuilding phase with both the company and her own life.

One of Tompkins's recent projects in what she calls "retail activism" is an advertising campaign in which the photographs and thoughts of some twenty-five customers are featured. Chosen from a poll asking the question, "What would you do to change the world?" the ads offer suggestions like "I'd reverse the status of educators and celebrities," and "Everyone would spend two days on the street without a cent."

Another Esprit endeavor is its new Ecollection, an environmentally conscious line of clothing featuring low-impact dyes, nontoxic handpainted or recycled glass buttons, and fabrics that have been recycled, respun, or rewoven. The company also has an environmental manager in its headquarters and plans to install counterparts in its other offices around the world.

Tompkins's ecological concerns are also highly personal. She loved the bucolic part of northern California, where her family had a home when she was young, and recently acquired forty-four acres of the last private wild land in the same area, to live on and preserve from further development.

Tompkins's career has been a series of letting go of old vines and grabbing new and challenging ones.

Finally, let's turn to the shining example of Winston Churchill, whose lifelong pursuit of learning enabled him to overcome an emotionally crippling childhood. Ignored by his parents, who packed him off to boarding school at age seven, he was a small, not very strong boy who earned poor marks and was treated harshly by his teachers. He rose above all this to become a leader, a prodigious orator, and a writer so skilled and prolific as to defy comparison.

Yet Churchill's public achievements could not satisfy the inner needs of a love-deprived "adult child." He was haunted by childhood insecurities that drove him to compulsive performance and arrogance. He also suffered from bouts of acute depression that he called his "black dog." For him it became a matter of necessity to step back from time to time, retreating to his country home and the avocations, including painting and bricklaying, that were his passions.

Churchill came to believe that new challenges were the key to his self-renewal. "Change is the master key," he wrote. "A man can wear out a particular part of his mind by continually using it and tiring it, just as in the same way he can wear out the elbows of his coat. There is, however, a difference between the living cells of the brain and inanimate articles: one cannot mend the frayed elbows of a coat by rubbing the sleeves or shoulders, but the tired parts of the mind can be rested and strengthened, not merely by rest, but by using other parts."

As with Odysseus, there is a vast difference between merely changing one's circumstances or surroundings and pursuing a life of deep learning. Most of us have experienced some major change in our lives without necessarily applying the skills of renewal to the process. Motivations for superficial change can be very straightforward: financial betterment, the status that goes with promotion, more pleasant surroundings, a boss who is a pain in the rear.

In contrast, a life of deep learning is the conscious pursuit of appropriate learning ventures that move in cadence with a higher purpose. Each of us forms an overarching vision of what his or her life ought to be, guided by beliefs and values that are often private and unstated. This vision provides a framework for the evolution of our personal dreams, channels to direct the energy we can liberate from the shadow. Happily, we need not dismantle our lives in the process of deep learning. Changes of career or location, radically refashioning relationships, or revamping life-styles may or may not be indicated. Such change is often more symptomatic of the desire to escape shadow issues than deal with them, and may prove unsustainable.

THE LUBRICANTS OF RENEWAL

Those who seek renewal will be helped by cultivating attitudes that may be unfamiliar. If you are to see clearly when you step back, and learn deeply when you go inside, you will probably need to relax certain expectations you have of yourself and certain limits that you unconsciously accept, as well as pay attention to concerns that you generally ignore. The following skills are the deep learner's equivalent of a mountain climber's ropes, pitons, and gummy shoes.

ADMITTING THAT EVERYTHING IS NOT OKAY

To begin healing yourself, you have to admit that you're in pain. The denial reflex is especially strong in successful people, and to break through that barrier takes courage, but mostly it requires an effort at awareness that keeps denial from occurring automatically. Ask yourself questions like "What's the worst that can happen to me if I admit that everything *isn't* okay?"

Letting go of denial is necessary for opening new learning channels. It gives you access to the less developed or suppressed sides of your character that, if given a little room to operate, can point you in new directions. It is also an admission that you need help and feedback in your search for renewal, sending a message to family and friends to stand by you.

Identifying the sources of your pain is just one part of the overall stock-taking that goes on when you step back. Ask yourself: "What's not working?" To prime the pump and break through your resistance, you may need to exaggerate the problem or problems. This applies to organizations as well as individuals. As one business strategist put it, "It's my job as a leader to pick a problem, an area that's just 'good enough,' and tease it into a protocrisis. I magnify that which others work to minimize. I do this in my own life, as well as in the organization I lead." He cited the following: "A problem of sexual harassment was elevated into a much larger examination of the company's overall attitudes, values, and policies that involve people development. We could have fought the harassment case, blamed the victim, and pushed on. As it turned out, by elevating the problem we found lots of new, fresh soil for growing stronger people for the business."

USE YOUR MISTAKES

It's easier to become a success than to *be* a success. The terrain of sustained excellence is a minefield of mistakes lying in wait. But errors and failures have much to teach us if we allow ourselves to acknowledge them. Too often an error provokes only the responses of shame, embarrassment, and self-loathing. We may mobilize our defenses and stonewall our critics, but when we do so, learning stops dead and the shadow swells with denial.

Our mistakes contain valuable information. They are essential to our education, showing us what can work by pointing out what has not. Leaders need to be reminded of this simple truth because they are under so much pressure not to acknowledge errors. Charles Handy says, "It's not the mistake that hurts us, it's the grace we employ owning up to it that counts."

There are many cases in which clumsy denials and attempts to conceal or downplay mistakes have resulted in damage to a company's credibility and profits: the Exxon *Valdez* oil spill, Procter & Gamble's gaffe in subpoenaing phone records to trace a leak, AT&T's slowness to admit problems in the computer shutdown that paralyzed East Coast airports in 1991.

Conversely, Johnson & Johnson's handling of the Tylenol poisoning case became a plus for the company because its leaders acted openly and decisively, and consumer confidence was encouraged. Warren Buffett, the investment genius called on to take over the restructuring of Salomon Brothers, practiced airing his errors. In a 1991 article, he confessed, "My first mistake was buying control of Berkshire . . . I was enticed because the price looked cheap." He goes on to explain what was wrong with his "cigar butt approach" to investing and what he learned from testing it.

The act of forgiving oneself, which futurist Don Michael calls "error embracing," is cleansing and strengthening. If we can't forgive ourselves, we will make only safe plans, rise to petty challenges, and waste energy searching for soft landings.

Any new learning venture requires a healthy dose of self-forgiveness. The late Gordon Sherman, a businessman included in *Fortune* magazine's Hall of Fame, took up photography seriously in his fifties, an age many feel is too late to begin anything but a hobby. Even though Sherman had learned the patient art of observing nature from years of trout fishing, his first efforts at wildlife photography resulted in many a picture of birds' rear ends. His greatest challenge in learning this new craft was being patient with himself. As he put it, "When I learned to forgive myself, the birds stood still."

Learning ventures unrelated to your primary career identity can encourage self-forgiveness. It's easier to accept mistakes made out of the spotlight's glare. Gordon, like most of us, wanted to be good at whatever he did. But in photography, he could allow the process of mastery to fascinate him more than the end product. He didn't have to be in the Nikon Hall of Fame.

GRATITUDE

"I've got mine—and I deserve it." Such lack of gratitude for talent, good fortune, and assistance along the way encourages hubris. If you cannot feel gratitude for what you have achieved, or what has come your way, you will always want more. Nor can you accurately direct your quest for self-renewal without gratitude. You must appreciate what you have in order to find out what you need.

Failing to acknowledge our blessings isolates and disconnects us from the larger contexts of life, from the community of feeling. For example, human beings are dependent on nature's benevolence, and gratitude is in order. A narrow definition of our "success" as a species encourages the illusion that we can dominate nature, allows the destruction of rainforests and the proliferation of acid rain. But a broad and sustainable human success would include gratitude for nature's bounty and action to protect her and ourselves.

We all need talent, time, and energy to accomplish difficult tasks. We need support and understanding from others. For this and more, gratitude is appropriate. It teaches us that interdependence does not mean loss of identity or giving up control over our lives.

OPENING UP TO NEW ROLES AND EXPERIENCES

A moment of truth in my public speaking engagements occurs when I tell audiences of hard-driving businesspeople that I practice meditation. The "confession" provokes discomfort in many. Reactions include averted eyes, sly smiles, shifting around in chairs. What's significant is not this particular issue, but that many leaders gradually close themselves off from new possibilities, rejecting experiences they come to consider inappropriate or activities that don't mesh with their self-image. This constriction of the possible could be the single largest obstacle in the way of renewal.

Finding out what impels you toward a new learning curve, in a new direction, comes largely from trial and error. Before you abandon your present comfortable situation, experiment in a safe context. Refresh the tired parts of the mind, as

Churchill recommends, by using other parts of it. Expand your boundaries a little. Make time for an activity that tempts you. Volunteer for a position that has nothing to do with your job. Change a tried-and-true behavior pattern or interaction with someone at work or at home. What you learn through these limited experiments could provide clues to what might lie ahead or give you confidence that you can perform outside your familiar milieu.

Ask yourself: What are my self-imposed limits? What are the things I've simply crossed off my list of possibilities, and why? What could happen to me if I (fill in the blank: meditate, take singing lessons, adopt a child, take a vacation somewhere where there's no phone)? And a related question: What is my security blanket—the financial prop, or perk, or routine, or symbol of authority I rely on—and what might happen were I to give it up or if it were taken from me?

Aretha Franklin singing in church as a young girl, Debbie Fields perfecting her homemade cookies, graduate students David Packard and Bill Hewlett working with electronics in a garage, and Bill Gates playing with new software ideas in high school were all experimenting with their future careers. There are many stories of experiments that resulted in new careers later in life. After years in business, my friend John Levy opened a storefront counseling center and now at sixty-something is traveling around the world as a counselor to wealthy families. Another friend, Deborah Szekeley, founder of the Golden Door and Rancho La Puerta spas, followed her heart and longtime community experience into the federally sponsored Interamerica Foundation.

Consider also the possibility that deep learning can go forward without any apparent purpose. It's hard for goal-driven people to get used to the idea that learning can be profitable in a sense that has nothing to do with immediate results. Step A does not necessarily produce Result B, but may have greater long-range consequences for physical, emotional, and mental renewal.

PRACTICING MINDFULNESS

Mindfulness is a heightened awareness of how we interact with the world—a highly developed form of observation. It is a familiar concept in Eastern spiritual disciplines, achieved through the practice of meditation. And it has also been studied from a Western scientific perspective, most notably by Dr. Ellen Langer. In her book *Mindfulness*, she identifies the key qualities of a mindful state as: "(1) creation of new categories; (2) openness to new information; and (3) awareness of more than one perspective."

Mindfulness is most easily understood by first seeing the effects of its opposite, mindlessness. Like some aspects of hubris, mindless behavior is caused by reliance on rigid categories, unquestioned mind-sets, and a limited perspective on people and situations. It is disempowering, inimical to change and innovation, creates a narrow self-image, encourages burnout, and damages relationships through misunderstandings and unintentional harm.

On a superficial level, you are acting mindlessly when you leave a movie theater and walk in the wrong direction for your car. Your mind is still wandering around inside the movie, disconnected from your errant feet. More serious kinds of mindless behavior result from the limiting categories that we put people into (including ourselves): male/female, old/young, handicapped/able-bodied, success/failure, and so on. Langer shows how mindlessness grows from a preoccupation with outcome over process (setting us up from childhood to fear failure) and a lack of awareness of context, how our behavior is controlled by surroundings and situations.

Cultivating mindfulness is a core skill of deep learning. Creating new categories (or metaphors or abstractions) lets us see tasks in a new light and offers a positive slant on things we are used to seeing negatively. Einstein turned a ride on a streetcar into a model for a theory that reinvented concepts of space, time, and motion—a spectacular act of mindfulness.

Langer uses the hypothetical situation of a man seeking a piece of wood three by seven feet for a scavenger hunt, in the middle of the night. There is no place open to buy wood, of course, but if the man were not trapped by rigid categories, he might have thought to take a door off its hinges.

Being open to new information and seeing the familiar in new ways means that you can receive and process important signals from the shadow rather than ignoring them, or absorb a piece of business news that is contrary to your expectations and turn it to good account. Being trapped in a boring environment restricts sensory receptivity; thus the repeated performance of a task after you have passed the peak on a learning curve can impair your ability to pick up on important signals.

Seeing the world from more than one perspective shows us how others see us, opens new windows on the world, and gives us more freedom of choice. "Every idea, person, or object is potentially many things depending on the perspective from which it is viewed," writes Langer. "A single-minded label produces an automatic reaction, which reduces our options." A flexible perspective can also help us change our behavior, giving a new slant to qualities that we are used to seeing as either negative or positive.

Mindfulness during a retreat allows us to use the regenerative powers of nature. It allows us to turn an afternoon of housepainting into a fruitful meditation. It can open us up to mysterious messages our inner voice delivers from the shadow. "In an intuitive or mindful state," Langer notes, "new information . . . is allowed into awareness. This new information can be full of surprises and does not always 'make sense.' If we resist, and evaluate it on rational grounds, we can silence a vital message."

Cultivating mindfulness may require some changes in your usual modes of thought. You may have to listen instead of talking, be thoughtful rather than reactive, put off decisions rather than displaying your ability to make them on the spur of the moment.

THE NEED FOR MEANING

When people tell me that they feel stale and need some sort of renewal, they almost always include the need to discover a larger meaning and purpose in what they do. This is especially true of the baby boom generation, who grew up in a socially conscious era. But much earlier Jung identified the urge to place ourselves in a larger context as a common trait of midlife.

You can find meaning in many contexts: family life, the contribution of your leadership qualities in public life, creative work that inspires others, or a spiritual framework that guides your actions. For men and women who have focused their efforts on reaching the top, cultivating the spirit of service can be a good way to discover purpose. The simple act of helping another person is often liberating and strengthening.

ALTERNATIVES TO LETTING GO: PARALLEL CURVES, PLATEAUS, AND THE SEARCH FOR DEEPER MASTERY

Our lives might be seen as a series of intersecting and parallel learning curves. Sometimes new curves replace earlier ones; others go on simultaneously, though rising and cresting at different rates. You may be peaking as a student while embarking on the learning curve of intimate relationships; beginning to lose energy as a trial lawyer just as your mentoring curve is getting hot; or in the rapturous phase both of learning tennis and learning to be alone.

We also can think of inner and outer learning curves, and how they relate. In successful people, the outer curve of public identity rises faster and peaks sooner than the internal one of personal discovery.

Learning curves are not a pat formula but a way of seeing your progress through life that points up the importance of constant renewal. Self-renewal is usually not a matter of jumping neatly off the end of one career curve onto a new one—

though some do this by dint of intense self-knowledge, decisive action, and good fortune. Sometimes renewal requires a bold leap to a new primary endeavor in work, but just as often it means that you need to explore an inner learning curve or develop an avocation that parallels and complements your job.

People with a high level of self-awareness and risk acceptance may pursue a deliberate pattern of changing jobs when the excitement of each learning curve diminishes. Author and statesman John Gardner is a good example. He regularly "repots" himself, as he puts it, to avoid getting stale. His intersecting learning curves are clear and distinct; he regards them rather like assignments to which he brings his gifts of intellect and management. Each contributes information and experience that are useful in the next phase. Throughout his varied life he has maintained a passion for self-understanding and a fascination with the challenges of leadership.

A more conservative approach is to begin working on a new learning curve while still actively engaged in your present one. More flexible work schedules often permit new career development to proceed parallel with an earlier track; for example, a woman who is moving from banking to medicine, starting with part-time training as a paramedic. Others can ease into a new field by doing some consulting in their existing field while learning their new work.

Another renewal strategy, used by those who are committed to a primary career or way of life, is to develop important, renewing avocations. Winston Churchill took his outside interests very seriously and derived immeasurable benefit from them. He was proud of his skill as a bricklayer and kept up his union card. He had a long-term vision of his estate, Chartwell, as a self-sufficient farm, and built elaborate fish ponds and gardens in furtherance of this vision. He authored fifty-six books, many of them while holding major posts in government service, including his years as England's Prime Minister.

Another way of fighting entropy involves flattening the top of the curve through a sustained effort to deepen your mastery of an endeavor. Extended, the peak of the curve becomes a plateau—a term that has gotten bad press in the working world in recent years. Many middle managers have been "plateaued"—stalled at a lower career level than they expected to attain—because of the economic downturn and intense competition for fewer top spots in the corporate world.

But philosopher George Leonard urges making the most of your time at the top of the curve. In the day-to-day struggle against entropy and the finely detailed practice of your craft, he believes, you can find sustained satisfaction and built-in renewal. "The achievement of goals" he writes, "is important. But the real juice of life, whether it be sweet or bitter, is found much less in the product of our efforts than in the process of living itself, in how it feels to be alive. We are taught in countless ways to value the product, the prize, the climactic moment. But if our life is a good one—a life of mastery—most of it will be spent on the plateau, that long stretch of diligent effort with no seeming progress. If not, a large part of it may well be spent in restless, distracted, ultimately self-destructive attempts to escape the plateau."

As long as you are learning—whether it is on fresh turf or in the dark recesses of your personal shadow, digging up demons you need to face—the results are the same: staleness, entropy, and hubris are defeated for another day. Most of us will need to use all these strategies at some point in our lives: letting go of an old learning curve, searching out new ones, fighting entropy on the plateau. Cultivating the attitudes and skills of renewal will aid you on all fronts.

CHAPTER 6

Deeper into Renewal: The Retreat

A PSYCHOLOGIST WAS ONCE SUMMONED for a delicate interview with a top executive who had been acting oddly. Every Wednesday afternoon this hard-charging company man would leave his office for a three o'clock appointment and not return. He never told anyone where he went, but because he was observed entering a nearby apartment building, it was assumed that he must be visiting a mistress.

The executive explained his habit to the psychologist quite easily. Inside Apartment 2B waited, not a luscious blonde, but a professional woodworking shop that he had set up, where he labored happily to turn out furniture and knickknacks.

He kept this special appointment with himself faithfully because it was his retreat from the demands he fulfilled so punctiliously day in and day out. He needed this chance to be alone with himself, engaged in an activity that took his mind far from his job and focused his attention in a calming way. The psychologist pronounced him eminently healthy. It was his retreat.

The deep learning that takes place during retreat is the heart of the renewal process. In retreat you can use solitude and introspection to mine the shadow for greater self-knowledge and vital clues to direct your future learning ventures, discover new sources of energy and creativity, find ways to rebalance your life, reset your clock, and redefine what success means to you. During periods of quiet reflection, the symptoms of hubris will stand out like a discordant noise; incipient puffery is more readily acknowledged.

Introspection is a hard commodity to come by in the rush toward success. It doesn't appear on most lists of typical leadership qualities—yet it is indispensable to sustaining success over a lifetime. To practice introspection and self-observation without distraction, busy people need to retreat in some manner from their workaday lives.

Retreats mean taking time to observe and reflect. The better you become as an observer, the better you will use your retreat time. Simply to stop and be quiet is a start, but retreats are an active process too.

WHAT IS A RETREAT?

You might think of a retreat as an ambitious, structured event in which members of an organization gather to plan and commune in a sylvan setting, or a situation in which you go off for months at a time to live in primitive isolation. This is only part of the story.

A retreat can be any amount of time you spend away from your usual productive round of activities, as long as that time is spent in pursuit of deep learning. A retreat can last twenty minutes or three months or three years. It can be a session of meditation, a walk in nature, or immersing yourself in dancing, music, painting, or any creative art. Some kinds of workouts would qualify. It can be any regular ritual that helps quiet the churning mind, allows you to journey inward, changes your level of awareness and self-knowledge—or an adventure in far-off lands that tests parts of yourself you have never known much about, someplace where old habits and skills won't be enough for you to get by on. A retreat is a refuge from a world in which you may have lost yourself and a place where you can find yourself.

Retreats can take place weekly, daily, or even more often. The location can be a fishing stream, a cottage at the beach, the Betty Ford clinic, an hour a week at a therapist's office, or simply a favorite chair in a peaceful room. The time, place, and circumstances vary as widely as your personal needs and resources, but the purpose is the same. Retreats are deliberately conceived opportunities to back off from the chase, attend to personal inventory-taking, and then go deeper—exploring what you normally neglect, getting better acquainted with whatever in you needs to be forgiven, nurtured, or germinated. To retreat, step back out of the spotlight and let your eyes adjust so that you can discern the shape of things in the shadow.

The business world is often suspicious of retreats, perhaps in part because of the word's military meaning: moving backward and possibly giving up. But for the aware leader, the long-distance winner, stepping back is anything but a defeat; it's a chance to gather new energy and ideas for the next campaign. Retreats can be thought of as a strategic pause, and such retreats have worked successfully in many human endeavors. As test pilot Chuck Yeager said, "I have learned to back up—but I never give up."

By serving the inner self on retreat, you serve the outer self as well. Yet it is often hard for me to convince busy, successful people that investing in personal growth through retreat will pay off on every level. They may acknowledge a need to get away now and then, but they try to pick a time when business is slow, and think of it as merely refueling for the job, or a chance to brush up on their serve or swing. Maybe, they think, some management insight will strike during a stroll on the golf course or the beach. And contact with the office is usually just a phone call or fax away.

The distinction between a Band-Aid getaway and a true retreat is subtle but important. The two can occur in the same place but produce very different results, depending on your attitude toward the experience and how you spend the time.

Pedaling an exercise bike with a sales report propped on the reading stand produces a different state of mind than a solitary ride down a country road.

Even a place specifically designed for retreat is only as effective as the attitude its visitors bring to it. I occasionally visit and speak at Rancho La Puerta, a health spa in the high desert of Mexico, and have had ample chance to observe how guests use and misuse their time there. Some use the Rancho as part of a long-term healing process. Others come full of purpose and promises: they work hard to lose a few pounds, get a tan, and feel better for a brief interlude. But they never really unwind and quiet down inside, merely transferring their usual frantic pace to this peaceful setting. The idea of just walking in the mountains or folding into a hammock never occurs to them. Their agenda is just to patch themselves up for the next battle.

People are often tempted to bring "just a little" work along on retreats—but work is as addictive as junk food and has no place in a healthy diet of retreat activity. In general, any activity not sufficiently disconnected from your normal routine will fail as a retreat; for example, being on call to negotiate a deal while on vacation. Hiking with a cellular phone is a very different experience from absorbing and quietly reflecting on your surroundings. The time element is important: anything done in a rush will only create more physical and mental tension, the opposite of what you're looking for.

Companions on a retreat should be chosen wisely: Those who know you in a certain context—that of work or organized sports, for instance—may have difficulty shifting gears, and conversation will tend to drift back to familiar subjects. A delightful tennis partner may be counterproductive on a retreat, where unstructured time and psychic exercise are the object, and no one should be keeping score.

Distinguish between retreat and recreation. While a boisterous game of touch football, a golf outing, or tennis match may relieve some tension, they won't promote introspection and deep learning.

WHY RETREAT AND WHEN?

Although the causes can be as varied as the human condition, a retreat might be prompted by a crisis in your work life, such as a corporate reshuffle that leaves you in an ambiguous or vulnerable position, by some event that has focused a growing awareness of boredom and nonfulfillment, or by unusually high stress that is bringing you perilously close to burnout. The need to retreat might arise out of a midlife struggle with changing roles, a confrontation with a troubled teenage child, or a vague, restless yearning for adventure—all potential symptoms of a need for renewal or rebalancing.

Retreats might have a specific, well-articulated purpose, such as taking time to ponder an important career decision. Should you hang in there and find mental refreshment wherever possible? Try to shake up the place? Or consider a more radical move like quitting?

Seeking answers to such questions is a legitimate goal for a retreat, but don't expect too much. Answers might fall into place quickly with just the right change of scene or perspective—but quick answers aren't always to be trusted. More likely, your search will unearth deeper questions. Probing into shadow territory may involve spending more time in the dark than you had hoped. But learning to live with ambiguity and doubt is an important skill.

Getting away from the situation in which you run the show is a check against ego-inflation, especially if the retreat involves learning a new activity or adjusting to a different culture. A woman, aged thirty-eight and head of a family-owned wholesale business, comments, "The people around me, my partners, tend to be like-minded and are not good messengers of change. I need to get away to find contrary opinions and ideas. In a way, I've limited myself by creating a company that values compatibility and congeniality. I need grit and friction, too."

Among the purposes of retreat, simple relaxation has a place:

improve your tennis, lose a little weight, or read that novel that's been gathering dust. Many people find that solutions to knotty work problems occur spontaneously in retreat settings. But these are side benefits to the core purpose of retreat.

True retreats involve some unstructured time, an idea that is foreign to many of us. A university administrator told me, "I've never known what 'unstructured time' means, at least since I started working. I simply wouldn't know what to do if I didn't have a schedule to meet." *Unstructured time is time spent mainly in your own company*, without distractions to come between yourself and your shadow. Devoting time to examining your inner self—your character, history, mistakes, regrets, values, and unadmitted impulses—is the primary activity of retreat, and what makes it indispensable to long-range renewal.

THE SHADOW-WORK OF RETREAT

Retreat should light the shadows that grow around every life and every successful endeavor, releasing the primal energy and passion, the unfiltered insights and raw creativity that reside there. A well-conceived retreat allows you to face guilt-provoking or "shameful" secrets. In a secure psychological harbor, you can haul out the craft of self, inspect it for damage, and tend to the barnacles that grow out of sight on the hull.

TRYING TO OUTRUN THE SHADOW

Success can give us many good things, but it usually fails to give us either time or the ability to enjoy it. Successful people often describe time as their greatest enemy and struggle to master it—only to discover that they are the ones mastered. A key element of hubris is the belief that every moment must be used, that our worth lies in our productivity and our aptitude for using time.

The revolution in information technology has worsened the

problem. When the mail wasn't fast enough, we resorted to overnight couriers; when it had to be there the next minute instead of the next day, the fax came along. Phones have invaded most of the places that once served as temporary refuges: cars, airplanes, hotel bathrooms; you can take your cordless model into the garden or a cellular phone just about anywhere. Laptop computers have made the portable office a reality, and inflight magazine ads for the SkyPager boast that your office can find you anywhere in the world with this magic device.

With technology turning up the heat in our working lives, the need for retreat has never been greater. Yet, opportunities for retreat seem to have dwindled; it's become harder to step back from the world. You may feel that you have come to an observation point and are ready to pause for a look around, but circumstances mitigate against it—physically and psychologically. As technology has encouraged the spillover from work time into personal time, we increasingly regard personal time as less sacred. The workaholic mind-set equates downtime with being left behind.

As time becomes an ever more precious commodity, the ante for how we spend it goes up. Our use of time must appear "valuable," both to ourselves and to others, or we feel we've "wasted" it. (The concept of "quality time"—those value-packed moments stolen by high achievers to be with their children—grew out of this mind-set.) Unfortunately, what we value tends to be frantic activity rather than stillness, society rather than solitude, accomplishment rather than contemplation. This is true not only in work but outside it. It's easier to justify time spent improving some external skill like our tennis game, harder to set aside the time we need for dialoguing with our deepest selves.

A 1991 *New York Times* feature called "Separating the Fugitives from the Stress Fighters" reported on the vacation styles of movers and shakers. The researchers identified four patterns, beginning with the *power players*, who don't even try to leave the office behind when they vacation. They sit by the pool talking on a portable phone to the office or spend an hour working each morning so they can feel productive.

Then there are the *stress fighters*, who spend their vacations frantically dieting and exercising. As the pollster notes, "They're on a mission, not a vacation." The *schedulers* feel compelled to structure their down-time, often opting for tours or other organized activities: "They want to be constantly stimulated so they don't have to think about what they left behind." *Fugitives* use vacations to flee job stress; heavy partying and staying up late are likely to be their distractions.

The article's author added another possible category: the *cheaters*, who invite business associates to a fishing camp, visit a client, examine the market by dropping into stores, or catch up on collateral reading.

Use your retreat to break the tyranny of time. Build in open-ended time and use your retreat time in unfamiliar ways. Several things will happen. You create space for your seldom-heard desires, needs, and notions to assert themselves, and you begin creating a model for a different, more friendly relationship with time.

Your job may benefit in unexpected ways, too. "I am always fighting time," says a forty-plus woman in publishing. "When I get away from my work routines, I can usually see how much of what I'm doing is wasted motion. Taking time away actually saves me time in the long run because I can see what's worth doing. I can move from time management to purpose management."

Unstructured time must be part of any retreat. Even on a weekend, you can build in some time "off the clock," where you have not scheduled any social events, errands, or organized recreation—some time when you can leave your watch in your room and simply exist in the present as much as possible. Take a quiet walk, meditate, or just sit and daydream under a tree.

Let the mood of the moment replace routines and habits. If you're feeling incredibly peaceful under that tree with your notebook or binoculars, or just a dog for company, don't break off your reverie just because it's twelve-thirty and that's when you always have lunch.

There are also activities that can take you out of your usual struggle with time.

OBSESSIONS

An aspect of hubris is the tendency for our vision to narrow as we pursue an old learning curve toward entropy. A winning groove is hard to climb out of, and methods that have worked for us can turn into obsessions, whether it's an accounting practice, a sales technique, or regularly scheduled meetings.

The most rewarding career will run out of juice if we maintain an obsessively tight focus over a long time. Pat Riley, the basketball coach who took the Los Angeles Lakers to four national championships, took a retreat from coaching at age forty-five. He says of his career up to that time, "Coaching is tough. There's a lot of pressure and the way I handled it was to take total responsibility. It just sort of consumes your life. It got to the point where I wasn't enjoying it like I did." Riley's retreat, which was mainly devoted to recovering from exhaustion (with a few forays into broadcasting) ended when he signed on to build a successful team for the New York Knicks—a parallel learning curve but one with plenty of room for growth.

Ellen Langer talks about how "mindless" actions can result when our vision becomes obsessive, our thinking locked into familiar, preconceived patterns and categories. "A single-minded self-image leaves both individuals and corporations dangerously vulnerable," she writes. Langer quotes Theodore Leavitt's classic paper for the *Harvard Business Review* entitled "Marketing Myopia": "The railroads did not stop growing because the need for passenger and freight transportation declined. That grew. . . . They let others take their customers away from them because they assumed themselves to be in the railroad business rather than the transportation business."

Retreats can help to make us aware of our obsessions and loosen their grip simply by putting us in an unfamiliar environment or context. We may need to stretch ourselves to deal with different cultural values, a changing frame of reference, a new vocabulary and skills, possibly a different language. When I spent a few weeks hiking in the Rocky Mountains one recent summer, it put me in contact with a whole new world of information, where knowledge of natural history and outdoor skills was given priority, and where the capacity to judge weather might be a life-or-death matter.

DROPPING THE MASK

Most leaders must wear masks. The public image cultivated by successful people, and reinforced by those around them, isn't necessarily false but it is usually incomplete. Significant pieces of their character and talents have gone undeveloped in the process of achieving what they have. So one of the main functions of retreat is to coax those less developed parts of ourselves—the lover, the playful spirit, the scholar, the craftsman, the daydreamer, the listener—out of the shadow.

Dropping the mask for a while and digging into your lost selves can benefit in many ways. What you discover of yourself in retreat could be the genesis of a major new learning curve. At the least, it could give you a new perspective from which to view your work and personal relationships.

The goal of this process—a fundamental goal of personality development—is to better integrate our private and public selves. Joseph Henderson, a protégé of Jung, says, "We must all have our public personas, those masks that we wear for others to see. Without such masks we would be overwhelmed by the demands and needs of the world. But, there must be an integrity between the two [the private and public selves]; otherwise, the stress of trying to hold conflicting feelings, beliefs and thoughts will make us sick."

Jung said that developing a "more spacious personality" is the most effective remedy for neuroses that stem from a tight focus on limited or "acceptable" goals. During retreats we can practice stretching to accommodate what has been compressed in the shadow. In examining the parts of ourselves that seem to threaten our public image, we may find ways to give them some space to operate—through conversation, writing about them, or exercising them in play or creative activities.

Ideally, these will be options we can use outside as well as within the retreat setting. Letting a latent gift out of the box while on retreat and then stuffing it back in when you return to "real life" is ultimately frustrating. I don't mean that you need to practice laying bricks or climbing mountains every day, but the attitudes and self-image you nurture through retreat-based activities you *can* take with you into any situation.

DOUBTS AND REGRETS ARE USEFUL

People to whom others look for leadership often have to suppress doubts about how they live their lives and do their work. Such people identify strongly with their enterprise and its image. The stories of corporations are told in quarterly reports, where the dark side of the picture is allowed into view as little as possible. But the stories of individuals are more finely shaded. If they are to be useful in guiding us, they must show the complete picture of a life with all its up- and downturns.

When we step out of the spotlight into a retreat, the doubts and ambiguities that we suppress in our public roles can come out of the shadow in a useful way. A banker in his mid-fifties told me, "There are times when I have to offer my employees and customers an image of strength and clarity when I'm actually feeling vulnerable and afraid. If I try to maintain that façade too long, I get into deep trouble. Only when I get away from work can I admit even to myself that I sometimes have doubts about my decisions or how I've handled a situation."

Doubts can serve as a form of intuition about what is needed next. Retreats give us the opportunity to follow these clues of feeling to their source. Have you been troubled by a vague sense of being out of sync with the goals of your company— believing you should care as much as your associates seem to, but finding it hard to muster any real passion for the tasks at hand or the next three-year plan? Here is a chance to look deeply into the fit of your values and the business's values.

The doubts and misgivings that seem so threatening when denied and kept in the shadow can provide excellent guidance when allowed to reveal themselves in the light of a peaceful setting. If you notice that you immediately dismiss doubts as soon as they arise, some retreat time is probably called for. Retreats allow you to defer decisions, to reconsider the path not taken, to grasp the full implications of your choices. They can provide a safe haven in which you can acknowledge mistakes in an atmosphere of honesty and forgiveness.

Regret and a sense of loss are also feelings we often shove into the shadow. It is easy enough to be sorry about a missed opportunity in business—a mistake that cost us money, an unmade move that could have benefited the company, but our regrets on this level may be only stand-ins for deeper regrets or losses in our personal account, which are harder to face. The difference has to do with what kind of insights we seek from our mistakes. What do our regrets say about our deepest fears and unmet needs?

Our deepest regrets are often associated with the failure to make full use of our talents or to the gradual erosion and betrayal of our core values. The decisions we regret the most often aren't those that hurt financially; they were the ones characterized by failure of vision and depletion of our "inner capital" of purpose. Time spent in retreat should allow us to examine these deeper losses and trace them to their sources.

QUESTIONS OF MEANING

The basic questions we encounter when we look deeply into the shadow are spiritual questions. They concern our place and purpose in the world, the significance of our lives, and our personal connection to whatever force keeps the world humming along. Most of us today have moved away from the religious structures that once supplied answers to these questions, but the questions have not gone away. Our compulsive busyness, our dread of unstructured time, and our reluctance to be alone with ourselves are rooted in the uncomfortable sense that our lives lack meaning, that we are disconnected and alone.

But the paradox of spiritual life, as seekers have learned for centuries, is that by looking deeply inside ourselves we discover our strong connections with other people, the physical world, and the spirit that moves it. In *Private Moments, Secret Selves*, Jeffrey Kottler quotes philosopher Fred Kersten: "One is always alone with or among things and others." Conversely, Kersten says, the experience of being alone is one of discovery—of ourselves and the world we inhabit: ". . . the self is always capable of experience and action—that is to say, is never isolated. Loneliness and solitude, therefore, discover rather than conceal the world, self, others, and things."

Living a spiritual life could be defined as living so that our most deeply held values and convictions are congruent with our actions. To have any hope of realizing this goal, we have to engage in deep learning—explore the shadow side of ourselves to find where unacknowledged beliefs and unquestioned values may be hiding, or where long–denied emotions may be pushing us to act in ways that are self-defeating.

We need not have any specific goal in mind when we set out on the path of deep learning. The only imperative is that we must travel it, engage in the process of simultaneous inner and outer discovery. If a symptom of hubris is action without reflection, then the antidote is understanding the forces that move us on the deepest level and are the true source of our power. All long-distance winners have discovered and pursued that understanding.

The Japanese have a tradition of bringing spiritual practice into the factory and boardroom. A legendary example is the late Konosuke Matsushita, industrial pioneer and founder of the giant Matsushita electronics empire. He directed his company's growth in pursuit of a social dream in which he believed deeply: to make modern technology available at low cost to every household in the world.

Matsushita's social philosophy and modest, down-to-earth style were inculcated throughout the company, giving it a solid foundation on which to continue growing in his absence. Late in his life, he gave over active management to others while engaging in long retreats in the mountains. Of his private spiritual journey we know little, but he often emerged with insights to contribute to the company's betterment.

WHERE TO RETREAT

Retreats can take many forms, but they usually require solitude, contact with nature, and the presence of ritual. The most effective ones contain elements of all these qualities.

THE ART OF BEING ALONE

In his book *Solitude*, Anthony Storr notes that psychology has long emphasized developing interpersonal relationships. He makes the case, however, that learning to be alone is equally important to human development: "It appears . . . that some development of the capacity to be alone is necessary if the brain is to function at its best, and if the individual is to fulfill his or her highest potential. Human beings easily become alienated from their own deepest needs and feelings. Learning, thinking, innovation, and maintaining contact with one's own inner world are all facilitated by solitude."

People whose lives are centered on creative effort—writers, musicians, painters—always have known that solitude is essential to achieving the highest forms of their art. Mozart said: "When I am, as it were, completely myself, entirely alone, and of good cheer, . . . it is on such occasions that ideas flow best and most abundantly."

But the same principle applies to anyone who needs to call upon his or her truest instincts and feelings, whether in the course of searching out new directions in life or creative solutions to day-to-day problems. Our inner voices usually cannot cut through the noise of our interactions with the world; they need periodic doses of solitude to make themselves heard. If your life centers on "doing," you will benefit by arranging retreats that involve time to be with yourself.

We are conditioned to be social creatures, and not much attention is paid to developing a child's capacity for using solitude productively. In fact, it is often associated with punishment, with chores like homework, or with parents who are absent or neglectful. People who kept too much to themselves were once suspected of witchcraft or sorcery—the dark impulses from the shadow manifested as black magic. Even now we tend to suspect the recluse of having done something wrong.

As adults, our resistance to being alone is compounded of all these things and many more, which can be summed up as fears from the shadow: the feelings, doubts, urges, memories, and regrets we would rather not face; the need for assurance that we are worthy and lovable; fear of the ultimate aloneness of death.

So we have developed endless distractions to keep from facing our shadow in solitude. The typical high achiever in almost any field crams a day dizzyingly full with work, and finds plenty of distractions in what little time is left between work and sleep: social and family obligations, spectator sports, volunteer activities, and just keeping up on the news. When the rare accidental moment of solitary, empty time occurs, we reflexively look around for something to do.

But those voices in your head aren't there just to criticize, or nag, or remind you of flaws, or run you through fruitless attempts to solve a persistent problem. Instead of trying to block them out or turn off the internal dialogue when it seems to be going nowhere, if you patiently nurture and guide your inner messengers, they can inspire, direct, and heal you. There are many pathways and techniques for doing this, and most of them begin in an environment of solitude.

A CEO in his early sixties who could afford any boat he wants tries to explain why he loves going out on his small day sailer. "It's one of the few places I can be alone, really alone. I like to keep busy, fully involved with the sailing so I can't begin to drift back to the office." He added that he experienced bursts of creativity—sometimes new approaches to problems he carried around, but also short poems and other creative expressions.

The more you practice being alone and using solitary time in different ways, the more rewarding and useful your experience of solitude will become. But whatever activities you choose, none is as important as the simplest: tolerating yourself. Theologian K. Rahner, quoted in *Private Moments, Secret Selves*, urges: "Have the courage to be alone . . . for once try to endure your own company for a while. . . . Don't speak, then, not even with yourself nor with the others with whom we dispute even when they are not there. Wait. Listen . . . Endure yourself!"

THE BENEFIT OF NATURAL SETTINGS

Being close to nature in quiet circumstances is enriching. Painter Georgia O'Keeffe returned again and again to the grand empty spaces of New Mexico so that she "could see." Through years of observing the work of glaciers in the Sierra Nevada, John Muir gained a long perspective on the efforts of his contemporaries to subdue the Western wilderness.

Uncovering the buried secrets of the psyche also requires quiet contemplation, which is why effective retreats so often take place in peaceful natural settings. Contact with nature refreshes our physical and aesthetic senses, resets our clocks to a healthier pace, offers an ever-present example of renewal, evokes gratitude, encourages introspection, and reminds us of our kinship with the rest of life. In nature our own nature can emerge. As Muir once remarked, "I only went out for a walk, and finally concluded to stay out till sundown, for going out, I found, was really going in." The natural world can transport us out of ourselves and our day-to-day preoccupations and simultaneously deep inside.

Among the symptoms of hubris are an obsessively tight focus on the challenges and problems of work and a decline in our powers of self-observation. While success sufferers may need to balance a life of action with greater introspection, it's also true that excessive introspection can lead to excessive self-criticism. Our internal dialogue can get out of control and become another form of obsession.

Spending quiet time in a natural setting, in an open and receptive state, can counteract such hypercritical attacks on ourselves. Most of us also need some form of instruction and support to develop a nurturing, forgiving dialogue with the self. A form of therapy developed by a Japanese physician uses structured periods of isolation in nature to bring a patient out of an obsessive focus on the self. In Morita therapy—or any effective retreat into nature—you must direct energy and focus outside the self, and by learning to observe with fresh eyes, you can break out of negative patterns.

A rigorous, extended retreat in a wilderness isn't for everyone, but for some it provides an unparalleled regenerative experience. A famous example is Admiral Richard Byrd, who in 1934 chose to live alone for many months at a remote weather station in the Antarctic. The pressures of his fame and fund-raising tours were getting to him, and he felt the need to escape into a simpler existence, in contact with elemental forces. The experience severely tested his health and endurance, but he never regretted it: "I did take away something I had not fully possessed before: appreciation of the sheer beauty and miracle of being alive, and a humble set of values. Civilization has not altered my ideas. I live more simply now and with more peace."

These are the words of a proud, hard-edged scientist and military man with a full set of macho traits. Yet the wilderness, with its awesome beauty, its capacity to crush the craftiest technology and the strongest will, softened him and brought out qualities he had not previously expressed. Those who opt for wilderness challenges often find that the testing they undergo—stressing the human body and mind in ways to which we are naturally adapted—provides an antidote to the less healthy stresses of urban life and careers.

Most of us have neither the inclination nor the means to pursue a retreat as ambitious and rigorous as Byrd's. An example closer to home is Gordon Sherman, the CEO-turned-nature-photographer. Gordon made retreat a major part of his life after learning that he had leukemia, and he pursued a love affair with nature in many forms: in his garden and orchid shed, at ponds and parks near his home that attracted wildlife for his camera, and especially on trout streams.

"The fishing changed it all for me," he said. "At first I was after the fish, learning the art and the paltry science, discovering the best places to catch fish. But later I became more interested in observing nature in all of its dazzling forms. Fishing was a way in."

Another acquaintance, an attorney and corporate dealmaker, notes: "It's always on the third day of backpacking when my shift occurs from doing to being. The idea of just being in the world, no goals or responsibilities, overwhelms me on these trips. I realize how little I need and how noisy, crowded, and polluted my normal circumstances are. When I go alone, the experience is different—it's deeper, quieter. Even when I'm with my wife, we separate for some time each day. We both crave the quiet and solitude."

It's no accident that most established retreat centers are located in unspoiled natural environments, with time to ramble outdoors built into weekend retreat schedules. But there are many other ways we can use nature in the context of retreat, from a trek in the Himalayas to a trip out to the backyard.

THE POWER OF RITUAL

Friends who have a summer place at a beautiful lake speak with special fondness of the first trip there each season, to open the house and begin their annual retreat. For them, the simple acts associated with preparing their living space and getting re-acquainted with their surroundings take on great meaning: bringing porch furniture up from the cellar, turning on the water, putting up screens. What in other circumstances might be merely a chore becomes a treasured ritual when it is linked in our minds with the gift of peace and quiet, the opportunity to step back from the routine.

Any retreat experience, whether short or long, undertaken for casual refreshment or deliberate self-exploration, is enhanced and set apart from everyday life by the presence of ritual. Deep learning can be difficult and scary at times and should be undertaken in circumstances that are as comforting, reassuring, and encouraging as possible. Setting up a ritual, whether it be going to a familiar place or engaging in a habitual pattern of activity, can reduce distracting anxiety and help quiet the mind so that we can focus better.

A mindful state turns a common chore or a simple physical act into a ritual. The breathing ritual of people who meditate focuses their attention on the present, aside from whatever biochemical calming effect it may have. Likewise the rituals followed by those who practice martial arts: putting on the garments in a certain way and bowing in ceremonial fashion before beginning a session. Some people who retreat by writing in a journal like to use only a certain kind of notebook or writing implement. For many, a familiar piece of music can serve as the entry point into a psychic state of retreat; for others a different sensory trigger like baking bread or the tactile experience of handling clay or stroking a cat or dog brings the mind to a profound stillness.

Retreat rituals can be quite simple: a particular route for a daily walk, or a certain friend who always accompanies you; a designated corner of the house for meditation; a bench in the garden; a pew in church you always sit in. Activities such as fishing that involve focused and repetitive actions like crafting flies and casting/retrieving the line are fruitful kinds of ritual.

Paul, a partner in a major law firm, took up fly-fishing in his early fifties because it seemed like an appropriate activity for the approaching "golden years." He soon came to enjoy the sport, but it was really the rituals surrounding it that he loved and that helped him bring up subterranean feelings. "The fishing digs are owned by a group of us, but each is allowed to reserve some time alone. I began to establish my routines during my first solo trip: setting up the fly-tying gear, checking the hatch and the river's condition, seeing where others were fishing, and settling down the dogs.

"Each day after the morning's fishing I like to reheat some coffee and tie flies. The tools and bits of exotic material seize my full attention. An odd thing happened on the third day of that trip: as I sat at my small bench working on a fly, a feeling of physical calm settled over me like sun warming my shoulders. A few snapshots of perfect moments from my childhood came back to me with amazing clarity . . . things I hadn't thought about for years, like early morning swims at our old camp.

"God, I felt good! I vowed right then to work out my life so that feeling of pure contentment was more the norm than the exception. It's been a crooked path, but I've been consciously working on changing the major sources of tension." Paul downsized his tensions and upsized his contentment by becoming the general counsel for a midsized company that had been one of the firm's clients. His wife has gone back to teaching, so their income depends less on him alone. He owns his weekends and, needless to say, goes fishing more frequently.

Organized, structured retreats usually contain prescribed rituals that serve to create a special atmosphere, draw the participants into an altered state of awareness. The drumming or chanting rituals practiced at men's consciousness-raising gatherings are a good example. They also illustrate why ritual is essentially a private matter even when practiced in a group.

It has always been easy to make fun of other people's rituals, and today the use of rituals to retreat briefly from the world is often ridiculed as a sort of belief in magic. If so, it is a magic that works, and has worked for thousands of years. If you decide that you need a retreat, give yourself permission to use any ritual that is effective. If you choose a solitary retreat, that is your concern and no one else's.

THE MANY FORMS OF RETREAT

Retreats are investments in a richer inner life, and like any other investment, the form they take will vary according to your needs and circumstances. *Find the retreat that fits* is the first rule of deciding where and how to pursue it, how much time and money you can expend, and what benefits you expect in return.

I encourage a variety of retreat experiences: benefits vary in short- and long-term retreats, in familiar and exotic environments. However, a consistent pattern of retreat has a deepening, cumulative effect. When you find something that works for you, pursue it until it stops working. The act of creating the time, place, aesthetics, and rituals of retreat is part of the healing they can offer.

THE DAILY RETREAT

Try cultivating the practice of retreating every day. Set aside a block of time that is yours alone, as inviolable as you can make it, and spend it in some activity that encourages mindfulness and helps to frame and order your day. It can allow you to reflect on events just past or soon to come, remind you of why you are pursuing your present course or what's not working about it. Such retreats offer a dependable, comforting sanctuary from the world, something to count on and look forward to.

The timing of a daily retreat is a matter of personal preference. Circumstances have much to do with the timing, of course; someone caring for a young child can take advantage of nap time to schedule a retreat, and a woman with a dog to walk has a ready-made excuse to retreat once or twice daily.

Meditation is an ideal framework for a daily retreat. It can be practiced anywhere that you can shut out the world for twenty minutes or so. But the range of possible daily retreats is very broad: from walking to gardening, practicing a musical instrument, swimming or going for a bike ride, writing in a journal, chopping wood for a stove, or preparing a meal in a mindful way. You might be able to learn to use commute time to retreat.

ULTRADIAN RETREATS

The term *ultradian* refers to a set of human biorhythms that take place during the course of a day (in contrast to *circadian* rhythms, those that repeat on a more-or-less twenty-four-hour cycle). Research indicates that our physical and mental energy fluctuates in a cycle of about 90 to 120 minutes of activity that peaks and then declines, followed by a "trough" of lowered activity during which the brain and body seek rest and renewal. *The 20-Minute Break*, by Dr. Ernest L. Rossi, suggests that by becoming more aware of these rhythms and planning our work efforts to synchronize with them we can reduce stress and improve health and performance.

Most of us have probably noticed times during the day when our energy and ability to concentrate seems to sharpen or wane. Instead of overriding the "down" signals by consuming caffeine or food, or forcing ourselves into attention, we can use some of these times as mini-retreats. When you feel the symptoms of a trough coming on—they could include the overpowering urge to stretch and yawn, or to daydream, or excessive tension or fatigue—Dr. Rossi recommends "putting yourself, as best you can, in a quiet, undisturbed environment. The lack of outer stimulation will enhance your mind-body's natural tendency to turn inward. Ideally, you might find a quiet place to lie down, or close your office door and relax in a comfortable chair. Even a short walk in a park or some other relaxing location will help. The goal is to eliminate from your environment as much as possible any ringing phones, chattering conversation, all those insistent demands of the typical workplace.

"The phone will wait; the work will still be there when you get back. . . . Your mind-body wants this time to do its internal housekeeping to optimize the metabolic processes of rejuvenation and recovery."

Sleeping and napping are forms of retreat. Sleep is the most universal and indispensable means of healing that our species possesses, and for many people the only entryway into the unconscious, the land of the shadow. Naps are often an appropriate response to ultradian signals. Winston Churchill, for one, was a great practitioner of strategic napping. Sleep is a retreat that we all engage in willy-nilly, so we will concentrate on retreats of the waking kind—just as important but more easily avoided.

WEEKENDS, VACATIONS, SABBATICALS, AND THE OPEN-ENDED BREAK

The opportunity for retreat is generally no more than five days away. Even a weekend can be restorative if we get it away from the busyness of usual activities. A new skill that we make time to practice on a weekend may turn out to be the seedling of a new life direction, as with the stockbroker-turned-boatbuilder or marketing-executive-turned-landscaper.

Retreating to a place where we have some history can provide continuity and perspective for our life story, a locus for all that we value and cherish. A real-estate developer and mother of two speaks of her front-porch retreats: "At our old cabin at the lake, there is a porch with a special chair that feels like home. When I am in that chair, life is remarkably serene and safe, and I don't know why. Our family has been going to the old cabin for many years. Perhaps we have marked it, like animals stake out a territory. I know that on early mornings, coffee cup in hand, feet up on the rail, the lake awakening me with its fragrance of pine, I can get quite poetic about it. In that chair I almost never think about work."

Retreating from the pressure and tensions of weekday life should feel as relaxed and unhurried as possible. Leaving on Friday, returning on Monday, enjoying the settling-in process, and responding to the rhythms of your body and nature, rather than the clock, are important to the regenerative experience.

Retreats of a week or more offer prospects not available from shorter ones. Most vacation styles have little connection with retreat; indeed, by and large vacationers are trying to avoid any time with themselves, rather than seeking it out. Not every vacation has to be a full-time retreat, but you can make excellent use of your vacation time by devoting at least some of it to that purpose.

If you are single, you might find it more rewarding to spend a week at a quiet bed-and-breakfast by yourself, with occasional others for company, rather than plunging into the social maelstrom of a singles-oriented resort. Couples might occasionally need separate vacations to manage genuine solitude, especially if they have kids, or can arrange to spend a little time apart and reunite later in the vacation.

Longer breaks offer the possibility of journeying far from home and immersing yourself in a new cultural or physical environment that makes you stretch and grow in unexpected ways. This kind of retreat sharpens your perspective on yourself in relation to the rest of the world.

Sabbaticals were once limited to the academic world, but in recent years they have been available to some people in professional or corporate life who feel the need for an extended respite from their demanding jobs. A retreat of several months' duration is a giant step back, providing real distance on our preoccupations and the chance to experiment at length with new learning ventures.

Finally, there is the interregnum retreat: times when you leave a job—voluntarily or not—without knowing exactly what you plan to do next. These seem to be becoming more common, in part because of the recent downsizing trend in corporate life, but also as part of the career profile of baby boomers, who are less concerned than earlier generations about lifetime job security. I know of several fortyish people who left excellent careers in the publishing industry with the declared intention of taking an open-ended break. They did not know their next move yet, but knew that getting away before they got more deeply entrenched had become their top priority.

This kind of "repotting" retreat often causes nervousness among friends and loved ones with their own needs and expectations. I well remember my family's reaction to the year off I gave myself some time ago. Yet it is undeniably becoming more common. If the trend-spotters are right, we are probably entering an era in which most people will pursue multiple careers over a lifetime, interspersed with period of retreat and readjustment.

WEEKEND WARRIORS: THE RADICAL RETREAT

The consciousness-expanding movements that have been developing since the 1960s have spawned a category of highly focused, often rigorous retreat experiences. Typically programmed around a weekend or two, most use the techniques of group therapy and psychodrama, and the stripping away and rebuilding of identity, to provide an intense encounter with the hidden self in a compressed space of time.

Radical retreats may not be for you. They are probably most useful if you have a fairly high level of experience and comfort with psychotherapeutic situations. Such group adventures may be recommended by your therapist as a way to extend or deepen your ongoing work with him or her.

Radical retreats are most useful when they are not just an isolated, one-time experience. You are more likely to integrate the results if they are followed up by further meetings with fellow participants and group leaders or independent study and practice of the principles and techniques involved. *Be sure to investigate such advertised retreats before committing yourself.* Is the content suitable to your comfort level? Is the event sponsored by an established human-growth center or run by a well-known leader? Personal referrals are helpful, though not infallible.

Perhaps the best way to approach the whole subject of radical retreats is to follow a simple checklist:

- Are the people or institutions well established and known for the high quality of their offerings? For example, many universities offer weekend workshops that are staffed by regular faculty or well-screened professionals. Places like Esalen at Big Sur, California, have many years of experience in organizing and managing first-rate retreats.
- Do the people who recommend the retreats serve as good models of the results that the advertising promises? Do the benefits of their work shine through?
- Are you clear about your expectations? If you are looking for this one-shot experience to resolve deep and long-standing issues in your life, you are not being realistic and it will probably not be a good experience.
- Finally, are you prepared? Have you done the studying and reading or taken other preparatory measures to fully benefit from the experience?

THE "HOW" OF RETREAT: PRACTICES AND PURSUITS

There is a wide range of activities that encourage mindfulness, calm the spirit, lead you to the shadow's gold, and point the way toward future directions. They include all of the following and doubtless more.

MEDITATION

The image of meditation has changed as serious scholars, physicians, psychologists, and members of the clergy have explored benefits of this practice. Herbert Benson's *The Relaxation Response* conveyed to millions of readers the power of a simple technique for deep relaxation and quieting the mind. A professor at Harvard Medical School, Benson and his research could not be shrugged off by skeptics. Perhaps more important was the fact that "real men" who had sneered at meditation found out that their hard-as-nails Japanese competitors used it regularly. So more and more persons in mainstream careers began to study Buddhism and other Eastern teachings and to practice meditation, and weekend retreats incorporating meditation grew in popularity.

Meditation offers an instant retreat anytime, anywhere. Once you know how to practice it, you can sit down and close your eyes in your office or car, on an airplane, or in the den of a friend's home. You need no extra props; a comfortable chair or couch will do. And with a few deep breaths you can let the world drop away, allow your mind to quiet down and your body to relax deeply.

Meditation can be a great gift. According to research that was begun in the 1960s by Maharishi Mahesh Yogi, who brought Transcendental Meditation to the U.S., and confirmed by later investigators, it can dramatically reduce the effects of stress by bringing deep relaxation to your bodymind. With long-term meditation, many of the effects of psychosomatic illnesses that are caused by stress disappear. Meditation also can help to synchronize the brain wave activity between the two hemispheres of your brain, enhancing your capacity to focus and to think creatively.

It can be easily learned by anyone. Today meditation teachers of all kinds are available in major U.S. cities, and T.M. teachers can show you how to use a mantra or meaningless sound to clear the mind.

A popular Buddhist practice called Vipassana teaches people to follow the breath. One teacher of this school, Thich Naht Hanh, writes in his many books about the quality of attention that arises from meditation, which can be brought to any activity, such as walking, writing, sitting in meetings, or even washing the dishes.

A regular meditation practice, such as once or twice a day, is an ideal way to insert regular retreats into daily life. It can also be used for problem-solving or to rehearse performances. Longer meditation retreats, such as week-long or month-long getaways, can bring even deeper rest and rejuvenation. They can be used in conjunction with shadow-work, visualization exercises, or support groups.

PRAYER

Prayer is a form of meditation for those of you who follow a religious path. Like meditation, it starts with a reverential attitude, a humble spirit that reaches out, listens attentively for answers, struggles with eternal mysteries, and seeks a community of others who likewise yearn for higher or deeper connections.

Praying is most commonly thought of as a direct dialogue with a supreme being, often in the form of asking for help or guidance, but it can lead in many directions. Prayer can draw us deeply inward to confront what is in our shadow or out of ourselves to praise and celebrate the works of creation. For some it is a kind of dialogue with the self, confessing errors and working through difficulties without imposing on friends or family. What makes it also a conversation with God is that this self is nonjudgmental and forgiving. Dean Allan Jones of San Francisco's Grace Cathedral notes that "prayer can be seen as attentiveness to the spirit without editing what's there."

You can pray without reference to an almighty being. You can speak out loud to yourself of what troubles your soul; you can confess to yourself, if not to another human, what needs to be said and heard, forgiven or remembered. You can introduce yourself to the spiritual dimension and get back from it the unexpected gift of self-healing and renewal. You can acknowledge what you have received and earned and find in that expression of gratitude new prospects and the desire to share yourself at work and with your community.

YOUR BODY

Retreats are an opportunity to refresh the muscles, skin, lungs, and libido as well as the soul, to observe the small signals we get from our body but too often ignore, to discover healthier ways of caring for it. People on the road to success often put the physical self in the shadow, and a neglected body will eventually cause all sorts of mischief. Neglect, shame, or denigration of the body can also be seen in eating disorders, especially among high-achieving women.

We are more aware of the connection between fitness and health today than we were fifty years ago. But many activities that promote fitness take a hard, competitive approach or are used as Band-Aids to temporarily cover symptoms. Don't go on a retreat to obtain tighter thighs or cardiovascular endurance. Seek the reorientation of the entire body as a source of information, pleasure, even miracles. Gentle practices such as massage and other bodywork therapies, bathing, stretching, yoga, and dance will probably be more beneficial to you than grueling exercise.

Emily was a major player in the fashion industry at forty. She worked literally in the spotlight, under banks of bright lights in her design studio. Along with her reputation grew a nagging sciatica pain that Emily thought she could get rid of by "working it out" at the gym. Six weeks later she was in agony, then in traction, and her doctor agreed to release her from the hospital only on condition that she take a long-overdue vacation.

I met Emily at the quiet ranch in the high desert of the Southwest where she had retreated. Within days she had developed a routine that included a solo walk each morning. "It was thrilling just to walk without pain, and I felt that I was healing myself. I found an appealing place to sit among a cluster of ancient rocks that were sacred to the Indians. One morning as I was sitting there, just spooning in the harsh beauty all around, not thinking of anything in particular, I started to cry. The tears were familiar and lasted a long time—they came from the shunned child I still was, under the skin of a successful adult."

She continued to use the rocky place as her shrine. Morning after morning she would "unzip" her shadow and try to face what was there, in the security of those timeless rocks. When she returned home to the daily grind, she continued the work of caring for her body and her gifts. She didn't just discover some good back exercises; she reclaimed her experience of being a wholly functioning person. She discovered the interconnecting pathways between the mind, the body, and the spirit. She learned how to delegate assignments and trust those judgments; with more time free of routine work, her creativity expanded. Each year Emily returns to her "crying rocks," her place for taking stock. Now, though, she goes with a sense of joy, celebrating the new life she found there.

During your retreat, try to assess how the components that make up your life are functioning. Do the parts seem to be in harmony? Take a close look at your diet. Exercise that is often abandoned under the very stress that a good workout could serve to ameliorate can be reintroduced. Mend broken connections with beauty and nature. Use solitude, prayer, or reflection to heal and integrate the parts of the self that seem to be fragmented.

THE HANDS-ON APPROACH

For brain workers, retreats that involve physical labor or manual dexterity are a wonderful way to rebalance. Seymour Cray, who founded the well-known producer of large-scale computers, retreats each summer to a lake to build a wooden boat from scratch, a retreat ritual as different from the intellectual work of computer science as one could imagine. Building a wooden boat requires hours of precisely cutting and fitting wood strips. Success comes from feeling the fit, not thinking about it. The practice is also an effective curb on the ego; a big reputation in the high-tech world is of no value in a small boatyard.

At the end of the summer, Cray gets rid of the boat in a ritual of his own devising, so there is no trophy. The purpose of this retreat lies in the process, not the outcome.

The managing partner of a Midwestern law firm found a retreat in performing a "Saturday purge" in her backyard. It began after she had hired a professional landscaper to lay out and plant her garden, and found she was unhappy with the results. She began to "purge" and redo parts of it to suit herself, studying horticulture and garden design as she went along. While her child napped or was looked after by his father, she built a greenhouse with her own hands and turned her space into a seasonally changing garden of delights. But clearing out old plantings is still what pleases her most. "The rest of my week is all about precision, using my mind, doing things carefully," she says. "On Saturday I'm free to root around, yanking up and discarding whatever pleases me."

A successful commercial artist has another hands-on weekend retreat. Saturday mornings, she shops for special ingredients needed for her Sunday cooking. After church she turns her house into an aromatic test kitchen, experimenting with a different ethnic cuisine each week. Everything is handmade from scratch, including the baked goods, and while working she listens to music that complements the menu, adding another sensory layer to the experience. Sometimes she invites friends over for a feast; or she may freeze her creations to enjoy during the week.

"I get completely involved in the tactile aspects of beating and kneading and shaping. The smells of herbs and bread baking combined with Mahler's First Symphony are intoxicating. I feel very peaceful in the kitchen on those days. I rarely use the kitchen during the week because I eat out or on the run, but on Sunday it becomes my sanctuary."

Whether your hands-on approach produces a usable product or just a pile of clay that goes back into a bucket doesn't matter. It's not the activity that counts; it is the inner result of the outer effort.

WRITING

Writing in a journal or diary is a creative and valuable way of using a retreat. Journal-keeping is not merely the routine recording of a day's events. Does it require a special talent for writing? Not so, says author Tristine Rainer in *The New Diary*. She describes how the journal form has evolved over this century into a practical and versatile tool for personal growth "that enables you to express feelings without inhibition, recognize and alter self-defeating habits of mind, and come to know and accept that self which is you. It is a sanctuary where all the disparate elements of a life—feelings, thoughts, dreams, hopes, fears, fantasies, practicalities, worries, facts, and intuitions—can merge to give you a sense of wholeness and coherence."

For example:

A middle-aged advertising director sometimes talks into her tape recorder during the hour she drives on the freeway to and from work. She finds it helps sort out her thoughts about her job, marriage, and her state of mind.

A country-western singer writes on planes and in dressing rooms to stay intimate with the private person behind his public image.

A businessman works in a leatherbound diary to examine the factors that complicate a major decision he must make.

A fashion executive goes to her diary when she needs to prepare for an important meeting. She imagines her client's point of view and rehearses what she wants to do and say.

Trying on different points of view in writing is a wonderful way of improving our understanding of relationships or of giving voice to hidden sides of our personality.

Rainer discusses how pioneers of modern journal-writing have expanded the form to make it useful for psychological exploration. Jung's major theories, for example, grew out of the self-study conducted extensively through his diaries. In *A Life of One's Own* psychologist Marion Milner (writing under the pseudonym Joanna Field) tells of using a journal to discover how to give her life meaning and purpose, and explores "free association in writing and drawing as well as diary-related experiments in meditation, relaxation, body awareness, and a number of other techniques." Jungian analyst Ira Progoff invented a systematic approach to journal-keeping, described in his book *At a Journal Workshop*, which allows even those unfamiliar with or intimidated by journal-writing to use it productively.

Self-conscious struggles with form hold back many people from using journal-writing effectively. Jungian analyst Joe Henderson found that in some cases writing kept his patients on the surface, so he favored more primal forms of expression, such as crude sketching or modeling in clay to encourage patients to unearth deeply buried emotions and experiences.

Advocates of journal-writing emphasize that there are many

proven techniques. TV's teenage medical genius, Doogie Howser, raps out his musings on a personal computer to start and end each episode of the show. Natalie Goldberg, author of *Writing Down the Bones*, favors the low-tech approach of a cheap fountain pen (for its tactile quality) on paper, and colorful spiral notebooks with cartoon covers. Most of the books about journal-keeping contain exercises that can help your thoughts flow freely, unhampered by self-editing or concerns about style.

Today's liberated, informed approach to journaling is a tremendous aid to the goals of a retreat. Your journal can be a place to record dreams and fantasies, provide healthy release from suppressed tension, clarify problems and solutions, help you understand your personal history, and much more. A journal's accumulated contents are, as Rainer notes, "a unique, unrepeatable story of self." You can find out where you are going by seeing where you have been.

DREAMS, DAYDREAMS, AND FANTASIES

Although it requires considerable experience in therapy to work with our own dreams, I mention them as a retreat activity because many of us find that the retreat environment stimulates our dreaming and waking fantasies. Sometimes this experience can produce a reconciliation with the most deeply hidden parts of the self.

Our dream production is beyond our control. We may prompt or participate in dreams to a limited extent, but the psyche determines how and when it processes the unconscious material we carry around. Our waking hours are broken into arbitrary fragments of time. Each has a conscious, limited purpose. But our sleeping hours are not ours to command, and our dreams are open-ended, freed from our usual relationship with time or logic.

Our dreams are nightly retreats into the unconscious, and we benefit from these journeys into the forbidden zone in ways that we are not even aware of. It is a basic principle of dream research, from Freud onward, that dreams function like a pressure valve, allowing repressed material from the shadow to surface in a nonthreatening way, rather than eventually erupting in a behavioral catastrophe.

But our dream retreats can be even more useful if we apply the conscious mind to interpreting and using them. As Freud, Jung, and their followers have shown, we can discover a lot about our psychological state, especially the shadow material that can be found in the symbols and archetypes of dreams, that we can use in our waking hours. A therapist can bring special insights to your dreams and help you relate dream content to your behavior.

One young entrepreneur found himself in considerable trouble in a new venture. To protect himself from being eaten alive by his ambitions, he turned to therapy and began to learn how to interpret his dreams. "Several of the toughest problems I faced came up in dreams," he reported. "They were problems that I had basically denied; my life's dirty secrets that I couldn't share with anyone, not even my wife. Dealing with them as dream materials with my therapist brought a great relief; I felt lighter and taller than I had in months. And it enabled me to tackle some other matters I had been procrastinating about. Once we started addressing these core problems, the business started to turn around. I had no idea how much of my energy had been going into avoiding these deep, dark problems which, once exposed, weren't as awful as I had thought."

He was no exception; again and again I see people locked into their business or professional problems as if they had grabbed a piece of frozen metal. The effort of denial adds still more weight and power to the shadows, but once they break through it, by whatever means, they experience a rush of relief and renewed energy.

To maximize the value of dream interpretation in exploring our shadows, we need to understand how much weight to give to certain dreams, what the archetypal messages are (the images that relate to universal human themes and concerns), and how the insights from dreams connect with other material from the psyche. Most people need help to do this. Though Freud called dreams the royal road to the unconscious, I am afraid it takes a skilled driver to navigate it.

Daydreams are the closest we come in our waking lives to accessing the rich material of our unconscious. Far from being a waste of time, they fulfill an important psychological function. They can deepen our learning from prior experiences by replaying them for further scrutiny, help us weigh decisions and rehearse options for our future, entertain and relax us, and provide important information about ourselves.

Fantasizing is a conscious, directed kind of daydreaming that is especially useful in sniffing out new learning curves. A good part of all human achievement originates in fantasy—the "what if?" questions that prompt exploration in science and the arts.

Many geniuses were notoriously poor or inattentive students, often chastised for woolgathering. Edison, Ford, and Disney were all champion fantasizers.

Daydreams tend to visit when we are engaged in an activity that is boring or when ultradian rhythms are at a low ebb, decreasing our ability to concentrate. So if you catch yourself daydreaming, it could be a sign that you need a mini-retreat. A retreat setting is the ideal opportunity to indulge in daydreaming without guilt.

THE ROLE OF PLAY

All play is a form of imagining. You and your best friend become deadly enemies facing each other across the tennis court. A group of children are the knights of the Round Table or the outlaws of Sherwood Forest. The teenager manipulating a video game is a fighter pilot or a sorcerer. Play can be an important ingredient in digging lost selves out of the shadow.

Most adult play is too organized and serious. As Witold

Rybczynski comments, "Play is beginning to look more and more like a kind of work." He notes an increasing emphasis on professional-level performance in the way Americans approach recreation: "The evolution from the simple to the intricate, from casualness to intensity, is visible in almost every contemporary American recreation, whether it's bicycling, roller-skating, cross-country skiing, or boating." Cautioning that we are in danger of losing the spontaneous, childlike qualities of play, he reminds us of the wise words spoken by Toad in *The Wind in the Willows*, "There is nothing . . . half so much worth doing as simply messing about in boats."

Retreats that include play are essential to tweak the imagination and break the patterns of rational thought. Pastimes that take us far from our normal activities can help. The fifty-four-year-old owner of a consulting firm each year chooses a Civil War battlefield, studies its history and characters, then travels there and imagines himself involved in it—a general for a day. "I get so absorbed I lose track of time, and for me that's hard. Some powerful feelings get dredged up. Crying comes naturally out on those battlefields—crying I needed to do as a child but couldn't."

Play can be both joyful and serious, not in the sense of winning or losing but its potential for self-discovery. For many people, men especially, some form of play may be the only time that deeply felt emotions find expression. Even if we see the emotion as negative, such as anger or the need to dominate, it is information we can use.

ARTISTIC EXPRESSION

Fanning a creative spark that has long lain dormant can lead to a new learning curve with tremendous potential energy. Trying your hand at an unfamiliar activity is also a way to bring an inflated ego back to earth.

Retreats are an ideal occasion to experiment with a creative endeavor that attracts you: painting, sculpture, ceramics, literary efforts, music. Daily practice of such activities constitutes a primary form of retreat for some; for others this window on self-knowledge may be opened only occasionally. Or the practice may serve to beguile a busy mind into a more restful state.

Winston Churchill used his painting to go inward, to care for his introverted side. Here's how he describes his discovery of painting: "Like a sea-beast fished up from the depths or a diver too suddenly hoisted, my veins threatening to burst from the fall in pressure—and then it was that the muse of painting came to my rescue."

As we learn more deeply and map the landscape of our shadow, we discover divisions or stress points between various parts of ourselves. Creative effort can help to heal these ruptures: between the kind and cruel, the shy and assertive, the gregarious and solitary parts of our natures. In *The Dynamics of Creation*, Anthony Storr suggests: "Man is a creature inescapably, and often unhappily, divided; and the divisions within him recurrently impel the use of his imagination to make new synthesis. The creative consequences of his imaginative strivings may never make him whole; but they constitute his deepest consolations or his greatest glories."

The American composer Aaron Copland wrote, "Why is it so important to my psyche that I compose music? . . . And why is the creative impulse never satisfied; why must one always begin anew? . . . The reason for the compulsion to renewed creativity, it seems to me, is that each new work brings with it an element of self-discovery. I must create in order to know myself."

The priceless solitude of retreat gives you the freedom to express yourself purely for your own benefit, without an audience—to dance alone, sing full voice or find your way around an instrument, paint, sculpt, perform alchemy, or play with words and ideas in poetry. When you allow such dormant sides of yourself to come alive, you open a direct path to renewal.

TEN QUESTIONS YOU MIGHT ASK DURING RETREAT

- How much distance have you put between your normal life and this retreat?
- Are you prepared to meet some aspects of your shadow?
- Is play feeling like work?
- How tightly affixed is your public-persona mask?
- Have you set aside some time to explore questions of meaning?
- Is solitude comfortable for you?
- Would you enjoy close encounters with flowers and other natural objects?
- Are rituals in place to support deeper explorations of your life?
- Is there professional help available if you want or need it?
- Do you feel free to act like a fool, explore something new and creative, get grubby?

CHAPTER 7

Home Again: Staying Renewed in the Work World

ALL RETREATS COME TO AN END. Sooner or later you re-enter the world you withdrew from, with its time crunches, value conflicts, struggles, and hassles. Even if your retreats have led you to a new learning curve, the momentum of that new curve will eventually bring you again to the point where you lose energy and purpose, and may get lost in hubris unless you pursue self-renewal on an ongoing basis.

This chapter is about sustaining renewal, converting the valuable lessons of retreat into the hard currency of daily living, and matching actions to insights. The goal is to take what you have learned from stepping back and move forward with it—to incorporate keen observation and mindfulness into your daily performance, and use your expanded self-knowledge to discern the shape of future learning curves. In this final stage, the participant self re-engages, but with greater awareness than before.

As we exercise our power of observation in the work of self-inventory and retreat, it becomes stronger, something we do naturally and automatically.

Marathon running illustrates how performance is directly

affected by observation. A top trainer points out that, "The winner is not necessarily the fastest or strongest or best conditioned among the top finishers. But she will know exactly where she is at every moment of the race; what pace is needed and what reserves she has for the finish. She uses what she has most efficiently, and constantly monitors her performance for data on which to base decisions."

In your professional and personal life, as you strengthen your observational skills and learn to match your actions to your insights, you will find that this feedback loop grows stronger. Your increased self-knowledge and awareness of others are reflected in your behavior, which you in turn monitor to increase self-understanding. As your public self becomes more reflective of your whole personality, including parts resurrected from the shadow, your internal critic quiets down and performance flows more smoothly.

There are obstacles to bringing home the lessons of retreat. We will first look at the difficulties that successful people typically encounter on the path to sustained renewal. Then we will explore ways to keep up the cross-fertilization of observation and action, to maintain that critical link with our hidden self. These involve making time and space for retreat on a regular basis, cultivating renewing habits of body and mind, understanding and integrating our stronger and weaker sides, and building support for renewal into our lives.

Personal change is both powerful and fragile; you have to keep at it. In retreat you plant and germinate the seeds of new possibilities, but they must be tended patiently. Profound change doesn't occur overnight, and if you're in a hurry, you can mistake a shoot of healthy change for a weed—or vice versa.

RE-ENTRY

The story of a friend who is starting to re-enter the world after a long retreat illustrates a healthy approach to the process as well as its hazards. Circumstances dictated a complete break from his former working life. But the same issues can arise for someone who has done the work of retreat in smaller doses and is determined to nurture the benefits resulting from it.

Spencer, a mid-forties entrepreneur, had recently sold his thriving retail business and had enough money to take as much time off as he wanted. He gladly turned his attention to parts of his life that he had neglected, such as spending extra time with his two sons and fixing up the house, while deciding what he should do next. Advice poured in from all sides; colleagues dangled attractive deals before him. He felt flattered but he was also gun-shy, fearful of making a wrong move, yet feeling compelled to do something. As much as he enjoyed the present, it was hard for an achiever like him to see it as an authentic life. He talked about these issues as we shared a favorite walk one day.

"There are lots of things to do," he began, "but I'm leery of leaping too quickly. I'm loving the time with Josh and Ben, and frankly I'm enjoying the freedom—this walk for example. But it doesn't feel real. Why am I procrastinating? Am I afraid?"

"Afraid?"

"Well, maybe I need an identity and a title more than I'm willing to admit. It's hard on the ego not to have a crisp answer to the question, 'What do you do?' Also, let's face it, I worry about not having a new challenge and wonder if I'm avoiding it. Maybe I'm deceiving myself about a next stage. Actually I may not have an encore left in me.

"On the other hand, I can't slip back into my old frantic life. I try to remember how crazy that was. Toward the end it was pure madness. I thought I could do anything. I remember sitting in an office in New York, talking about a huge deal with a person I didn't respect and thinking I could straighten him out. The guy was crazy and immoral, and I must have been pretty far gone myself to think I could change him. My wife [his partner in the business] finally put a stop to it."

We ambled along in silence for a while, our boots kicking up the red dust. Then I asked the obvious: "Are you seeing any projects that are truly challenging?"

He grinned as he answered, "Not yet. The real challenge is the one inside me. I'm finding that much more difficult than I'd anticipated. It's not just the issue of who am I outside my work, it's also the confusion—the lack of any structure except the one I create each day. Business had a discipline to it, work to do, decisions to make. I miss that. Part of me feels embarrassed about making self-discovery my primary occupation. Also, I feel guilty at times. What am I contributing? How do I justify my life? This looks like retirement, my friends are calling it retirement, but I'm not nearly ready to retire."

I admired Spencer's ability to distance himself from public success and grapple with his shadow issues. How much of his sense of self-worth came from what he did, the badges he wore, and what others thought or said about him? How much did his personal stock tick up or down when his public performance changed? How high did he rise (inflation) or sink (depression) based on worldly success? And did such success pose a threat to his personal well-being?

Spencer still hasn't resolved the questions he raised, but they are out there on the table, playing a role in every decision he weighs, every opportunity he chooses to explore or bypass. He knows himself well enough to avoid pursuing another business endeavor, trying to top his own success; he has a healthy fear of falling into another inflationary pattern or simply work without meaning. Yet he sweats over his self-definition and outside opinions about his choice not to chase conventional trophies. So he looks for challenges that bring growth but not hyper-inflation.

STUMBLING BLOCKS TO SUSTAINED RENEWAL

Spencer is a typical Type A, self-motivated, successful entrepreneur. Such people have often spent most of a lifetime developing patterns of behavior that are very hard to change: fierce competitiveness, a compulsive attachment to work, a dependence on the high of the next conquest or promotion.

The vise grip of habit and the comfort of the familiar conspire to make us cling to old patterns. Physiology apparently plays a role as well. As we grow older, the neural pathways that regulate behavior are less quickly formed, so it takes longer to reprogram ourselves out of unwanted behavior. But psychological factors are the chief demons on the path to staying renewed. They include:

Fear of what you may lose. It is hard to listen to that quiet voice urging you toward a new learning curve. Beneath your attachment to the benefits of success lies the fear that if you give up what you already know how to do, you will lose your identity. Spencer enjoyed seeing himself as a father, in a new role, but he was haunted by the possibility that his real self had been left behind when he sold his company. Where was he to exercise the aggressive, creative, productive go-getter that resulted in his prior success?

Fear of isolation, of not being at the center of things. Not long ago I did some consulting work with a progressive manufacturing firm. Jake, the veteran VP for human resources, was worried about the results of a follow-up study on executive training retreats, in which participants expressed mixed feelings about their experiences. In particular, many reported that it was upsetting, even frightening, to be away from the action. A top engineering executive, who had never taken a vacation longer than a week since he worked for the firm, reported that he didn't sleep or eat well the whole month he was out of the office. He'd heard rumors of a reorganization and wondered what moves his competitors might be making. Such anxiety reactions make it difficult to sustain the benefits of retreat and to contemplate retreat on an ongoing basis.

The discomfort of change. While it is exciting to feel that you are going through an important, positive change, it can also be disquieting. A young comptroller in Jake's firm, rumored to be the successor to the VP of finance, found his time away stimulating yet disorienting. "I liked the experience; I felt opened up to new ideas and values. But since being back, I seem to be more discontented or uneasy, and others say I'm more critical. I just don't fit in as well. For instance, I really resent going to the same old meetings that rarely raise important questions." He felt pressure, not just from outside but from himself, to remain the cooperative guy who did things by the book and never made waves even though in retreat he had seen the possibility and benefit of acting in other ways.

The benign conspiracy. Also drowning out the voice we can hear in retreat are the voices of those around us. Friends, loved ones, and associates may not welcome too much change. A product manager in Jake's firm reported, "Others saw me as different when I returned. No matter how much I tried to downplay my experiences, people keep bringing it up, implying that I've changed, become more distant from them." She mentioned that her boss teasingly referred to her as their new egghead. Established relationships and procedures are reassuring in a workplace, but can be anathema to personal (and organizational) renewal. Familiar roles in a personal relationship can be even more obdurate: they often have a longer history and the emotional stakes are higher.

Such reactions in the aftermath of retreats, whether voluntary or sponsored, are not only normal but valuable. Retreats are such a powerful tool because they *do* stir up feelings that people normally put aside. The time away from the fray often engenders confusion and restless energy that you simply need to live with for a while, paying attention to any clues and signals you can glean. Too often, individuals and companies regard retreats as mere tune-ups, after which the participants will jump happily back into harness and carry on as before. If you are prepared for the strong feelings that arise from retreat, you will feel less threatened by them; if you try to deny them, they will lurk in the shadow.

How you experience re-entry after retreat is affected by what prompted you to retreat in the first place. Those who are cut off suddenly from their working life—for example, losing a job in a downsizing or merger—feel the symptoms of re-entry more acutely than those who step back deliberately and gracefully. We resist being pushed, even if change is needed, and resistance wastes energy. In contrast, those who retreat voluntarily are well positioned to sniff out productive new learning curves. Success sustainers step back before push comes to shove.

MAINTENANCE RETREATS: MAKING TIME AND SPACE FOR RENEWAL

To build on the work of retreat and remain free of hubris, we must maintain access to the hidden self that we contacted in retreat. To do this, we need to visit the shadow often. We may open up a dialogue with ourself during planned retreats or short-term therapy, but unless it is encouraged on a regular basis, it will fall silent.

Maintaining an open channel with our shadow is hard. We cannot command the unconscious to obey or use reason or charm to coax out its secrets. We can only try to leave our egos behind and follow practices that encourage deep learning and hinder the growth of inflation. Maintenance retreats—those you can pursue on a regular basis, thereby deepening their effect—are essential.

THE GIFT OF TIME

To sustain a spirit of renewal, we must create the time necessary for working with our shadow. I have discussed how time tyrannizes successful people and how they can use a retreat to obtain glimpses of a more harmonious relationship with it. David Cooper describes the challenge this way in his book *Silence, Simplicity and Solitude*: "The biggest demon we encounter when thinking about taking a retreat is our sense of lost time. . . . When we are focused on this feeling of lost time, some part of ourselves is expressing itself. It may be the part that constantly pushes us to achieve something, that measures our self-worth by our actions, or that is afraid of being alone."

A key to long-range renewal is finding a more permanent, nonadversarial way of relating to time. Therapist Joe Henderson, when asked what he had received from his analysis and training with Jung, said, "Jung helped me to reset my inner clock." He explained that he had gone to see Jung while a medical student because of anxiety he experienced about never having enough time. He had been told that his career would be jeopardized if he didn't publish by a certain age, but he didn't feel ready. With Jung's help, he came to accept that good writing comes when it will, when it is worth doing. Well into his eighties, he is still publishing.

In *Time and the Art of Living*, Robert Grudin comments on this phenomenon: "Time is endless when it is adequate. For in one sense time exists only in relation to what is willed and done; and the act of completing something is like closing a circle in nature." He is saying, in essence, that if we shift our focus to what we wish to accomplish rather than the time we have to do it in, we gain a little freedom from time's grasp.

Like Henderson and other success sustainers, we can leave the prison of linear time behind by total immersion in the activities practiced in retreat, such as painting, gardening, meditating. The experience is akin to what some athletes report at the peak of performance: time seems to expand to accommodate the necessary motion or compress to a blink to carry them through painful or boring stretches.

Gardening became very important for Joe Henderson, allowing him to see his own life in seasonal rhythms. He speaks of changing his garden each year, adding some plants and discarding others, never rushing nature. Many things happen only in the fullness of time. Plants coming to harvest cannot be rushed; nor can rain, or trust in a relationship, or incorporating a sport into muscle memory, or gaining self-understanding. Some things never happen at all while we anxiously wait and watch for results.

Making time for regular retreats often seems hopeless to those engaged in a day-to-day struggle to find enough time to meet their obligations. But our sense of time is greatly a matter of perception, as Robert Grudin points out: "[W]hen we try to manage our own time, setting new goals, cleansing and rearranging the little houses of our days, time gently mocks us— not so much because we lack wit as because time operates on a deeper psychological level than conscious effort can ever reach."

Though it seems to defy logic, we may simply need to accept that taking time to retreat will ultimately give us a more comfortable relationship with time in all our endeavors. When we reach a point where mind, body, and surroundings are in harmony, where we focus with true intensity, time magically seems adequate to our needs and energy flows unimpeded. We can discover this powerful key to performance through regular retreats and later incorporate it into everyday routines.

MAINTENANCE RETREAT RITUALS

Closely observed commitments to private time—even if only a weekend—are essential to making retreats part of our lives. Jean-Louis Servan-Schreiber, the French authority on time management, shared a simple technique when I asked how he maintained his extraordinary productivity. During the work week he uses one briefcase for work-related material and occasionally adds items to another: his retreat briefcase. Every available weekend, he and his wife escape by high-speed train to their farmhouse in Provence. On such weekends the business briefcase is opened only on the train. Once in the country, Servan-Schreiber returns to his creative writing, to which the special briefcase is devoted.

A retreat scheduled annually or at some other regular inter-

val can augment more frequent maintenance retreats and serve
as a touchstone in your life. Many people use the New Year's
holiday, or Rosh Hashonah, as a one-day retreat to step back
and put their lives in perspective; others have evolved an annual ritual around their birthday or another date of personal
significance.

One dear friend of mine spends his New Year's day review-
ing in writing his own development and what he feels he has
achieved for his family, friends, and community. Business accomplishments no longer count in his scheme. He then makes
a list of goals for the coming year and puts it aside, to check a
year later. Taking the time to write things down instead of
making a couple of vague resolutions in your mind is an act of
commitment to personal growth.

Even a meal can become a time for renewal. A ritual I
cherish is taking my brother to a special long lunch once a year.
We see each other at other times, but this is an event carefully
set aside for just the two of us to review where we've been and
where we're headed, against the backdrop of our shared family
history and prior commitments.

Develop retreat rituals that guard you from encroaching
ego-inflation, encourage self-exploration, and help keep your
life in balance. They should deliver lessons (and sometimes
errors) to learn from, quiet space in which to listen, and new
vantage points for observation.

CULTIVATING RENEWING HABITS OF BODY AND MIND

Sustaining renewal is largely a matter of closing the gap between the self that functions in the world day-to-day and the
self we can access on retreat. Renewing habits of body and
mind help bridge the gap and bring home the spirit and benefits of retreat. They encompass many activities, and they can
be cultivated.

THE MIND-BODY LINK

Recognizing the mind and body as a integral unit and caring for the health of both is fundamental to sustaining renewal. As many studies have shown, the benefits of physical exercise go well beyond cardiovascular fitness and improved self-image, affecting our cognition, psychological equilibrium, and emotional state through complex biochemical processes. The outer work of considered physical exercise enhances our access to our inner life. Testing and stretching our neuromuscular systems also teaches us about our capacity to learn and grow.

Among those investigating this connection is Michael Gelb, whose High Performance Learning seminars are based on learning how to juggle. This has proven to be a great way of making people aware of how their bodies react to the challenge of learning something new. "I deal with seasoned, thick-skinned executives," Gelb notes. "Yet you confront them with this playful challenge, and you can see the change in their bodies—and they can *feel* those changes!"

Tim Gallway's *The Inner Game of Tennis* is based on his discoveries about physical awareness, mindfulness, and re-framing in the context of improving at a sport. A player of great natural gifts, he was also very self-critical and tightly strung, obsessed with winning every point. His book traces the transition from that harsh and frustrating approach to an appreciation of the process, an ability to really get inside what's going on when racquet meets ball. He learned to find joy and satisfaction in the feeling of hitting the ball well, regardless of whether it went in or not.

Exotic or strenuous forms of exercise are not essential. Walking is an activity most people can do on a daily basis. Note the difference between ordinary and mindful walking. Your feet might be carrying you through beautiful country, but if your brain is still enmeshed in the usual tangle of problems and projects, you might as well be riding a subway.

There are many ways of walking mindfully, all involving the

effort to draw our attention outside ourselves and into our surroundings. We can borrow the simple "walking meditation" technique of a Zen teacher named Thich Nhat Hanh, who suggests:

- Stroll without purpose or direction, breathing rhythmically.
- Count the steps between each breath.
- Each step is taken mindfully.
- A natural smile will emerge as you observe beauty and release time concerns, worries, and sorrows.

Hanh notes, "Often after a few hours of serious practice you will find that the breath, the counting, the steps, and the half-smile blend together in a marvelous balance of mindfulness."

Higher education executive Patty Mullen swims and rows in San Francisco Bay to start her day. The combination of solitude and challenging exercise works to balance her demanding intellectual and management responsibilities. Whenever possible, she takes longer retreats by backpacking in the Sierra Nevada, but she needs her daily fix in the cold morning bay.

Access to the inner self is not aided by practices that chafe, create tension, or feel like work. A good example of a non-renewing ritual is the workout room in the New York hotel where I occasionally stay, a stark gray-and-white cell lined with exercise bikes constantly whirling away. The riders, still wearing their closed street faces, stare grimly at high-tech readout panels flashing data on progress or regression, simulating competitive conditions, or at papers resting on eye-level racks. The room reeks of sweat and earnestness.

Some forms of fairly strenuous exercise *can* create mental space for the inner voice to be heard. Beautiful natural surroundings make a difference, but a mindful attitude is even more important. Even riding an exercise bike can be a form of retreat, if approached in a mindful way, rather than bringing our performance obsessions into the workout room.

HANDS-ON WORK, PLAY, AND GOOD TALK

Maintenance retreats are the ideal setting to exercise creativity through our hands, which stimulates inner dialogue and enriches our interactions with others. An advertising dynamo named Sam has a Saturday morning ritual in which he and a neighbor get together for some mundane project like cleaning out the garage. The rules are few: it must involve simple manual labor and not take too long. In describing the value of this practice, Sam says, "I get lost in the work and my mind wanders. We don't need to be talking all the time, but often Homer and I talk about things I never discuss in my so-called 'normal' life."

For Steve Allen, playing the piano is both a professional skill and a renewing ritual. "When I'm performing or writing songs, the piano is an instrument of work. But for some time each day, I just sit down and let my hands wander on the keyboard. I lose myself in melodies that come automatically. My fingers seem to be connected with a different part of my mind, and when I finish these playing reveries, I feel quite refreshed." These moments, Allen told me, encourage him to trust his nonverbal side. Anyone whose primary strength lies in wit and intellect will benefit from experiences where an instinctive, physical function asserts itself.

C. West Churchman said, "The excellent leader possesses the art of good conversation," and good conversation springs from the inner resources of the participants. Dull inside: dull discourse. A natural and beneficial result of maintaining an inner dialogue is that it enhances the quality of your interactions with others. Good conversationalists draw on a rich trove of feelings, stories, facts, impressions, concepts, even dreams. They dig for the stimulating question and can bring disparate or conflicting views into a manageable synthesis. Their words ring with humor and resonate with an integrity that inspires confidence.

By the same token, the more you enrich and deepen your

discourse with others, moving your inner dialogue into conversation, the more substance you derive for your private musings. If you have friends who are willing to share the contents of their shadows, that gift will help illuminate your own. For example, if someone confesses to you that he is troubled by envy of a colleague, it may surprise you. Later you might start to wonder what unacknowledged feelings of your own might be easier to live with if shared with a trusted friend.

Rich conversation flows from the experience and curiosity of the participants, yet the topics need not be lofty. This is a secret women have always known. Kakuzo Okakura, the author of *The Book of Tea*, offers another viewpoint: "A special contribution of Zen to Eastern thought was its recognition of the mundane as of equal importance with the spiritual. It held that in the great relation of things there was no distinction between small and great, an atom possessing equal possibilities with the universe. . . . [Simple work] formed a part of Zen discipline and every least action must be done absolutely perfectly. Thus, many a weighty discussion ensued while weeding the garden, paring a turnip, or serving tea."

Quiet work with the hands often seems to open up the flow of dialogue, internal and external. Men and women today have fewer opportunities for such conversation-provoking activities, but anyone who has enjoyed rich talk while tying flies or building models or painting a room knows instinctively what the Zen thinkers have articulated.

DEEP LEARNING CONTINUED: BALANCING OUR PERSONALITIES

As we have seen, our shadows contain not only negative emotions that hold us back and encourage hubris, but less developed parts of ourselves that hold the key to sustained renewal. We may glimpse these neglected potentials when we first begin to retreat, but they will emerge and flower only with ongoing attention. Undertaking this deeper shadow-work is equivalent to embarking on a sharp learning curve about ourselves.

Each of us tends to favor some aspects of our personality and some ways of operating over others. Reflective persons may deny their feeling side, while those prone to emotionally based decisions may not recognize their inability to reason through a situation. Our shy self fights against our gregarious tendencies; our rational side finds our intuitive side a threat; our masculine attributes tend to overwhelm our feminine ones, or vice versa.

To grow and adapt, we need to observe our weaknesses and strengths, encouraging the development of weaker functions while maintaining our natural strengths. Such rebalancing will benefit both our working and personal lives. For example, if someone who relies mainly on an analytical approach to problems works at bringing her emotional side into the equation, unexpected discoveries will result. Similarly, if a creative type needs to master business skills to succeed in an entrepreneurial effort, he will be energized by taking the first steps toward mastery.

Jung believed that rounding out the personality into a whole was the goal of psychotherapy and of personal development in general. The lifelong process of understanding our unique, complete, individual self he termed "individuation." This occurs by integrating all the elements of the psyche, bringing to consciousness the less-used parts and reconciling them with the stronger parts of our self-image. Joseph Campbell describes Jung's concept thus: "The aim of one's life, psychologically speaking, should be not to suppress or repress, but to come to know one's other side, and so both to enjoy and to control the whole range of one's capacities; i.e., in the full sense, to 'know oneself.' "

Jung describes his idea of individuation as "self-realization" and notes that it "aims at a living cooperation of all factors."

Thinking of personal evolution in this way is especially useful if you have focused strongly on success in one limited area.

JUNG'S BASIC TYPES

Jung proposed a psychological typology as a means of observing our preferred way of approaching life or solving problems. His typology is made up of two pairs of opposites: thinking vs. feeling, and intuition vs. sensation. If your most conscious side, or the way you approach life, is thinking, then you see the world through ideas—intellectual constructs. Intuition and sensation may be developed in varying degrees (for example, as an intuitive thinker), but feeling—the relational, evaluative mode—will be your inferior function. Many people have met clear thinkers, even visionaries, whose emotional lives seem to have been cut short, who have no access to the joys of intimacy.

The converse is also true: feeling persons tend to have underdeveloped reasoning faculties. Highly emotional persons often seem unable to think in a straight line, for their feelings sweep them away. An effort at rational explanation of a situation may have little effect if their feelings are totally in control.

People whose intuition is primary—who see patterns of connection and move on hunches—may have varying degrees of feeling and thinking developed. Their least-developed function, according to Jung, will be sensation. They may be able to fly high, see the big picture, but their feet are not planted in the world of things. They may have a hard time replacing a light bulb.

Conversely, sensation types will be at home in the world of objects, noting details and comfortable at moving things around in space. They may seem more embodied than others, more grounded or stable. But they cannot soar to the heights like intuitives or express deep emotional responses like the feeling types.

Each of us has all of these qualities; they develop to different extents according to our natural character inclinations and our early childhood. Jung and one of his chief followers, Marie-

Louise von Franz, linked the inferior function to the shadow. If we use only what we develop easily, they said, only those capacities that emerge on their own, then the others remain in the shadow. The result is an imbalanced life—whether overly intellectualized, overly emotional, overly intuitive, or overly earthbound.

Another set of opposing traits in Jung's typology is the introverted and extroverted, either of which can also languish in the shadow. In business and public life, those who extend their extroverted natures are usually encouraged and rewarded. But relying too heavily on extroverted behavior and ignoring the need for contact with the inner self can tilt one dangerously toward hubris.

A case in point may bring Jung's ideas closer to home. Thomas, a well-known media figure, a handsome, personable man of forty-three, once leaned across our breakfast table and confided that he was "losing it." On occasional earlier meetings he had complained about overwork, not having enough hours in the day, but this time his tone held a more desperate note. He spoke of "coming apart . . . I'm out every night; I'm drinking too much. I'm afraid of being alone, but I'm also afraid of stopping. In fact, I don't know how to stop."

We spoke at length about his inability to get off the treadmill. At the end of our talk he decided to seek professional help. Thomas began therapy with the partial aim of nurturing his neglected introverted side. A year later he said to me, "The more I know myself, the more I like what I find. I like my time alone now and seem to need less approval from others."

If you are uncertain about identifying your stronger and weaker sides (called superior and inferior functions), you can ask trusted friends and associates for their impressions or do a little reading on the subject. If you want to go deeper, you might take a Myers-Briggs inventory or similar test arranged by a psychologist. However you go about it, this work aims at a "recovery of the self"—the complete, whole self that you are capable of being.

SELF-KNOWLEDGE AND LIFELONG LEARNING

All success sustainers seek new learning journeys. The journeys begin as we revive parts of ourselves that were in the shadow—the intuitive or feeling person, the craftsman, student of music, ecologist, or writer—parts or roles that may have been put aside in favor of "serious success."

The less-developed sides that we bring forth from the shadow must stretch their wings, like butterflies emerging from a chrysalis. They need fresh learning ventures to feed on, and they will move toward the kinds of learning they crave. As we pass through life, hidden sides of our character continue to emerge and unfold, hungry for new nourishment. John Gardner says (of course speaking of women as well): "Exploration of the full range of his own potentialities is not something that the self-renewing man leaves to the chances of life. It is something he pursues systematically, or at least avidly, to the end of his days. He looks forward to an endless and unpredictable dialogue between his potentialities and the claims of life."

Do not think that focused, purposeful learning belongs to your past—before the claims of life asserted themselves. I hear people in business speak wistfully of how great it would be to go back to school, to have the leisure to learn for the joy of it, as if school were the only possible context for learning. Do not fail to see your potential for lifelong learning because you are stuck in the notion that learning equals absorbing and regurgitating information handed down from on high. As Ron Gross points out in *Peak Learning*, "Many people have trouble at first with the idea of self-directed learning because they have been trained by society to equate learning only with what is taught in educational institutions."

Do not undermine your hopes by setting up an either-or choice: retreating to the ivory tower or grappling with the world. As Gardner astutely notes, the conflict between new prospects and life's demands produces a creative tension. This interface is where growth takes place.

BUILDING SUPPORT FOR RENEWAL

Much of the work of renewal is solitary, growing out of the busy achiever's need to spend time with him- or herself. It is also frightening and likely to raise doubts, questions, and confusion that we need help to sort out. Especially in resisting the siren song of hubris—probably the hardest part of sustaining renewal—most of us need a support structure.

Surrounded by people, the leader is nonetheless alone. The best safeguard against hubris is to nurture strong, honest relationships and solicit the input of friends and mentors. You need friends who are loving yet blunt, who ask rude (honest) questions, who don't let you off the hook. If you find yourself seeing less of such friends, hubris advances; if you defend yourself too well against their prods, hubris wins.

A recent report by a top researcher on male development came to the truly tragic conclusion that most men simply do not have many friends. My own experience with men in leadership positions is that they often feel isolated, cut off, and mistrustful—rich in acquaintances yet poor in friends. In *Renewing the Leader's Creative Task*, John Gardner writes: "The leader needs something that doesn't appear on any organization chart: a circle of associates who are willing to be both supportive and critical. Pity the leader who is caught between unloving critics and uncritical lovers. Leaders need . . . advisers who will guide them lovingly but candidly through the minefields of arrogance, overweening pride, fixed ideas, vindictiveness, unreasoning anger, stubbornness and egotism."

A friend is someone we can count on for understanding, support, discretions, and, if we're lucky, insight, wisdom, and well-timed foolishness.

Leaders' lives are enhanced by the presence of a sage-fool. One dreadful aspect of self-inflation is the tendency to limit foolery. There is a vast difference between humor that comes at the expense of others and real humor. Leaders who chide, tease, and ridicule others often find that their own skins have become too thin when barbs fly their way. The long-distance leader welcomes the "fool" who democratically deflates all puffed-up egos (including their own) at the right moment.

Medieval kings and queens sometimes used their court jesters as confidants and even advisers on matters of state. Perhaps these court fools were like early, unlicensed therapists for rulers wise enough to heed them. The fool took the risk of holding a mirror of honesty up to the ruler's face. Who else in the court could be counted on to tell the truth when it was necessary? The fools of old thus focused on shadow material that others refused to see, or, if they saw, refused to name.

Modern leaders who are secure in their position can also play the fool to everyone's advantage, by their role-playing exploding the pent-up gases of an overripe success. Churchill loved to play the fool when it suited him to do so, and especially relished exploding the pretentions of the uppercrust. Great leaders like him know how to play the fool in order to shatter the stifling gridlock of arrogance, stuffy earnestness, and self-consciousness that plague organizations and groups.

Learning expert Edward De Bono writes in his book *Six Thinking Hats*: People do not mind "playing the fool" so long as it is quite clear that they are just playing a role. . . . [A] role gives freedom. We might have difficulty in seeing ourselves being foolish, wrong, or outsmarted. Given a well-defined role we can act out such parts with pleasure in our acting skill rather than damage to our egos."

Even if you play this role only in private or with those you trust implicitly, it can still be refreshing. Few things are more liberating for a leader than to be able to play the fool for a loving and uncritical audience, your grandchildren, for instance.

Humor in general is an effective weapon for fighting hubris; if we can't find something to laugh about when we look in the mirror, we haven't looked hard enough, and every long-distance winner can tell stories of gaffes and pratfalls.

The following questions should help reveal whether your

support structure includes friends and "fools," and how well you nurture them:

- Do you complain that no one understands you?
- Have you reduced the time you spend just hanging out with friends?
- Do you tend to lay the full burden of serving as truth-teller and confessor on your spouse or life partner?
- Are you working to recruit more friends and "fools" into your life, or are you satisfied with those you have?
- Have you created a reward system for the "friendly fools" in your life (or your company)?
- When did you last thank those who talked straight with you? What did you say?

I can often tell when a leadership group is healthy by the sounds of their meetings. The more cohesive and trusting the group, the more open they are with one another, the more open, the richer the humor. In such groups secrets don't survive, and shadows get exposed. The players in such groups have the capacity to shift roles from supporter to critic to sage to "fool."

Support from Coaches, Teachers, Mentors, and Therapists

Sustained deep learning requires vigilance, courage, practice, timing, and motivation. People in various roles can provide guidance and help you nurture these qualities. They can be supportive yet objective, using their outside perspective to help you see the larger pattern of your development. Such relationships can be informal or prescribed, ranging from the wise friend who is willing to serve as a coach, to a closely directed therapeutic situation.

Our chosen guides can help us explore the unknown territory of the shadow, especially if they have done such exploration themselves and can reassure us as to its value. They can gently draw our attention to behavior that encourages or exhibits hubris. Sometimes they can provide information, encouragement, or instructions about life that we didn't get from an absent father or an overprotective mother.

Friends too can be excellent coaches, if chosen and used well, observing a few key guidelines. If you ask a friend to act as your coach in personal growth, you need to make an overt agreement with that person so that there is little room for misinterpretation in their new role. You should ask straightforwardly for his or her time and be specific about the kind of exploration you want to do and feedback you desire. You must prepare to risk intimacy that will change the character of the relationship you have had. You should establish clear reciprocity so that the relationship does not become uncomfortably unbalanced. And you shouldn't expect too much, particularly as you start on this course. Don't ask for more than you know the friend can give, in time, skills, generosity, wisdom, and emotional range.

Women seem to be better trained at friendship from an early age; they know more about how to use friends as advisers and confidants. Perhaps the men's movement will help to make men more aware of their need for friendly coaching and their obligation to provide it for others.

Studies show that caring teachers and firm, wise coaches greatly influence the course of many young lives. Once out of school, we largely do without the aid of teachers, but the need remains. A teacher in adulthood (as distinct from a coach or a mentor) is usually someone whom we have sought out to help us master a particular skill: it may be golf, music, painting, writing, meditation, or a martial art, but it can be the art of living too.

In helping us bring out and develop capacities from our shadow, any teacher is contributing to our sustained renewal. Some, in addition, may possess life's wisdom that they are willing to share, or offer insights about us based on a growing personal relationship. Anytime you place yourself in a learning situation, personal discoveries over and above the targeted goal are likely to emerge.

Another form of support is an experienced older person who takes on the responsibility for guiding us along a career path— it may be a supervisor or a professional working in a related field. Historian Page Smith, in a 1991 *San Francisco Chronicle* article, recalls: "I was extremely fortunate in my mentors. They were quite simply and practically my teachers, men who loved me and cared for me and encouraged me and who refused to let my inherent laziness and general drollery discourage them. . . . I cannot imagine my mature life without them."

Smith goes on to lament the modern dearth of mentors. His context is the knowledge factories of contemporary academe, but it applies equally to the world of commerce and the professions. Much is said about the need for mentors in career development, but the transient and highly competitive nature of business today does not make a fertile environment for producing them. Witness the manager of an investment banking team, who gave this answer when asked what his company did to protect its young bankers and traders from burnout: "We don't," he said. "We know that by the time most of these guys are forty, they're pretty much useless to us—too much emotional damage, probably a divorce or two. But hell, they've made plenty of money . . . they can go retire to a ranch and never work again."

Nonetheless, good mentors are out there if you know how to ask. The guidelines suggested above for finding coaches in friends can be applied here as well, with some modification to fit the workplace.

If you are at an appropriate stage in your career development, consider being a mentor to someone else. It is a learning curve that can contribute greatly to renewal at the right time. People often fear that if they take on the role of teacher, they may stop learning themselves—as though their well of learning would be emptied rather than replenished by a mentoring experience. I reacted with some unease the first time a younger man explicitly asked me to be his mentor: it felt awkward, maybe "ageist"; it was both flattering and threatening.

Thinking over the request, though, I realized how much I had gained from the examples and guidance of older men. I began to feel more comfortable with the idea, as long as certain limits were established. Mentoring does have its hazards, such as overdependency: a too-close connection usually ends in a struggle to separate after the relationship has lived out its purpose. But would-be mentors should know that it isn't a one-way street. You give back something, certainly, but at least in my own case, I received so much from the interchange that it hardly seemed an act of generosity.

Working with a therapist, either on a long-term basis or for a specific period devoted to a particular issue, is partly a way of acknowledging and focusing on your need for support. Therapeutic sessions are like short, intensive retreats, and they can help you process the feelings and discoveries that come out of longer retreats. A skilled therapist can gently pry open the door to the unconscious that you closed to avoid dealing with guilt or rage or fear of inadequacy or a wound of rejection, and work with you to sort through, interpret, and resolve this shadow material.

If you're hesitant about the value of therapy, or wonder if you really need it, or if you feel that such a commitment might be okay only if you were close to falling apart, a remark of Joe Henderson's may be comforting: "The best results come for people who are healthy enough to see the need. Truly sick people can get rather limited benefits from therapy."

SUPPORT FROM COLLECTIVE MYTHS

Our life stories flow from our personal history. They are also profoundly affected in both reality and our understanding of it by the prevailing myths and social trends of our time. Both personal lives and institutions will reflect social change. Mass change can be frightening or a source of hope, expanding or restrictive. You can be in line or out of phase with, ensnared or liberated by change. And you can respond by swinging freely or hunkering down and clinging to an old pattern. Veteran deep learners recognize and shed the dead weight of faltering myths and relish the buoyancy of emerging ones. Sensing that you are in sync with a powerful emerging myth—for example, caring for the environment or engaging in community service—will reinforce the inner messages you hear in retreat.

Your personal myth should be flexible enough to grow in response to social changes but not alter course at their whim, in violation of your own needs and dreams. On the advice of a longtime mentor who convinced her that a career in finance was stifling, a forty-year-old woman left her solid position to pursue a new chapter in academe. After teaching business school students for a year, she knew it was not what she was after. Each day felt more burdensome, and at first she blamed her dull students.

Eventually she realized that she had been trying to live out her mentor's ideas rather than her own. With this awareness, she began to revise her story. Remaining in the academic community, she first turned her studies to the problems of upgrading Third World economies; later she progressed to teaching and consulting with visiting leaders from those countries. Her career began to feel much more open and adventurous. It was taking shape in response to an urgent sociopolitical phenomenon, but it was very much her own.

Each of us is part of the collective; we add to it and draw from it. Yet we must construct personal myths that are as individual and distinct as possible. Leaders are leaders rather than followers because they are alert to the pulse of the world around them, yet, in most important things, they act according to their internal rhythms and instincts.

When I consulted with the founder of a recently sold company, he was flailing around trying to find his next chapter in whatever was current and hot. "Perhaps I should start up a new company in the environmental sciences sector," Ed speculated. "That's a play for the future, don't you think?"

I looked at this energetic fifty-year-old engineer and avoided his question. "I'm not sure—what do you see yourself actually doing? What dreams do you want to pursue?" After a long pause, he answered, "I'm too young to stop working and I'm too old to play baseball."

I interjected quickly, "Let me say it another way. You have lots of choices: why limit your consideration to what you have already done? Would running another company thrill you as your first one did?" He looked surprised, and then laughed and said, "I really do love baseball. Maybe I could try out this spring."

Ed did try out the next spring—not as a player but as an observer writing about spring training and what it's like to be fifty and unemployed. He had two pieces published and was as thrilled as if he had hit a major league home run. Well, almost. He is now pursuing a career that combines writing and video production, and makes time to follow the Giants to Arizona for spring training each year.

REVISING YOUR PERSONAL MISSION STATEMENT

A life of never-ending learning and renewal is guided by a compelling vision of how your life should be, what you want to spend your time doing—what is worth doing. The information you gather from the shadow during retreats should coalesce over time into a clear picture of how your needs and values are evolving.

I have suggested that early in the renewal cycle, when you have reached an observation point and are ready to step back and take inventory, you draft a personal mission statement. This may involve stating one overarching purpose in your life, or a ranking of priorities, or a word portrait of how you envision your life at its best. The time following a retreat or a series of retreats is a good one to revise your mission statement in light of the discoveries you have made. You are tracking any changes in what most fascinates and compels you, based on messages that flow through the open channel to your inner voice.

You may also choose to revise it at some regular interval, such as annually. There is no ideal interval for such a revision, though if your values seem to change frequently, you may not have spent enough time exploring in the shadow—you are probably reacting to external pressures rather than tuning in to your inner voice. If your values and goals do not change at all, it's likely that you are overriding and denying some internal signals urging change.

The point of working at your personal mission statement is to help you articulate the insights of retreat and thus successfully match your future actions to them. Your deepest sense of purpose may be hard to capture and commit to paper, but I have seen substantial payoffs result from the exercise. When we cast our hopes, dreams, and ambitions into words, it helps to solidify our intentions.

Sustained deep learning, aided by the passage of time, usually leads us to an important discovery. At some point in life our desire for wealth, position, recognition, and power lessen in importance as the need for a larger purpose emerges. This larger purpose often takes the form of an urge to give back to the world—what developmental psychologist Erik Erikson calls the "generativity urge"—and may be expressed through child-raising, mentoring, volunteer work, and other altruistic activities. John Gardner speaks eloquently about this in *Self-Renewal*: "Despite almost universal belief to the contrary, gratification, ease, comfort, diversion, and a state of having achieved all one's goals do not constitute happiness for man. . . . The storybook conception [of happiness] tells of desires fulfilled; the truer version involves striving toward meaningful goals—goals that relate the individual to a larger context of purposes."

Expanding your personal mission to include altruism is both a sign of maturity and a powerful incentive to learn. The baby boom generation seems especially inclined to seek a higher purpose as they approach the middle years. The formation of the Social Venture Network—a group of successful entrepreneurs, investors, and other leaders who work to infuse the business community with a sense of social responsibility—is a direct outgrowth of this phenomenon.

One of SVN's members is Ben Cohen of Ben & Jerry's ice cream fame. After the partners had established a progressive business with solid community roots and forward-looking employee relations, Ben grew restless. He became interested in the issue of rainforest preservation, and combining this concern with his marketing talent, he developed Rainforest Crunch, a confection made with nuts bought directly from Amazonian natives, who could thereby continue to live off the land. Ben recently embarked on a voluntary retreat, and his self-renewal work may well result in new ecological ventures.

On the international scene, we can see how a larger purpose lends dynamic energy to the learning curves of many leaders who have returned from enforced retreats as political prisoners—the victims of repressive regimes in Latin America, South Africa, and Eastern Bloc nations. Their language is remarkably clear, and an integrity runs through their ideas and visions that is missing from most political rhetoric. Their words carry a refreshing optimism and sense of commitment that reduces the vocabulary of sound bites, spin talk, and photo opportunities to absurdity.

Vaclav Havel, the playwright who became Czechoslovakia's president after his release from prison, spoke thus to the U.S. Congress: "Without a global revolution in the sphere of human consciousness, nothing will change for the better in the sphere of our being—we still don't know how to put morality ahead of politics, science, and economics. We are still incapable of understanding that the only genuine backbone of all our actions, if we are to be moral, is responsibility—responsibility to something higher than my family, my country, my company, my success."

Not all of us need to find in ourselves the commitment level of leaders who took enforced retreats in prison, or devote our lives to fighting for a cause. For most of us, our mission will find expression in something close to home: improving the community, pulling a scattered family back together, making safer products, teaching others what we know. Whatever motivates us most deeply will be a product of our efforts toward renewal, and the actions we take on its behalf will further propel the renewal cycle.

Whatever the vision that pulls you forward in search of a new learning curve, keep in mind that renewal lies in the *pursuit* of larger goals rather than in their *attainment*. "For that reason," Gardner says, "the self-renewing man never feels that he has 'arrived.'" The poet Robert Louis Stevenson expressed the same idea in his famous aphorism: "To travel hopefully is a better thing than to arrive, and the true success is to labor." Of course, we need attainable goals as well—but as on a rising learning curve, energy and motivation live in the approach rather than at the peak.

In the last chapter, we will begin to redefine the concept of success for the leaders and organizations of the future, applying the lessons of retreat and renewal. Leaders will be dealing with paradigm shifts in how corporate structures organize and manage human resources, how people manage their time and life rhythms, and how growth and productivity interact with finite natural resources, among others. Concepts of balance, ethics, and aesthetics will be important in our redefinition of success, and perhaps most important, in finding our ability to deal with shadows. Leaders and organizations that can open and explore shadow issues will be those best able to sustain success—for themselves and those they serve—in a world of rapid change.

CHAPTER 8

The Long-Distance Leader and the Self-Renewing Organization

MOST OF THIS BOOK has explored what enables a person to sustain success—the wisdom, skills, and practices that characterize the long-distance winner. Many of the persons it cites are leaders, with responsibilities to further the growth and development of an organization. In business, the professions, public service, and education, we need many more long-distance winners who are also long-distance leaders.

The current leadership deficit in America is far more serious than our fiscal deficit. The demand for healthy-minded, wise, and ethical leaders far exceeds the supply. Many young people possess the raw materials of long-distance leadership—intelligence, drive, organizational skills, and the will to lead—yet never make it to maturity. And, as we've seen, many of their mature counterparts derail or self-destruct at the height of their success. Both of these failures are due to a larger failure to identify and promote the most fundamental qualities of leadership—which are also the qualities of the self-renewing person.

Out of the endless debate about leadership essentials has developed a short list of prerequisites: energy; stamina; curiosity; persistence; common sense; the capacity to trust and engender trust; a balance of self-assurance, compassion, courage, and natural modesty; the ability to listen closely and to communicate effectively; a commitment to ethics and aesthetics; and a high regard for individual differences.

For the most part, the institutions that are supposed to mold leaders are not teaching these prerequisites. Peter Drucker, the grand master of management science, has declared publicly that high-status business schools are anachronistic. Popular opinion about the products of law schools indicates that they are not doing the job either. Professional training has come to place too much emphasis on skill acquisition and positioning for career advancement, on competition and individual achievement; their range of inquiry has narrowed along with the increasing specialization of careers.

Skills training is a necessary part of the leadership curriculum, of course, but is not sufficient in itself. What's needed is education that teaches young leaders to work collaboratively, struggle with value conflicts, learn from mentors, promote creativity, prize errors, and think globally and cross-culturally. Warren Neal, dean of the School of Business at the University of Tennessee and a respected innovator in business education, believes that future leaders must learn to be good citizens and "servant leaders"—a term that implies the value of altruism as well as an awareness and a rejection of hubris.

Formal education could do much more to advance leadership excellence, but it is not the only source. The fundamentals of leadership can be learned in virtually any setting. Farming, printing, and teaching were among the endeavors that honed the designers of the American federal democracy. To answer our present needs, long-distance leadership must be taught through the example and practice of existing leaders who have absorbed the lessons of self-renewal through hard-won personal experience. This chapter is devoted to examining and describing the characteristics, attitudes, practices, and impact on organizations of those robust survivors, the long-distance leaders whom we so desperately need.

QUALITIES OF THE LONG-DISTANCE LEADER

The leaders of a sustainable organization must have a deeply internalized knowledge of renewing practices and their value. They must be committed to the values they wish to communicate and to the worth of the endeavor they are engaged in, and be willing to take the risks needed for growth, including the probability that they will look foolish on occasion. They must take the long view: many fledglings fail because they embrace the smart-game mentality, a cynical view that shaves ethics for short-term profit and treats people as a disposable commodity.

Above all, they need the ability to go inside and access whatever is in their shadow, driving their behavior. The most gifted and successful leaders, if they lose the capacity to go beneath their surface persona and face shadow demons, put themselves and their organizations in danger. But once familiar with the personal benefits of shadow-work, they can spot ways to light and explore collective shadows that are damaging the organization.

THE LEADER AS SHADOW-LIGHTER

Long-distance leaders honor the power of the shadow in their lives, and have learned how to read the hidden messages encoded there. By modeling shadow-lighting themselves and by promoting it in their organizations, leaders can help to defuse toxic secrets, release productive energy, reclaim creativity, and reveal directions for future development.

Once the shadow takes hold in an organization, its grip is hard to break, so leaders should aim to prevent the buildup that comes from perpetuating secrets and taboos, from denial, projection, and scapegoating. The leader must probe the shadow by investigating and correcting rumors, provide a model of self-revelation and clarity, fashion policies that promote open dialogue, and institute prompt and personal responses to errors.

The benefits of lighting shadows are not limited to public relations. When I meet with leaders who are in trouble or feel trapped in some hush-hush problem, I often begin by asking how much time and energy The Problem is consuming. If they can imagine what it would be like to let the beast loose and recapture the lost resources devoted to it, they can begin shadow-lighting. They can see the issue in terms of a cost/benefit analysis: Keep the monster in the dark, cover it over, and hope it will vanish. Or light the problem quickly and free up the psychic and real assets that the cover-up is consuming. When they can sort out the competing interests, costs, and benefits, most leaders go for the light.

The basic principles of shadow-lighting in organizations are:

Break secrecy codes. Members of the board of an old, family-run firm complained about "communication problems" that characterized meetings and clogged decision-making. At the root of the problems was an elaborate silent code covering which subjects were appropriate to discuss. By persuading the head of the family to reveal a dark, never-discussed secret, the code was broken; others gained courage to bring up once-forbidden topics, and business moved briskly forward. Now at each annual family retreat, they make it a point to air out the warehouse of secrets and skeletons.

Humor or organizational play can be a gentle way to air secrets. A law firm with two very self-aware senior partners puts on an annual follies in which members poke fun at group secrets and assumptions in spoofs or parody inflated practices.

Hire a critic. Long-distance leaders recognize the value of an objective, tough-minded critic who is not afraid to point out what others would keep hidden. This may be someone within a company, but sometimes more usefully an outside consultant. The consulting business is full of spin doctors who paint happy faces on bad news, often making things worse, but others are valuable in helping their clients face facts and get through crises as quickly and cleanly as possible.

Bring sunshine to darkness. Deliberately spotlighting a problem to see what can be learned from it is an excellent way to avoid shadow growth. When a client of a large accounting firm went bankrupt, the firm's head took it as a signal that they needed to refurbish their practices, procedures, and ethics. He initiated a project using focus groups of front-line employees and selected clients to arrive at a clearer picture of what was going wrong. Videotapes from these sessions often contained strong criticism of management and excellent suggestions for improvement. The company has since undertaken an annual "audit of internal practices," using such focus groups to bring in sunlight and keep them on track.

Wear a comfortable mask. Leaders should be mindful that the persona they adopt fits the inner self as well as the role they have chosen. Wearing a mask of unflawed success is stressful to the leader and deceptive to those around him or her. Wearing a mask of unwarranted failure is no better. A woman I consulted with, the president of a small liberal arts college, typically spoke and behaved in a self-deprecating way about her achievements, perhaps because low self-esteem made her feel undeserving of her position. Whatever the cause, this public face was in conflict with her leadership role, causing internal stress and loss of confidence among those who looked to her for strength. Both the too-ambitious leader and the too-cautious one may be unwilling to face issues arising from the shadow.

Seek support and use it. Wise leaders seek support in dealing with shadow issues in their personal and working lives. Leaders all too often become isolated in their lofty posts, trapped in an image of strength and control that can be maintained only at a high cost. Perceptive colleagues and board members can serve as sounding boards and provide new ways of looking at work-related problems; family members, friends, and sometimes a therapist should be sources of support and ideas that contribute to personal growth.

THE LEADER ADMITS MISTAKES

Long-distance leaders learn from their bad decisions rather than sweeping the results into the shadow. They learn in two ways: first by doing things differently the next time and second by learning to disentangle errors (and successes) from the ego. A leader suffering from hubris, however, will thrash about awkwardly in a situation that calls for openly embracing error.

Errors buried in the shadow are learning opportunities lost, yet it is sadly true that many leaders are too pumped up with ego to take advantage of this. I have observed that leaders who are oriented toward the fast buck or too image-conscious usually deal with mistakes by denial or stonewalling; for them, all bad news must be given a positive spin. Corporate spokesmen and lawyers admit nothing, and public relations flacks grind failures into pixie dust to fling in the eyes of the press and public.

Lack of the capacity to acknowledge error can have grave consequences: people at every level begin to hide mistakes, and secret-keeping becomes a sideline. The need for an error-free environment leads to risk aversion. Short-term thinking (tighter controls and small plans) prevails over bolder long-range initiatives.

Arthur Colman, a Jungian analyst and consultant, says, "In organizations that are really sick, there is so much blaming, denying, and scapegoating that little work is done, and all the decisions are fail-safe—which usually means too little and too late. Such an organization chews up and spits out leaders before they can begin a true healing process."

In a 1991 *New York Times* article, crisis management consultant Gerald Meyers discussed the major telephone network failure that shut down several East Coast airports that year. "AT&T was paralyzed by its misfortune," Meyers writes. "Officials blamed innocent technicians, then babbled shockingly poor explanations to the press.

"The boss didn't help. At first AT&T's chairman, Robert E. Allen, remained invisible. His effort to minimize his company's error is the knee-jerk reaction of any unprepared executive confronted by a sudden, grave mishap. He neither apologized nor acknowledged error, and hid behind other company executives. . . . And [two weeks later] AT&T still hasn't said exactly what happened. If it doesn't know, it should say so and not guess, try to find scapegoats or fabricate."

Meyers goes on to cite other companies that suffered from engaging in denial and obfuscation: Audi and its acceleration problem, Drexel Burnham's insistence on its innocence in the face of mounting evidence of wrongdoing, NASA burying its head in the sand after the Challenger explosion. And he points out the benefits of admitting errors and taking action to correct them, using other examples. His advice: "Be the source of bad news, not the victim of it."

The error-embracing leader does not fear risk. He or she takes valuable lessons from mistakes, uses the learning opportunities they offer, and is skeptical of reports that are too perfect and optimistic. Self-forgiveness, which is implied in accepting your own mistakes, is a key nutrient of renewal. And the self-forgiving leader can extend that tolerance to others.

Other guidelines for dealing with errors include:

Reward the messenger. One CEO established a system of rewards for those who bring to his attention those policies that are *not* working. The reward is doubled if a suggestion for an alternative policy is tested and works better.

Publicize errors for the general good. Scientists frequently publish information about failed experiments as a means of helping colleagues avoid similar traps. In health care, at its best, studies of how cures made things worse (iatrogenics) are highly prized. Other professions and the business world could do well to follow a similar practice.

Scan recent history for losses as well as wins. A veteran board chairman told me that he begins every annual meeting with a list of decisions that he'd like to rescind. A steel company plans to review the elements of a just-ended three-year plan, focusing on which elements failed and why. The head of a fashion firm who, in analyzing her own mistakes, has become willing to acknowledge those of her organization, has brought some of the best of personal shadow-work to the boardroom.

THE LEADER AS EGO-INFLATION FIGHTER

At AT&T, a study under the supervision of leadership scholar Bob Greenleaf identified a second-level plant supervisor who had produced a crop of top leaders for the system. When questioned about his techniques and curriculum, he could recount only two things: "First, when they get too full of themselves, I trip them up, dust them off, and let them try again. Second, I tell 'em, if you're a son of a bitch, stay that way, unless you really change. Don't try to be something you aren't, because then you wind up being a son of a bitch *and* a hypocrite—and that's twice as bad."

From my own experience, here are several behaviors that curb ego-inflation in leaders and their organizations:

Be your own "fool." The leader who can acknowledge foibles and use humor at his or her own expense is practicing healthy ego-deflation and encouraging others to do likewise. Honest, gentle, well-timed humor can ease tension and stimulate dialogue in meetings, and encourage risk-taking by showing that the consequences of mistakes need not be disastrous.

Keep a sense of perspective. The perks and privileges that accompany success are highly ego-inflating when overindulged, and maintaining a balanced and moderate life-style will help you keep a clear perspective on success. A good example is Wal-Mart founder Sam Walton, who created a retailing empire out of his drive and ingenuity and became the richest man in America. Yet he never allowed power, wealth, and publicity to undermine his personal integrity.

Walton disliked being listed at the top of *Forbes'* wealthiest people in America, saying, "It's just paper." He lived in a modest home a few blocks from one of his warehouses, drove an old pickup truck, kept an austere office, flew coach, and stayed with friends when he traveled. Perhaps more important than such details, he remembered to give good fortune its due when recounting his success.

Share the credit. Worthwhile achievements are the result of our own efforts and those of many others: pioneers in our field, teachers and coaches, co-workers, and critics. A mentor once told me that business letters should never begin with the word "I." It seemed like a small point, but his advice has served to remind me that I am part of a team and that a swelled head—hubris, if you like—lies in wait for the unwary.

THE LEADER AS DEEP LEARNER AND TEACHER

The long-distance leader uses the techniques of deep learning to avoid hubris and cultivate personal growth and renewal. He or she encourages others throughout the organization to do likewise. Through self-observation and retreat, such leaders attain a high level of self-understanding and perspective on their situations. By holding a part of themselves outside their success, these leaders can question directions and values without abandoning the battlefield. The long-distance leader must develop the capacity to be a full participant while also being a wise, detached observer-coach; to be an active player in the immediate game while understanding that other games lie ahead.

Long-distance leaders are learning-hungry, using the challenge of the new to fuel their own and others' capacity for performance. They know that the most nourishing part of any learning curve is the lower to middle region, when new learning is proceeding rapidly, and that near the top of the curve they are dancing just ahead of encroaching entropy. Therefore, deep-learning leaders are, like Tarzan, always on the lookout for a new vine to catch hold of. Sam Keen, author of *Fire in the Belly*, once told me at a meeting about a new project: "I can hardly wait to teach this subject. I will learn so much."

Learning-hungry leaders are easy to spot.

- They lean into a discussion without cynical sniping or protective posturing.
- They listen and question—then listen again.
- They cultivate outside interests: cultural, political, or social.
- They often seek out persons who are out of their mainstream but who have something valuable to pass on.
- They try to avoid situations characterized by pretense, flattery, crudeness, or pettiness, even when the persons involved are rich or famous.
- They return from vacation overflowing with stories about the history, arts, and customs of the places they visited.
- They welcome the opportunities to teach and serve as a mentor to others.

The curriculum for a leader's deep learning can range far and wide. It will probably focus on the following areas:

The shared pursuit of mastery. The ability to envision future learning directions while focusing on mastering the present one is a key leadership art. It is the responsibility of team leaders to convey to their team members the pleasures of doing something truly well, the creative excitement that lies in the process. George Leonard says: "Life is filled with opportunities for practicing the inexorable, unhurried rhythm of mastery, which focuses on process rather than product, yet which, paradoxically, often ends up creating more and better products in a shorter time than does the hurried, excessively goal-oriented rhythm that has become standard in our society."

Chef Wolfgang Puck, whom I had the pleasure of observing at work in his Santa Monica restaurant, Chinoise, is an example of the shared pursuit of mastery. He is a pure joy to watch, constantly moving, observing, commenting to assistants while fabulous creations emerge from his kitchen. He is in command, yet seems part of the team that surrounds him. Few endeavors are as subject to rapid entropy as running a fine restaurant, and Puck enjoys the challenge of opening new branches.

A corporate leader in full stride, working with a closely knit team, achieves much the same efficiency of movement as do Puck and his crew in assembling inventive and delicious meals. The leader moves from scene to scene, assembling just the right characters for each scenario and making decisions that often involve high stakes. The decision-making process may be slower and the goals more distant, but the integrated, hands-on approach to planning and management is much the same.

Generative Learning. In my experience, most of today's leaders seem to be too impressed by technique per se, especially the quasi-scientific sort that lends itself to quantification. They are enchanted by the latest computer program for "guaranteed" long-range planning, the psychological test that promises "safe" employees, the newly discovered accounting loophole that will allow a profit to appear in the quarterly report. This sort of learning helps the leader keep score on the current game, not expand and change the game itself.

By contrast, generative learning demands the willingness to plunge into the creative chaos of unexplored territory. To be a generative—a creative—learner, the leader must take a more intuitive approach, synthesizing new input from outside the established system. Generative learning can be stimulated by play or by imbuing work with playlike qualities. Computer games and "groupware" networks encourage this sort of playfulness and reduce inhibitions in searching for answers to complex problems.

Another fascinating set of activities uses gamelike rituals to help change thinking patterns. Giving work an element of play can be as simple as giving yourself (or your employees) the challenge of approaching a task in a new way, thus making it a game. A corporate leader in the chemical industry described to me the pleasure of learning to play tennis left-handed. He experienced it as a venture away from his predominant power side—the way he usually plays the game in both work and tennis. This scientist knows that mindless ruts are the bane of research projects. His left-handed tennis was achieving what his science and business experience had taught him: to break up patterns of inquiry by employing the playful side of his mind.

David Bohm and F. David Peat write in *Science, Order, Creativity*: "If science always insists that a new order must be immediately fruitful, or that it have some new predictive power, then creativity will be blocked. New thoughts generally arise with a play of the mind, and the failure to appreciate this is one of the major blocks to creativity."

Another tool for generative learning is the *annual learning curve checkup*. Most annual performance evaluations are about meeting goals, improved productivity, or profit—easily measurable material. One success sustainer conducts a separate, deeper self-evaluation that focuses on learning. He brings into this process three close friends and associates and reviews such matters as new ventures undertaken and their risks, his failures and how they affected him, and non-work-related subjects such as books read, old and new relationships, retreat experiences, where he is in his life development, and how his career is aiding or retarding his personal growth.

I recommend that all leaders put themselves through a similar annual process, especially if they are also given a formal performance appraisal in the workplace. A comparison of the results will clarify the picture of how others' expectations of us match up with our own expectations and goals, and may suggest that some invigorating new learning is needed. Leaders can also urge that some form of self-evaluation along these lines be incorporated into the performance appraisal process for all employees.

Encouraging and celebrating diversity. Nothing in a leader's life is more stultifying than monotonous safety. The need for a diverse mix of people and cultures in organizations becomes clearer each day as the concept of a global economy moves closer to reality. To function optimally in a working world in which plans and decisions may be based on assumptions and experiences very different than their own, leaders need exposure to the broadest possible range of backgrounds and points of view.

Even more valuable is the energy and fertility that diversity brings to thinking, planning, and value creation. In work environments that prize and encourage diversity in ethnic backgrounds, ages, and gender, old assumptions are often pushed aside and employees are allowed to use their special vantage points and experience. Leaders in such environments are blessed with many advantages in generative learning because diversity challenges tidy stereotypes that are laden with shadow projections. It stretches our comfort zone, our conviction that there is only one way of doing things. Diversity provides new patterns of language, thinking, and behavior, and brings a richer cultural texture to discussions and planning exercises. It gives our minds a larger stage to play on and demands agility in performing our roles.

THE LEADER AS SHAPER AND TRANSMITTER OF ORGANIZATIONAL CULTURE

Every system has its own set of ethics and aesthetics, its sense of what should and should not be done, and with what kind of style or quality. These values, along with various organizational myths and traditions, are the main ingredients of corporate culture. They are derived largely from its leaders. Is your organizational priority to get the job done fast or to do it exceptionally well? Is its style conservative or flamboyant? Is the office environment relaxed or frantic? Are decisions made by consensus, following long debate, or by fiat?

I agree with Max DePree that a prime function of leadership is building and preserving certain values that become associated with an organization, qualities that make the place special, and effectively communicating those values throughout the organization. Max DePree, longtime leader of Herman Miller Inc., compares the leader's role in this effort to that of the tribal storyteller, usually a tribal elder. Part of the challenge is to evaluate how corporate ethics and aesthetics are put under stress by external change, and to identify those values that are worth keeping.

During hard times, for example, the leader who fails to protect employees, or lowers the standards of customer service, or mistreats suppliers, or plays fast and loose with community or environmental responsibilities may damage the organization's immune system. A solid, healthy organization can recover from a loss of market share or a period of low earnings, but the one that compromises or harms its core values may never get well. Leaders must occasionally assert their sense of what is right against the accepted wisdom of marketing or business trends.

Creating a self-renewing culture through rituals. Effective leaders understand the power of ritual events to shape organizational culture. Ritual can have a negative impact, as with certain kinds of meetings that many of us have learned to dread. But they also can work positively to draw people into the spirit of an enterprise, acknowledge work well done, and build a base of shared values and assumptions. Here are a few such practices:

- The monthly information-sharing meeting, in which management reviews with employees the current performance and problems of the company;
- The one-on-one talk between the head of an organization and an employee, focusing on the value of his or her contribution. This kind of conversation can be enabling and productive;
- Team-oriented adventures such as Outward Bound trips, ropes courses, and the like can enrich the organizational myth, promote a spirit of interdependence, and allow employees to experience an enhanced sense of self;
- Celebrations of individual and team task-fulfillment mark moments in the company's history. Recognition is a powerful motivating tool as well as a way of noting the interdependence that sustains success;
- An affectionate gesture such as hugging can be a renewing ritual that expresses caring, support, and enthusiasm. Women leaders tend to feel more comfortable with such gestures, and males could take a cue from them and from the easy physical camaraderie shown by teams of athletes.

Organizational retreats. An effective retreat is not just another off-site planning meeting. Time should be built in for unhurried conversations and private reflection. Agendas should be clear (and hidden agendas, if any, aired), and procedures developed and agreed to by the participants. Group discussions need sensitive management to avoid the dangers of scapegoating or defensive withholding of information. Above all, leaders must make it clear that they value this kind of interchange for its learning potential, that it is not a gimmick to shore up sagging morale or a perk for work performed.

One successful retreat was planned so that the leaders lived together in adjacent beach houses. In addition to stimulating, provocative talks by outside speakers and discussions on a variety of topics, a communal feast was planned for the second night. Each house was given a recipe and the ingredients for a special dish. With the help of roving expert cooks, everyone learned about recipe reading, and cooking. The results included lots of laughter, surprisingly delicious food, and warm memories of fellowship and community.

THE LEADER AS PROMOTER OF HUMAN GROWTH

The company that encourages the development of its employees as complete human beings is investing in its own future. This means finding the skills and gifts of employees and encouraging them to use them, allowing employees creative leeway in solving problems, and providing space to explore new directions when they are nearing the end of a learning curve. It means valuing employees for their long-range learning potential as well as for the immediate benefit they may bring to the organization.

Max DePree tells a story about visiting the widow of a recently deceased millwright who worked for Herman Miller, and learning to his surprise that the man had also been a poet. This led Max to think about how little leaders really know about their employees, and how much more of a contribution those men and women might make if the whole person were valued and developed by an organization. By providing a forum where everyone in an organization can share nonprofessional aspects of their lives, leaders can discover connections and enhance intimacy that might never come to the fore on its own.

We are said to be passing out of the Industrial Age, when workers were seen as troublesome, interchangeable parts, into the Information Age, which demands highly autonomous groups of nimble-minded workers. In this context, leaders will want to abandon mental attitudes forged in the past and become active promoters of human growth. Their present and future tasks include developing:

- teams with shared values, whose members participate in creating the organizational mission and setting appropriate goals;
- a work force that can analyze its own thinking and decision-making styles and determine what new learning is required for improvements;
- extraordinary systems for sharing knowledge and information, and interpersonal communications that are both functional and educational.

Meeting these challenges will mean investing in in-house training programs and human resources departments that do much more than keep files and process claims. This requires a leadership mind-set that promotes learning at every level of management. Some leaders and organizations are in the forefront of promoting human development, among them Pacific Gas & Electric. Under chairman Richard Clarke, PG&E devoted several years and vast resources to creating a "Blueprint for Learning," aimed at transforming the company into a "learning organization." A chapter in the company's 1992 *Guide to Learning Resources*, an elaborate catalogue of in-house training offered by the company, states the issue that every organization must face: "To succeed in the 1990s and beyond, PG&E's people must not only have the skills to do their present and future jobs well, they must also be equipped to think critically, share a vision, solve problems as a team, and make decisions based on a broad understanding of the business."

The metaphors of Industrial Age organizational life were drawn from war and sports: predominantly male and fiercely competitive activities. But as increasing numbers of women and men with more balanced perspectives enter the ranks of top leadership, the language, images, and practices of organizational life are changing.

Even the aggressively male world of professional sports is finding that a fuller view of human capabilities is both ennobling and productive. Most sports managers have accepted Vince Lombardi's dictum: "Winning isn't everything; it's the only thing." They treat athletes like cogs in a well-oiled machine, valuable only for a specialized ability, rather than encouraging development of the whole person and the players' innate leadership abilities.

A few people, however, believe that there are better paths to winning. Phil Jackson, the coach of the 1991-1992 NBA champion Chicago Bulls, is "dedicated to the totality of keeping body/mind/spirit as whole as possible." The players respond to his more nurturing style and the results speak for themselves. Ex-rugby star Tony O'Reilly, now CEO of H. J. Heinz, says of the Lombardi winning-is-all ethic: "I absolutely reject it. It's vulgar. It carries the seeds of its own destruction. People are more than winning machines."

OTHER WAYS TO PROMOTE HUMAN GROWTH INCLUDE . . .

• *Building a learning organization.* Put learning high on the organizational agenda. Make employees aware of learning deficiencies and offer remedies. Publicize learning achievements.

• *Annoying the complacent and comforting the unhappy.* When employees have dug themselves into deep grooves, leaders should take note and come up with ways to shake them up a little. Giving them tough new problems is a good method. On the other hand, someone really trying to crack a mind-busting problem might be helped by some sympathy and reassurance.

• *Evaluating Deeply.* Offer insights about performance that go beyond numbers. How much deep learning is the employee engaged in? Is she aware of gaps in her knowledge that are holding her back? The long-distance leader can set an example of self-criticism and the passion to learn. Learning and development goals should be part of any formal evaluation process.

• *Assigning stretches.* Cross-training is vital to any organization run as a network. Some employees need to be stretched more dramatically than others, shifted to a milieu that at first seems daunting and even chaotic. For example, an introverted employee might find even minimal public contact stressful at first, then experience dramatic growth. Every personnel shift should be analyzed for growth potential.

• *Rewarding growth.* Most compensation plans are based on numbers. Establish rewards for learning that expands mental capacity as well as measurable competence. An idea that has proven useful is to reward supervisors for growth demonstrated by their subordinates.

• *Demonstrating commitment tangibly.* Mere lip service to personal growth will be met with an equally meaningless response. Add human growth as a goal to strategic plans and annual reports. Institute mini-sabbaticals and retreats for renewal.

HOW WOMEN ARE CHANGING THE LOOK OF LEADERSHIP

The long-distance leaders of the future are likely to be persons who are comfortable in multiple roles and who can shift easily from learner to teacher to planning team member. They will not be strictly defined by their educational or ethnocultural backgrounds, families, professional associations, or work settings. They will keep organizational boundaries flexible and permeable, to provide incentives and meaningful opportunities for as many employees as possible.

This description already applies to many of today's women leaders, who embody many qualities of long-distance leadership better than men. Women are generally more accustomed to self-observation and introspection, willing to seek support, to laugh at themselves occasionally.

The accomplishments of Anita Roddick, the British-born cofounder of the Body Shop products empire, are remarkable. The business she and her husband, Gordon, run generates millions in profits. But she has become an international celebrity through her support of indigenous peoples and environmental causes. Her success and personal interests are part of a broad, value-textured vision. She and other women are fashioning a new style of leadership that is based on the values that give their lives meaning, and they do not shrink from integrating their private concerns with their working lives. When Anita mounts a petition drive for an improved environment and invites fellow employers to do likewise, she is speaking volumes about passion, courage, individual power, and organizational impact.

Sally Helgesen, the author of *Female Advantage*, searched for the special qualities that women executives bring to their work. She found that her subjects had the capacity to be inclusive, to weave networks; were gifted in interpersonal communication and in creating inviting visions. Helgesen quotes Roddick on the elements of leadership as practiced by women. This leadership is based on "principles of caring, making intuitive decisions, not getting hung up on hierarchy; . . . having a sense of work as being part of your life, not separate from it; putting your labor where your love is; being responsible to the world in how you use your profits; recognizing that the bottom line should stay there—at the bottom."

Women tend to be skilled at articulating their values and visions. They know how to empower others, in the process developing networks that in turn become powerful agents for change. They have a compelling need to learn and a strong work ethic vis-à-vis learning. "There is a seriousness with which these women approach their tasks of leadership. They are learners, students about themselves and the process of leadership," according to authors Helen Astin and Carole Leland.

This wisdom is beginning to surface in many companies, and not only those run by women. A number of leaders, many of them familiar to me from the Social Venture Network, try to act on similar principles. These are people who have gone through an early stage of stressful striving, big wins, and occasional flops. They speak of paying back, or making a difference, and devote time and energy to worthy causes. This should be the norm of leadership rather than the exception, and it is the direction long-distance leadership must take.

QUALITIES OF THE SELF-RENEWING ORGANIZATION

"An institution is the lengthened shadow of one man," wrote Emerson. Over time, an organization will usually outgrow that shadow, but it will always bear the imprint of a strong leader. Individuals and organizations also share developmental issues, such as problems that grow from material kept in the shadow and the need for continuous learning. For both individuals and organizations, effective responses to those issues will determine whether they stay the course.

The self-renewing organization is not driven by its leaders to buy and ingest other enterprises in order to constantly expand its resource base, market dominance, or shareholder profits; it is energized by a long-range vision, looks inward to develop its human capital, regularly engages in self-scrutiny, and periodically changes direction on the basis of shrewd observation.

In every solid organization we will find a long-distance leader at the helm. But, rather than imposing his or her ideas from the top down, such leaders encourage the development of leadership qualities on many levels of the organization: the willingness to open and explore its shadows, to embrace errors and discourage a culture of secret-keeping, an appetite for new learning, a mind-set that encourages the personal growth of employees.

The easiest way to understand a self-renewing organization is to see how it differs from the typical pyramidal structure:

Decentralization of power. In large, pyramidal structures, the brain (the decision-making capacity) is located in suites at the top of an office tower. As one wag commented, there isn't much oxygen at the top of a pyramid. In self-renewing organizations, knowledge and decision-making power are dispersed where the action takes place.

Adaptable leadership. The old organizational model featured the "cowboy" leader—lonely, isolated, resourceful, action-addicted, and restless. Self-renewing organizations develop and nurture large numbers of leaders who know how to work alone and in teams, swarm around trouble, and retreat to think deeply and plan carefully.

Flexible structures and procedures. Yesterday's and many of to-day's organizations are massive, hard-wired with policies and procedures, specialized by department and function, and slow to respond to change or mistakes. Tomorrow's successful organizations will be light and flexible, situation-responsive, quick to adapt, and generative in planning. They will thrive on partnerships and strategic alliances, continuous learning, and an awareness of shadows.

NETWORK FEDERATIONS

"How many leaders will one organization need?" asks British management expert Charles Handy. "A lot, must be the answer, lots of them, all over the place and not only in the center." The old structural model for organizations had many levels, a few top managers at each, lots of workers at the bottom level, and very few near the top. Many companies are still run this way, which encourages fierce internal competition and the belief that the very top is the only really worthwhile place to be.

The successful organization of the future is more like a network, with fewer strata. In place of vertical ladders leaning on pyramids will be broad planes in which people can operate and grow in a variety of ways. Within these large "fields" will be many self-managing groups combined in different ways for various assignments and linked by networks.

The network principle is already in place at innovative corporations such as Apple Computer. These are the new expressions of federalism—independent units that gain strength through affiliation and through networks that encourage collaboration. In a nutshell, there will be lots of opportunities for leadership at every level.

The business world recently was amazed by the announcement that IBM would reorganize into self-directed units linked in a federation. The amount of autonomy to be granted each unit was not specified, but the prospect included separate units making alliances with other companies and even seeking outside capital. IBM's news came soon after the breakup of a much larger and even more entrenched monolith, the Soviet Union. Interestingly, both chose to reorganize into federations bound by a network of agreements about sharing economic and other mutually beneficial activities.

Both the former USSR and IBM had secrecy fetishes. Under the guise of preventing leaks to competitors and protecting themselves against enemies, their controls over information became wasteful and destructive to morale and creativity. IBM, the citadel of capitalism, and the USSR, the fortress of communism, both carried heavy, enervating shadows full of secrets that allowed them to deny serious problems.

Many theories are offered for the breakdown of monolithic, pyramidal, rigid organizations, but the causes seem to be simple. The collapse is a response to the new information technology, the growth of a global economy, and the increased pace of social and political change: smaller units can act more quickly, respond to adversity and opportunity more easily. It is a response to human needs and demands. People do better in smaller, self-organizing units that maximize their potential to grow and change, to exercise creativity, and to express their capacity for initiative and collaboration.

To nurture network federalism, the long-distance winner will need to become a network leader, focusing his or her observation skills on the strengths and needs of all the players. So when you, as a leader, find people with entrepreneurial gifts, you will need to give them space and freedom to operate independently. Those with a high need for community acceptance can be encouraged to take leadership roles in staff development and morale-building functions. Many organizations also have employees who prefer to detach themselves and exercise their creative gifts in solitude. They too can be functional leaders by articulating corporate culture through written communications or graphic skills, conducting research that aids the organization, or simply by setting examples of work excellence.

The ability to detect, even anticipate, where energy and resources are needed, and to deploy them quickly, can mean the difference between survival and slow death in today's fast-changing business climate. That is why network federalism is an appropriate response. The leaders deployed throughout the system are like specialized cells in the body's autoimmune system, capable of reading and assessing new information and sending the right message to achieve the desired result.

Network federalism is based on the premise that each element must be healthy enough to sustain itself and to serve the organization as a whole. Individual networks are often flexible—expanding, contracting, or reconstituting themselves to suit project needs. The loyalty of employees is focused on the project team.

Old Organizational Systems vs. Network Federalism

EARLIER MODELS	NETWORK FEDERALISM
Hub-and-spoke systems. All information gathered at the top (or center), secrets sorted, then sent out. Prone to censorship and secret-keeping.	*Open systems.* Information flow to units as needed; secret-keeping discouraged.
Individual rewards. Rewards go to individuals who amass power and protect it.	*Unit rewards and incentives.* Positive reinforcements for managers who empower others and foster collaboration.
Control and elitism. Knowledge is the province of the elite. Workers informed, not asked. Middle management proliferates.	*Control and self-management.* Information and experience convert to knowledge as fast as possible. Knowledge acquisition and sharing become the backbone of self-managing groups.
Thinking from past success. Thinking is both provincial and rationalized to capture and hold past successful strategies. Tendency for self-inflation and rigidity.	*Mindful thinking style.* Local and global interconnects are part of all planning. Values of diversity, ethics, and aesthetics permeate policy deliberations. Learning highly prized. Hubris watched and moderated.

SEEDBEDS FOR HUMAN GROWTH

Leaders in network federations empower others to respond to people's needs, rather than trying to solve problems from the top down. Charles Handy calls this the "post-heroic leader:

[Such] leaders ask how every problem can be solved in a way that develops other people's capacity to handle it. It is not virtuous to do it this way; it is essential."

Harold Geneen is an example of the failure to build leadership on all levels—Geneen, the business genius who built ITT into a conglomerate with delayed-action self-destructive propensities. In his shadow life were mistrust and a compulsion to keep power to himself, which destroyed his company's seed corn for the future. Anthony Athos and Richard Pascale, in their comparative study of Japanese and American leadership, noted that "Geneen's overemphasis on his own independence too often left others captured within such constraints that they were unable to develop the kinds of skills they would need when he retired. . . . When subordinates can't grow, institutions do not develop long-term mobility. Without good mentors, the next generation doesn't mature well."

The self-renewing organization also must take advantage of the extended working lives of employees and their increasing tendency to have several discontinuous careers in the course of a working lifetime. Downshifting, in the sense of shortened hours, can be a significant way of allowing people to rebalance their lives and grow without having to leave the company.

A still more profound change would be in how people *feel* about their work—how organizations can help employees get the most satisfaction from their working lives. If money and power are the sole or primary ends of our efforts, work will be merely never-ending competition, with no long-range winners. The experience of millions proves that these values do not make a fulfilled life.

The more enduring purposes of work were described by E. F. Schumacher in *Small Is Beautiful*: "To give people a chance to utilize and develop their faculties; to enable them to overcome their ego-centeredness by joining others in a common task; and to bring forth the goods and services needed for a becoming existence." These rewards can be accessible to many more people than now enjoy them.

Schumacher and others have also observed that work and relaxation are complementary parts of the same process. Neither can be appreciated in the absence of the other. A balanced life doesn't mean simply doing less of one thing and more of another—getting larger doses of leisure as an antidote to career stress. It means approaching work with the same joyously energetic spirit we bring to play, and applying the same dedication and seriousness of purpose valued in the workplace to our personal lives. The organization that encourages this approach to working life in its employees is actively nurturing self-renewal.

Working on a personal level toward a balanced, integrated life and helping others within the organization do the same is a worthy goal for any long-distance leader. Those in positions of influence have the best opportunity to demonstrate this potential synthesis of work and play in their own lives—to lead by example toward a deeper excellence. They have the power to affect many other lives. By modifying their organizations, they can encourage working environments that feed creativity and channel competitiveness into action for the common good.

TOWARD A SELF-RENEWING SOCIETY

As we learn, one by one, to apply the skills and principles of self-renewal to our lives and careers, our organizations and institutions will change, one by one. If this happens on a large-enough scale, we will be on the road to a self-renewing society. In spite of the apparently overwhelming dimensions of global problems, solutions will be found if enough long-distance leaders are developed and take charge soon. I have shown how courageous, pioneering leaders are building open, network-federation organizations in which employees are encouraged to grow and to enjoy meaningful work. These same leaders are also tearing down the barriers that separate families and communities from the workplace.

You can join the ranks of the self-renewing leaders. Those of us who have attained some measure of success, encountered its dark side, and profited from the experience have a golden opportunity.

Index